The Crown Rights of the Redeemer

Dedicated to
Professor Sir Neil MacCormick

The Crown Rights
of the Redeemer

The Spiritual Freedom of the
Church of Scotland

THE CHALMERS LECTURES OF 2007

Marjory A. MacLean

SAINT ANDREW PRESS
Edinburgh

First published in 2009 by
SAINT ANDREW PRESS
121 George Street
Edinburgh EH2 4YN

Copyright © Marjory A. MacLean, 2009

ISBN 978 0 7152 0877 9

Published with the support of The Baird Trust, The Chalmers Lectureship
Trust and The Hope Trust.

British Library Cataloguing in Publication Data
A catalogue record for this book is available from the British Library

Typeset in Sabon by Waverley Typesetters, Fakenham
Printed and bound in the United Kingdom by Bell & Bain Ltd, Glasgow

Contents

Acknowledgements

This book is offered to the Church community in Scotland as a contribution to our thinking about current constitutional questions affecting us. The material was prepared originally as a doctoral thesis completed in the University of Edinburgh in 2004, which turned out to be rather an unsatisfactory end-point because it fell before the conclusion of the most celebrated recent Scottish case in this field, *Percy* v. *National Mission*.

A little over three years later, the material was brought fully up to date, and its arguments much more satisfactorily concluded, to be presented as the Chalmers Lectures in autumn 2007 in the universities of Aberdeen and Glasgow. The Chalmers Lectureship Trust supported that exercise financially, and the trustees' assistance extends to the partial funding of the publication of this much longer text.

Two trust funds routinely and quietly support the ministry of the Church of Scotland as a community of scholarship, and especially encourage those preparing for the ministry to acquire the habit, and resources, of regular and life-long study. The Hope Trust and the Baird Trust have each significantly supported this publication as it comes to final fruition, making it possible to make available to the Church's ministry a monograph designed to provoke thought and debate, without any fervent expectation of a single conclusion or a ready agreement with the opinions expressed in these pages.

Finally, the Principal Clerk of the General Assembly, Very Rev. Dr Finlay A. J. Macdonald, has been an imaginative and kind supporter of this prolonged exercise for the ten years elapsing from first matriculation to final publication. His flexible attitude to the fuzzy overlap between the work of this project and the work of his department has benefited both, and certainly benefited the author.

M. A. MacLean
May 2009

Introduction

Christian people try to obey God.

That simple sentence describes something immensely difficult to do in practice. There are many difficulties and many challenges. Perhaps the first of these is the challenge of working out what God wants, what are the commands, the Divine Laws, the religious rules that a believer should try to obey. And perhaps the second challenge is the difficulty of obeying them even once they are recognised, when human frailty and sinfulness obstruct good intentions.

In countries like Britain, another problem is created because Christian people also try to obey the law of the land. In a country which most people believe is free and democratic, religious people are just as respectful of civil and criminal law as anyone else is. Most religious people, almost all of the time, have two sets of rules to obey and do their best with both of them without suffering any conflict.

Sometimes, though, the law of the land seems to the Christian to conflict with God's commands. Legislation may allow things to happen which some people cannot believe are pleasing to God: recent examples clearly include issues of human sexuality, embryonic research and nuclear weapons. Occasionally, those laws will directly challenge the principles, priorities and behaviour of those individuals and give them terribly difficult decisions to make. Faced with conflict, many believers will regard the Divine Law as a greater mandate than human law, and will choose to obey God, as they understand such obedience, and if necessary, therefore, to disobey the human law. The clergy who have obstructed the roadway outside the Faslane Naval Base have been doing exactly that.

So far, so simple: not easy, mind you, but straightforward enough in legal terms.

The first complicating factor, which begins to indicate the scope of this book, is that Christians do not always act strictly as individuals in moral and legal isolation from each other. They all belong to the Church, which describes itself as the Body of Christ; and the Church is a corporate body for secular legal purposes just as much as it is for internal, spiritual ones. The difficulties and conflicts besetting the individual believer beset also the Church corporate. The Church is subject to the divine authority and, for many purposes, is subject like any big institution to the law of the land. Sometimes, the Church has tough moral decisions to make which are forced on it by uncomfortable decisions of Parliament or the courts.

A second complicating factor arises from the fact that the Church exists in part to act as a spiritual body with religious authority. In its teaching ministry, and in the light of its calling to declare God's forgiveness and call to people everywhere, the Church has its own authority, its own rules and principles, and its own regulatory systems. The Church does not just obey the law of God: the Church largely administers the law of God in the world. The Church finds itself trying to resolve every tension between divine and human law, because it is the guardian of the law and doctrine of Christian faith.

If the Church could simply organise the whole of human law, it would be possible to ensure there were no conflicts between the two systems. Alternatively, if human authorities were trusted to know the whole mind of God and legislate accordingly, again things would be simple. These suggestions are not facetious: both of these models of law have existed in the Western world at different points in history. Neither model describes most democratic societies today, so all the difficulties and rubbing-points remain, to be puzzled over by the Church as it faces up to the problems of its own constitutional position. That is the third complicating factor: the loss from modern institutions of human authority, of their sense of subjection and obedience to God's laws. Another way of expressing that is to say that the Church can no longer presume that secular rulers will accept that their sovereignty is divinely derived, with all the implications which would flow from that belief.

This book looks at these fundamental issues from the contemporary Church's point of view. Its themes include spiritual freedom of and within the Church, the extent of the rightful authority of the Church, and its duty to represent authentically the ultimate sovereignty of God in a legally regulated society. Chapter 1 presents an attempt to classify human theories of sovereignty from a theological perspective: it is a self-contained essay which may be useful for Christian students of jurisprudence who wish to identify different ways to express the relationship of Church and State.

A book like this one could be written from within the tradition of any one of the range of Christian denominations, all answering similar legal and moral questions, questions that are profound and technically demanding. The answers might vary from one denomination to another, and certainly the historical materials examined would differ among them. This monograph comes from the tradition of the Church of Scotland, and addresses all the pertinent questions entirely from that denomination's experience. That is, as it happens, an especially apposite location for the debate. Reformed theology, from Calvin's *Institutes of the Christian Religion*[1] onwards, has always reflected on the place and responsibility of what the tradition calls the 'civil magistrate' within the structures of a world ultimately subject to God's authority above all else. Scotland is a country whose political history – especially for the four centuries following the Reformation – has often overlapped entirely with its religious history, the key events and personalities forming equally part of both kinds of narrative. Chapter 2 describes most of that post-Reformation period and the tussles and tugs between the two jurisdictions, secular and ecclesiastical, in Scotland. The most basic, unanswered questions always were: how is the authority over people's lives allocated in a Christian society, and which sorts of topics belong to each authority?

Chapter 3 describes the principal attempt, in the early twentieth century, to establish a model that would answer those questions of distribution of authority. As the very close cultural ties of Church and society were on the brink of dissolving in the secularisation phenomenon of the twentieth century, an Act of Parliament in 1921[2] enshrined in law a formalised version of the classic Reformed relationship between a national Church and a civil magistrate. The first of the perennial questions mentioned above was to some extent answered, with an apparent method for allocating authority between two very different jurisdictions; but this happened just as the moral authority of one of those jurisdictions was about to slump in modern Scotland. The second question was, this book will argue, answered only inadequately, with far too little specification of the scope and content of each type of law. Chapter 4 describes the current situation, of great complexity and frustration, where the hard questions enshrined in legislation force the courts to address them head on in case after case, and the uncertainties provide constant problems for executive agencies of the state and the Church alike.

This book is not intended to provide a narrative of the process of gradual secularisation that might arguably be traced back as far as the Reformation or even beyond it to the European Renaissance. That is a task that can be traced in many written histories, and often they are written as if looking through a particular thematic prism. One history might trace the development of worship, another of doctrine, another would focus on the professional ministry, and still another would tell the story from the point of view of musical composition. There would be many others, each with its own flavour or theme. The parts of this book which trace Church history do so only to the extent of noting the struggles over legal sovereignty that arose frequently but patchily through the centuries; and no apology is made for the resulting selectivity of material.

The end result is an argument designed to identify an irreducible minimum of law and authority that belongs properly to the Church, the area which cannot appropriately be conceded to a purely temporal regulation. Put in terms of the very simple question with which this Introduction began: when must Christian people be allowed to obey God without finding any worldly rules applying to their spiritual circumstances? What should be the Church's area of freedom from any other law? If this book generates some debate, it should be because it argues, in Chapter 5 and the Conclusion, that this area should be as small as it can possibly be, and that the Church should concede to temporal authority everything in which it is at all possible for Christians to obey the law of the land, or at least to bear the consequences of that law where it conflicts with their religious consciences. Many people in the Church will have far greater ambitions for ecclesiastical authority, and so will take the opposite view from the one expressed in these pages; and in that case good will come out of this publication, because debate and discussion will surround a vitally important question facing the Church of Scotland.

Equivalent questions face other churches all over the world. The conclusions reached here would need to be translated into their very different conceptual frameworks, historical narratives and legal systems, before they could be applied in those traditions. Even in Scotland itself, for example, no other denomination has the same constitutional status as the Church of Scotland; and it can only be guessed at how the differences multiply when the theological and legal arguments here are applied to a different Church polity or a different civil legal system. Such an exercise is perfectly achievable, and would provide a fascinating test of the validity of the conclusions in this book. That is why these pages began with the simplest and most universal questions about Christian obedience expressed as plainly as it seemed possible to do. The conclusions of all the arguments that follow, whether they are wise or woeful, will perhaps bear some kind of relevance far beyond this one Church, which was arbitrarily chosen for study merely on the grounds of intimate, life-long acquaintance, professional association, and visceral emotional attachment.

Notes

1 Calvin, J., *Institutes of the Christian Religion*, trans. Henry Beveridge (London: James Clarke, 1962).
2 Church of Scotland Act 1921 c. 29.

Chapter 1

Sovereignty and Authority – a Reformed Analysis

This chapter attempts a general definition of the legal and intellectual concept 'sovereignty' and then classifies the principal ways in which it has been appropriated and applied in political science and church–state relations. To the contemporary mind the generality of political science seems very different from the specialist discipline of church–state relations, and there is no direct connection between some aspects of legal authority and the sovereignty of God over the Church. The legal relations between the Church and the world in which it is set have changed a great deal, however, in the period since the Scottish Reformation. Church and state have at times been so tangled together, politically and legally, that it is not possible or appropriate to distinguish purely 'secular' or purely 'sacred' elements of the topic until the most recent times. The features, limitations and locations of sovereignty described in the following pages provide a classification of the characteristics claimed for sovereignty over many centuries, and that will be an important resource and lexicon of terms for the historical examination of the Church that will follow.

The Meaning of Sovereignty

The Definition of Sovereignty

The legal concept 'sovereignty' has been described in so many ways and located in so many places, as this chapter demonstrates, that a simple definition can be only a point of departure, not a summary of the whole argument. Broadly speaking, sovereignty may be taken to be a quality of legitimate authority that is not subject to any greater authority, in other words the ultimate authority within the society or institution in question. Scholars have amplified this in various ways. The sixteenth-century Carmelite historian and lawyer Jean Bodin offered a fivefold list of the functions of the sovereign: appointing magistrates and determining their duties; ordaining and repealing laws; declaring and ending wars; hearing appeals from the magistrates; and exercising the power of life and death where the law gave no provision for clemency.[1] The list suggests that the tasks of the sovereign power include routine elements of government but also extraordinary responsibilities at moments that are far from routine. Theories of sovereignty are particularly useful in assessing the non-routine periods in the life of a community, as this exploration will demonstrate in the life of the Church. Carl Schmitt, an admirer of Bismarck, regarded sovereignty as the ability to decide when to exceed normal powers. Rational government deals only with normal circumstances, he pointed out, and so hardly demonstrates a uniquely authoritative competence. He preferred to ask: 'Who is responsible for that for which competence has not been anticipated?'[2]

Schmitt was suggesting that the characteristic that sets apart a sovereign from some lesser kind of authority is the ability to determine who has what power, what is known in jurisprudence by Schmitt's phrase *competenz-competenz*, the legal competence to determine other powers' competences.

Another property vital for a legal sovereign is the ability to ensure that one's will prevails. Legal sovereignty, if necessary, must be able to wield sufficient coercive power to overcome challenges,[3] and sometimes the unanswerable force is the only realistic identifier of the sovereign power. Bertrand de Jouvenel, who wrote on power and sovereignty in the mid-twentieth century, described the exercise of this power as the suppression of any alternative states that might spring up within the state and damage its internal network of social relationships.[4] The ability to compel the behaviour of others, by use of violence if necessary, is normally a necessary characteristic of a legal sovereign authority.

The general definition above may be described as the internal or vertical aspect of sovereignty, because it is entirely concerned with the relation between the highest authority and those inferior authorities and individuals subject to it. Regarded horizontally or externally, in contrast, sovereignty is the extent to which the supremacy of one sovereign power holds sway before encountering the presence and authority of another sovereign power. It is sovereignty as the extent of jurisdiction, whose most common political measure is geographical. Limits are provided through public and private international law, treaties, conventions and contracts; and other constraints arise in the form of wars and other conflicts that thwart the exercise of sovereignty whenever it is claimed but disputed.

Writers on sovereignty have often used the spatial metaphor of the 'sphere' to describe the extent of a sovereign's authority, and it is a description associated with the Dutch Reformed theologian (and Prime Minister) of a century ago, Abraham Kuyper. This might describe a territorial area (e.g. Great Britain), but it might equally describe a community of people (e.g. the worldwide Jesuit order) or an area of life (e.g. the financial services industry). Inside the sphere the sovereign has supreme powers, and at the same time expects not to be subject to conflicting powers from outside that sphere: those are the vertical and horizontal aspects of their powers.

This metaphor usually presumes a 'zero-sum' model, as if human sovereignty is a fixed and quantified commodity that can be carved up between different competing authorities by contract or conquest or cultural norms, but it cannot as a whole be enlarged, reduced or duplicated. In reality, though, human life is dynamic and always changing; new areas of endeavour develop (e.g. the internet) and new communities emerge (e.g. a new religion). New figures of authority and new sources of rules and protocols need not be in competition with existing sovereign authorities, and need not reduce their powers. In the mid-twentieth century, the jurisprudential writer Hans Kelsen criticised too limited a concept of sovereignty, judged in only in a finite horizontal manner. It is a mistake, he argued, always to divide sovereignty into artificial territorial pieces, whereas in reality some kinds of authority transcend nations.[5] This is where a spherical model of sovereignty is inadequate to describe the contemporary world, but it is a model that has been used too frequently in understanding the Church as a legal institution, and that this has been to the Church's detriment as a spiritual organisation.

This book focuses on sovereignty because the Church of Scotland, since the Reformation, has consistently tried to acquire authority that fits the description above of complete power over a number of people in a particular sphere (within the spiritual life of Scotland) and subject to no interference from another sphere (the civil authority). One problem is the inadequacy of the particular, spherical, model of sovereignty; but another difficulty from the outset is that *sovereign* authority as described above is not the only kind of authority an institution may have. Many professions, associations, companies and voluntary organisations have some degree of internal regulation, but they are entirely subject to the civil law or to the regulation of other authorities and bodies too. This chapter explores with a theological awareness the characteristics of sovereign power, laying the foundation for an analysis of the history of Church and State in Scotland. It cannot be presumed that a Church's spiritual or temporal authority must be naturally or invariably 'sovereign', though that was the presumption within the Church of Scotland in the early part of the twentieth century.

The Limits of Sovereignty

The horizontal aspect of sovereignty described above demonstrates that any sovereign power is likely to encounter external limits to its extent. There may also be limitations on the sovereign in its vertical exercise within the community. The kinds of vertical limits that may exist include the restrictions of religious duty to obey the Divine Law of God recognised in the Bible or from the Church, the law known in the Middle Ages as the *ius gentium* (the law of nations), and Natural Law.

Natural Law theory is the most common version of a theory of limited sovereignty: it is a strand of jurisprudence founded on the belief that some laws are inherent in nature or community and cannot be altered by any human authority, even a supreme one. The substantive beliefs of Natural Law theory have always included such axioms as appear in any system of law that has a category of self-evident propositions. Natural Law is the normative element of whatever objective truth *can* be reached by the exercise of human rationality, though it might *happen* to be delivered also by religious revelation alongside God's commands (Divine Law). To put that another way, it does not require a religious mind to find Natural Law, but religion may affirm its content. The principal intellectual authority for this tradition of thought is the thirteen-century Dominican friar St Thomas Aquinas. In his magisterial work of theology, the *Summa Theologiae*,[6] he maintains that a sovereign is not exempt from the law,[7] and that the positive human law derives from Natural Law[8] by a process of reasoning he calls *synderesis*.[9] Natural Law is not just a restriction or mitigation of the effect of human rule, but it is the central positive influence shaping political institutions to benefit the whole people.[10] For Aquinas, obvious examples of Natural Law principles included the avoidance of intemperance in various forms, relating to food, drink and sex.[11]

Natural Law theory has been used to qualify many ideas of sovereignty.[12] Before the Reformation, the theory provided notions of restraint for temporal rulers aware that there was an authority higher than their own jurisdiction and sitting in judgement over them. The ideas of Natural Law theory were conveyed for their edification in a kind of writing known as *Speculum Principis*, or 'Mirror of Princes' literature.[13]

In the writings of the Reformers, though a greater emphasis lay on the revealed law of God in Scripture, Natural Law was not forgotten. It was resorted to, for example, by George Buchanan, one of the intellectual leaders of the Scottish Reformation. To the extent that his *De Iure Regni Apud Scotos*[14] is an apologia for the removal of Mary Stuart's authority, it marshals arguments from history and Natural Law. To the extent that it is a work of secular political philosophy, it derives social unity also from Natural Law and builds upon it a compact between crown and people. For Buchanan, society does not exist merely for purposes of utility, but it derives from God and serves the good as defined by God. The ruler of such a society does not have an arbitrary authority, because he or she has a duty to promote and restore the health of the social body, and must be qualified with the necessary abilities to fulfil that responsibility. The main constraint upon the king is law, which acts as a moderator upon his public actions, and to which he is ordinarily subject in his private capacity (that is, for purposes like property-ownership). Buchanan's is a thoroughly public-law model of monarchy, in which Natural Law controls the monarch's rule that is exercised through positive law. In the next chapter, Buchanan's role in the Protestant Reformation will be further described.

For Jacques Ellul, a modern proponent of Natural Law theory, Natural Law had an important function in the transition from the medieval world to the classic state. It enabled the separation of Western law from Catholic religion and, in due course, the provision of common substantive beliefs that came to be enshrined in the positive law of nation states.[15] Natural Law is for Ellul the enemy of sovereignty, because it always serves to limit the otherwise completely free exercise of power.

In the struggle between the Church of Scotland and the civil power for authority over religious affairs, both parties were aware of the constraints on their own authority and on that of the other party.

The Locations of Human Sovereignty

The shape of sovereignty is largely determined by its location, as that affects how it is exercised and regarded. Before the Reformation there developed two competing sorts of theory: hierocratic ideas that placed sovereignty at the point of ruler-ship and usually regarded it as conferred from above; and theories of popular sovereignty locating it within the general common weal which conferred authority on its ruler from within, or perhaps from below. In either event, sovereignty was regarded as deriving from God: in the former case as a divine right to rule, and in the latter as a divine authority to a people to select and empower its ruler.

The Sovereignty of the Ruler and the Divine Right of Kings

The idea that the sovereign power in a community lies with the ruler, the person who wields day-to-day authority, is the political theory of monarchs and oligarchies that do not believe their authority has come to them from the people at large, or from any other human authority within the community or beyond it. The theory was articulated intellectually at times when it came under attack from forces contending that sovereignty belonged somewhere else. In the two centuries before the Reformation, this debate was joined inside the Church, between the Conciliarist movement, which argued that authority was derived from the community, and the Papalists, who were the traditionalists. The early sixteenth-century French theologian Jacques Almain was a proponent of Conciliarist theory,[16] and argued in his *Libellus de Auctoritate Ecclesiae*[17] that the community had a natural right to uphold the common good and to confer or recall political power. This version of the argument was to influence Scottish thinking in due course. In practice, however, the papal monarchy held sway against the growing power of the College of Cardinals and the ambition of secular princes.[18] The ecclesiastical setting of the pre-Reformation argument is instructive, because it demonstrates that a spiritual power may claim to be a sovereign ruler, and that is significant for post-Reformation Scottish history.

The Conciliarist controversy concerned the *spiritual* power of the papacy, and the question of whether the pope should behave as a monarch without reference to other possible sources of authority. The better-known Investiture controversy[19] concerned the *temporal* power of the Holy Roman Emperor and other European monarchs, and the question of whether *worldly* power was conferred by God through the Church. The rather radical fourteenth-century rector of Paris University, Marsilius of Padua, argued in his *Defensor Pacis* that the state existed to facilitate the use of human powers to enable people to live well and in moderation. He boldly claimed that only the state – not the Church – could exercise coercive power, so the secular power is alongside but different from any spiritual power.[20]

Secular rulers, when they would no longer tolerate deriving their authority from the Church and the pope,[21] traced it instead directly from God as a divinely given right to be the monarch. The main elements of the theory were: (1) the belief that monarchy is a divinely ordained institution; (2) the belief that the hereditary right is indefeasible; (3) the belief that kings are accountable only to God; and (4) the assertion that God enjoins passive obedience and lack of resistance by the subject.[22] By the ceremonial of kingship, the mystique built around it and its continuity, their sovereignty was credited with an atmosphere of the daimonic, a quality of indefeasibility and a presumption of accountability only directly back to its divine source.[23] This theory, known as the Divine Right of Kings, may constitute a claim for unlimited sovereignty, or as noted above it may utilise a concept of final authority that is limited by law, Natural Law, personal responsibility or competing rights.

One Divine Right thinker who influenced Scottish political thought was Jean Bodin (1530–96), whose writing informed the ideas of James VI.[24] Bodin, a member of the French Estates during the reign of Henry II, treated public law as a scientific discipline.[25] A contemporary of George Buchanan, Bodin could not conceive of a people being sovereign over their lord,[26] and concluded that a ruler so limited was not truly sovereign. For Bodin in his *De Republica*, sovereignty could not be limited 'in power, or in function, or in length of time'[27] and it was logically indivisible. Bodin's belief that monarchs were directly appointed by God produced the conclusion that the rights of the Crown could never be relinquished or alienated.[28] A prince so indivisibly sovereign that he could not distribute his sovereign powers to others was nonetheless limited by Natural and Divine Law.[29] He was limited too by private positive law, in that he would inherit the private contractual obligations of his predecessor, like any heir, with no royal exemption from private bonds – the same point made by George Buchanan in the Scottish context.[30] James VI, in

his *True Lawe of Free Monarchies*,[31] echoes Bodin's ideas
when he talks of mutual duties of prince and people and stops
short of a theory of absolutism. A historian of the Stuart age,
Glen Burgess, concludes that the divine right was considered
by Bodin and others to be unconditional but not unlimited:
unconditional in terms of human accountability but limited
by Natural and Divine Law.[32]

Classic writing on sovereignty, like that of Harold Laski in
the early twentieth century, regarded the Glorious Revolution
of the late seventeenth century as a watershed time when
the notion of absolute kingly right finally faded away.[33]
Other accounts claim its continuing importance, especially
in England during the Orange and Hanoverian dynasty, and
as an ideal of High Anglicanism thereafter.[34] The theory
of Divine Right, limited or not, remains a fiction in the
ceremonial elements of modern monarchies, with religious
elements in the accession or coronation of a new monarch.
Its significance is its staying power in the imagination as one
of the 'mystical preconceptions of sovereignty'.[35] As a model,
divine right was a form of power claim[36] with more than
one application, not just to monarchy. In the next chapter,
Scottish Church history will appear sometimes to consist of
a struggle between the divine right of the king and the divine
right of the Presbytery.[37]

The Sovereignty of the Ruled

> The conflict between the papacy and the conciliar thinkers
> was fundamentally one between the defenders of the idea of
> sovereignty in the ruler and those who sited it in the community
> at large ...[38]

Sovereignty has not always been seen as a quality only of
rulers. In France, for example, the 1789 *Declaration of the
Rights of Man* declared the principles of popular sovereignty
to be 'equality before the law, collective sovereignty of citizens

of *la patrie* (nationalism), and the rule of law'.[39] Though sovereignty is not divisible, political power is conferrable, and a ruler may have received his or her authority ultimately from some or all of those ruled, who – according to this sort of theory – are truly the sovereign power. In the discussion below of theories of popular sovereignty, the concept of sovereignty will be located in places other than the powerful and those set apart to command.

The idea that sovereignty resides not with the ruler but in the community was (like the theory of ruler sovereignty) first articulated in an ecclesiastical setting. Marsilius applied the idea of popular sovereignty to the Church itself. He distinguished ecclesiastical from secular rule but, by crediting both with sovereignty that was ultimately popular, he succeeded in maintaining a single sovereign body in both spheres. In a society where membership of the Church was for all practical purposes universal, the indivisible sovereignty of God, conferred whole upon his people, created a sovereign populace that could devolve the power to rule upon different, chosen authorities for sacred *and* secular purposes. It is a theory with as much a divine mandate as the Divine Right of Kings, but here the route of conveyance of the power is thoroughly different, through the totality of society.

Applying this same theory to secular rule, Aquinas used a threefold scheme of authority:[40] its *principium* was its ordination by God, its *modus* was determined by the people and its *exercitium* was conferred by them on their ruler or rulers. The kingdom of Scotland has always been notable for operating under a simple version of that principle. The title of her monarchs has traditionally been *rex Scottorum* not *rex Scotiae*, in other words king *of* – *belonging to* – all the people, not king *over* a realm. The Declaration of Arbroath in 1320 made the same point in describing Edward as *rex Anglorum*, and asserting that Robert Bruce, as the king of Scots, ruled subject to the assent of the people.[41] The contrasting, English model of sovereignty was described by the Victorian economist and political theorist Walter Bagehot.[42] Bagehot argued that the Crown in Parliament was the location of sovereignty in the British constitution, and dismissed the notion that sovereignty was distributed among different institutions and authorities in Britain in the same way that it was in a federal country like the United States. He believed that the ultimate authority was a newly elected House of Commons, and founded his constitutional theory on the principle of 'choosing a single sovereign authority, and making it good'.[43] The difference in emphasis between the language used in pre-Reformation Scotland and the language of Bagehot is the question of whether the people doing the choosing can be said to be the ultimate location of sovereignty, or whether it lies only in the ruler so chosen.

The former, Scottish model was substantially the vision of Samuel Rutherford, whose *Lex, Rex*[44] was written in the covenanting ferment of the 1640s at around the time of the Westminster Assembly. For him there was no naturally self-evident form of rule, but authority came immediately from God and was mediated through the whole people. The divine origin of human power meant that any form of jurisdiction of one person over another was artificial and the product of positive law, not an inherent, God-given right. He retained a trace of Divine Right theory by maintaining that the people carry out God's choice in establishing their government,[45] but in doing so they gather the sovereignty that is scattered among them and transfer it to a single person, or parliament or political authority of some kind.[46]

> May not the sovereign power be eminently, *fontaliter*, originally and radically in the people? I think it may and must be.[47]

Rutherford's vision was the transfer of a fiduciary dominion (an authority entrusted by the people to a chosen ruler), not a masterly nor an absolute one (assumed or imposed by a ruler). The people did not give up their liberties: the powers of the king extended only to the execution of his responsibilities and not to the arbitrary compromise of his subjects' liberty.[48] To the people he credited a power of government (i.e. the appointment of it), but distinguished it from the power of governing, which belonged to the ruler once established.[49] In this respect, Rutherford's theory is characteristically Scottish, free of any sense of the inherent superiority of the ruler. He pointed out that the people could not confer any power above the law, since they did not have such unqualified power themselves. If the ruler then risked acting as if he were above the law, he could do so only in the service of the *salus populi*, and subject to the people's approval.

The discussion so far has addressed the ownership and conferring of sovereign power. An important argument within popular sovereignty theories was whether the people could revoke their action, recover their own power and reinvest it elsewhere. Whenever a people were in conflict with their ruler, their residual power to retrieve their original authority was an important matter.

A medieval dispute raged over the question whether the *lex Regia*, as it was known, was an irrevocable conveyance or a revocable delegation of power.[50] Marsilius, for example, believed that the popular conferring of sovereignty upon a ruler was retractable. Likewise, the Conciliarist Jacques Almain (who was taught by the same teacher as George Buchanan) believed that kings held power communicatively from the people, but that sovereignty was only delegated, not alienated. Those monarchs who believed in the Divine Right of Kings, in contrast, could not countenance such a revocation argument, because they did not believe the sovereignty they exercised was the people's to retrieve, but it was given to kings by God who alone could remove their power only by death or conquest.

The answer to the disputed point was important for the Reformers who were leading popular revolutions and frequently had to face the question whether the civil authority could be opposed, ignored, resisted or even overthrown. The biblical record seemed to support the theory of the Divine Right of Kings, not least in Romans 13,[51] so Knox and others had to find a way to be faithful to scriptural authority without thwarting the enterprise of reform. In the wars of the Reformation, Lutherans were forced to develop theories of resistance against the Catholic Emperor, arguing that the relationship among the Empire's ruling Electors was a contractual one and that as fellow magistrates they had the right to replace the secular authority above them.[52] As far as ordinary people were concerned, however, the prevailing teaching until the mid-1550s was that the only right was passive resistance to the commands of evil rulers. Bodin believed it was not legitimate to resist even a wicked prince, though the subject should refuse to obey any command contrary to the laws of God or nature.[53] There was no avoiding the punitive consequences of disobedience of a ruler, even where the disobedience was morally inspired and the ruler was wicked. God had appointed the ruler; so all vengeance was left to God.[54]

As spiritual power passed back and forth between ecclesiastical and civil authorities in post-Reformation Scotland several times, each side behaved as if it was legitimate to prise power over the Church away from the other, to recover authority they each believed was fundamentally theirs to exercise.

The Sovereignty of the Individual as Right-Bearer

The theories of sovereignty that recognise limitations on the powers of rulers normally include among those limitations the rights and privileges held by individuals. Some individual rights prevail against almost any other kind of legal claim.

A society that recognises rights is one that regards the interests of the common weal as served by the protection, at any cost, of certain individual interests above the will of the majority.[55]

This is true of even simple societies, if they observe the principle of private property. The individual enjoys the *ius in re* (the right is located in the legal interest in the property) which by force or legal authority is exercised *ad personam* (against another person). The feudal system was little more than a multi-dimensional network of such rights operating under a communitarian model of law that did not yet recognise more sophisticated, inherent personal rights.[56]

With the humanistic jurisprudence of the twelfth century onwards, the individual became the basic unit of legal activity[57] and subjective rights *in persona*, rights that are the property of the individual and not attached to property or legal relationships, were recognised. These were the kinds of rights argued for by the Franciscan friar William of Ockham in the early fourteenth century. Sometimes rights have been regarded as inherent, natural and self-evident; and this view of rights is a branch of Natural Law theory. Otherwise rights have been seen as artificial legal advantages, albeit desirable ones, which are conferred by positive law or political authority.

After the Reformation, rights came to be a starting point of political reflection.[58] One view equated the liberties of the citizen with the possession of sovereignty. De Jouvenel, for example,[59] described liberty as a kind of personal sovereignty that works as if the individual is in the centre of a circle surrounded by other people in their circles. The touching radii of different circles are the legal relationships between persons, and the circles are imperfectly round wherever the sovereignty of another limits an aspect of personal liberty. One's right trumps all else, and gives one what Sir Neil MacCormick calls a sphere of sovereignty.[60] This does not comprise a strong theory of duties, since it treats them as nothing more than an absence of right, or the compromising of a personal liberty. This is the model of sovereignty as a sphere of unassailable power (as already described), but here it is attributed to each individual. Every human has, for this purpose, a spherical bundle of personal rights and can use it to trump any lesser kind of legal entitlement or possession; and these rights constitute a fundamental constraint on the jurisdiction of the recognised sovereign of the community. Furthermore, the spheres must sometimes collide when the interests of their different possessors cannot be compatibly accommodated. That is one model, which takes an extremely high view of individual rights.

A second model distinguishes rights from sovereignty. Sovereignty theories that locate sovereignty in the ruler or in the whole body of the ruled community suppose that there is an authority that prevails over the rights of the individual, but that sovereign has a primary obligation to promote those individuals' rights. Rights exist, but they do not rely on the sovereign authority of their owners: instead they are protected by the external powers of authority and government that are called 'sovereign', and those powers preserve the physical security of their subjects, administer justice, and determine and guarantee personal rights for everyone. Rights are recognised as very high-ranking legal claims, and their guarantee has a priority among the tasks of the sovereign. In this model, however, individual rights are not absolute trump cards in conflict with each other or claimed against a sovereign power. They cannot be, because hard political choices have to be made among conflicting interests, and political society cannot operate if every individual citizen believes his or her rights are absolutely supreme over everyone else's.

The real power of that model of rights lies in its practical implications: that democracy must be more than merely the prevalence of the will of a majority, that the civil magistrate has to take people's rights into account, and that justice cannot be dispensed or disposed by anything so partial as a vote. Bertrand de Jouvenel qualified the idea of democracy in this way:

> Liberty of opinion is the basic principle of the political institutions of the West. It is an obvious mistake to regard majority decision as the criterion of the regimes which we call 'democratic'. So far from massive majorities in favour of a government and its policy giving us a feeling of the excellence of a regime, they render it suspicious to us ... [61]

The attraction of natural rights theory is its protection of the interests of tiny minorities against the 'tyranny of the elected majority',[62] and the persecution of the unconventional few.

Later in this chapter, the sovereignty of God will be discussed. The second of these rights-based models is more consistent with the Reformed belief in the constant sovereignty of God over the world and the Church. If relationships between people are viewed in the light of their mutual relationship with God, the billiard-ball image of independent spheres of sovereignty is inadequate because it does not describe a relationship that is triangular (including God) or to any extent spiritual.

The Sovereignty of Society and of the State

Popular sovereignty places the supreme political focus on a large number of individuals. For some purposes, especially political and religious ones, the recognised 'actor' is a group of people and not its constituent individuals. The medieval debates addressed the question whether the people could be a single, organic whole in the same corporate manner for political purposes as for religious ones (where the people 'is' the Body of Christ). If not a corporate body, the people could only be a group of individuals, with no common personality or single legal capacity.[63] At a philosophical and legal level the answer was not clear, though corporate life of many kinds was commonplace in the Middle Ages, in religious orders, trade guilds, etc. Were people able to associate in a way that produced a new being that was something other than the sum of its parts? If they were, was that association irrevocable, so that individuals once committed to each other were forever bound to that particular form of society? Did the sovereignty of the people belong to a loose confederation of individuals or to a single societal personality? How would such a corporation operate: how would it decide its own will and welfare, and what would become of those who belonged to a minority of opinion or circumstance? How would it exercise sovereignty, and how confer power?

For as long as constitutional thinkers have regarded political society as a complex and secular institution (in other words, since the Renaissance), the concept of 'the state' has been the inclusive term to describe the political machinery of a nation corporate. Two ways of understanding the state have to be distinguished, which parallel the two ways of regarding rights, described in the previous section. Just as one model of individual rights regarded their bearers as sovereign to the extent of having and wielding the rights, while the other model preferred to regard the sovereign power guaranteeing the rights as lying somewhere other than in their individual bearers; the same difference is found in the two models of the state.

One definition,[64] then, regards the state as being sovereign, because it concentrates all power in its own hands and rules, without superior, over the people who live within its geographical jurisdiction. This definition distinguishes the state from the ruler, because the state is a legal entity that is not limited in the way that the personal authority of the monarch is limited; so the state is able to reach further with an ever-increasing machinery of law or coercion. This definition also attributes national sovereignty to the state, which provides its moral legitimacy and political supremacy.

When the essentially private, feudal power of medieval rulers was transformed by the appearance of a public, legally legitimated, sovereign authority, civic loyalty was directed to something other than the personality of the monarch.

[A]n authority *de facto* becomes an authority *de jure*, when a convention intervenes to supply the loss of personal loyalty.[65]

The earliest expression of the state as a single personality appears in Marsilius' *Defensor Pacis*[66] of 1324, in which he defined the efficient cause of the state as the soul of the whole body of citizens. This provided a mystical solution to the problem of the basis for common action of citizens in establishing, correcting and deposing of a ruler. The language of 'soul and body' was used in due course by Hobbes,[67] who described sovereignty as the soul of the state.

As early as Machiavelli, an overemphasis on the coercive element of the state exalted the instrument above its function[68] – the state began to be treated as if it were an end in itself. (The pathological extreme of such exaltation is the totalitarian state, which is not only an end in itself but also the end and purpose of everything and everyone within it.) The new kind of legal authority extended over the whole territory of the nation state and ruled it by public laws not private contracts. Its multiplication of enactments of positive law weakened the authority of Natural Law and Divine Law, and this process was encouraged with the strict separation of the secular and the religious in Lutheran-inspired political thought.[69]

The other definition of the word 'state'[70] does not claim that it is a thing, or end, in itself. It is merely a term for the recognition of the existence of ordered government and law within some territory, and the relative independence of that government from outside interference. This theory of the state regards it not as an organic thing in itself, but as the shape and framework of political life, a matrix upon which the law is arranged, and the apparatus of the country's bureaucracy.[71] The network of social relationships that makes up political and social life is served by legally recognised structures, but those are integral to national life, not sovereign over it.

> [T]he State, in this sense, is above all things, not a number of persons, but a working conception of life.[72]

Bertrand de Jouvenel, talking of justice, described it as 'a certain configuration of things in social geometry'. 'Social geometry' is understood to be the framework of the state in this second sense of the term.

These latter theories have prevailed since the Second World War, when the pathology of an absolutist state, acting without constraints or the limits of Natural or Divine Law, fulfilled earlier fears about the totalitarian model of the state as itself a sovereign power. For example, the theologian Emil Brunner's writings on justice emerged partly out of a horror of a state absolutism that rendered everything else relative.[73] If a state is not a *rechtsstaat* (law-state), if it is subject to no external standards of objective justice, its internal decisions are nothing more than expressions of personal preference without any independent means of judging between them. Brunner conceded that the state was necessary to regulate community, though he believed it was imperfect because of its inevitable resort to coercive power. For Brunner, the authority of the state was not composed of the individual liberties of its members sacrificed for social ends in a Lockean contract model; members of society submitted to the discipline of the state in exchange for its protection by a kind of contract that did not absorb existing individual rights.[74] This theological vision countered the sinister promotions of state primacy that Brunner detected around him.

Even more recently, the notion of the state as a framework of social geometry, rather than as a sovereign power, has been supported by writers who narrate the mutation, diversification or fragmentation of old nation states and the emergence of other shapes or sources of power in a global society. For example, Samuel Huntington's *Clash of Civilizations* provides a narrative of re-alignment as the 180-plus states of today lose elements of their sovereignty and come to be replaced in importance by seven or eight major civilisations, in ways that echo ancient empires and civilisations.[75] These may be characterised by religion or race, but the clash of cultures and religious systems is as important as the clash of political ideals has been in the past.[76] In some cultures, there has been no equivalent of the fading of the ideal of Christendom, so that in Islamic states, for instance, social care is built directly on religious principles that shape political decisions.[77] For Huntington the controlling criterion of communal self-assertion is often religion: a cultural alignment means more to people than an administrative one, and the restless urge to recast state borders is often strongest in places with a strong religious influence or revival. A sign of this motivation for change is a situation where the official law of the state does not correlate with the moral and legal intuitions of its people.[78] Either the law is imposed by force and re-education or the political network is reformed. Neither of these two outcomes indicates a stable society.

Religious and supra-social boundaries are not the only parameters of secular sovereignty.[79] Globalisation and technology force the reconfiguration of sovereignty because technological activity overlaps conventional physical boundaries and decentres the vertical and horizontal relationships of political institutions. E-commerce, international popular culture, offshore companies and many other contemporary phenomena put in question traditional claims that a monolithic nation state really has total legal powers of regulation. Saskia Sassen[80] describes this as a reconfiguration not a removal of sovereignty, with the erosion of the state in favour of the individual. This is reminiscent of the medieval state-less pattern of multiple allegiances and private commitments in a non-territorial framework under the feudal system. In the contemporary world, the single person may submit to different authorities for different purposes, and this is quite the opposite of totalitarianism. The territorially bounded community need no longer confer an all-purpose sovereign power to a single ruling authority.

This monograph examines the relations of two types of ruling authority in the peculiar context of Scotland and Calvinism: one is the traditional state acting as the civil magistrate and the other is a different kind of authority within the same territory, that is, the Church.

The Sovereignty of God

> Where God is truly known, man ceases to be lord over himself and his determining and willing take place no longer through his own freedom but in the freedom of the Holy Spirit.[81]

Each of the four theories of power and government so far considered involves the location of sovereignty somewhere in the human order. Hierocratic theories locate it with the power to rule, while popular sovereignty theories locate it in the ability to recognise and concede that power in others. Rights-based and other individualist theories, while not directly theories of political sovereignty, may find an inalienable authority inherently within each human, while some state theories abstract public sovereignty into the process or personality of the political system. Consequently, each of these legal theories has to be measured somehow against a Christian assertion of the sole sovereignty of God, which is a primary theological and doxological foundation of Reformed Christianity.

> There is only one limit to the sovereignty of the State; it is the knowledge of the sovereignty of God.[82]

Located in God, sovereignty is self-evidently non-negotiable and inalienable. It is an aspect of Providence and of the divine rule. It is absolute, because God is subject to no greater power, but it is not arbitrary,[83] because God acts true to other attributes of divinity: to the faithful, the sovereignty of God is fulfilled in predictable and lovable ways. To the Christian believer all human powers are subject to the sovereignty of God, though an atheist with power will not be conscious of being so constrained. Since this book will ask how the sovereignty of God can be honoured by the Church in its relations with the civil order, the characteristics of divine sovereignty are now explored.

The Mode of Divine Sovereignty

Diakonal Sovereignty

The sovereignty of God has an unexpected nature, characterised by service and love of the world and not by compulsion or coercion of behaviour. The biblical record of the covenants of God and people do not present a sovereignty based on coercion or sheer power. In the experience of Noah, Abraham and Moses, and in the life and death of Christ, God loves and serves the world and the people of God within it. The self-giving of God is greater than the demands of God. God who is Sovereign is God who is Love. This Christian model of sovereignty is thoroughly unconventional because it locates sovereignty in the place of love and covenant, in the service of the infinitely loved world. It is sovereignty of the servant, what I shall term 'diakonal sovereignty.'[84] Diakonal sovereignty commands by attraction not compulsion. It is the ultimate expression of 'soft power', a cultural appeal that wins consent, in contrast to 'hard power', a manipulation of economic or military power to command.[85] It is Oliver O'Donovan's 'objective correlate of freedom',[86] because it does not compromise the freedom of its subjects, unlike humanist versions based ultimately on coercion.

The Scottish contemporary theologian Ruth Page builds her Christology on the idea that God is 'with' us alongside, and is not a commanding power above us.[87] Using metaphors like parenthood, friendship and especially companionship, Page resists the idea of the sovereignty of God being a claustrophobic or dominating characteristic, but talks of God's friendship as an 'uncoerced concurrence'.[88] She also makes a theological remark that illustrates the point made earlier in this chapter about the artificiality of a 'fixed-sum', quantitative idea of sovereignty. Page describes a shift in the theory of power between a high Calvinist view (in which God has 100 per cent of the power in a quantum calculation) and an Enlightenment view (in which humans have claimed more and more power, and God's seems almost to have disappeared).[89] She suggests that a more profitable model of the power of God is a relational not a percentile one. Applying that Christological understanding to her experience of the Church, especially in Scotland, Dr Page criticises every example of 'top-down' authority within a rigid institutional denomination, and offers a renewed vision of spirituality, ecclesiology and missiology, all transformed by her distinctive image of the sovereignty of God.

Not only does this kind of diakonal sovereignty model transform the Reformed understanding of the sovereignty of God: it provides a revolutionary way to grapple with the powers of this world, including the powers of the Church. Walter Wink, an American New Testament scholar, is best known for his trilogy of books[90] on the powers of this world, what New Testament scholarship refers to as *exousia*. Especially in *Engaging the Powers*, Wink makes a similar argument to Page's, as he describes the artificial and arbitrary emergence of the system of domination as the method of ordering the affairs of the world and of the

Church. Christ's purpose, especially the purpose of his execution, was to break the spiral of domination[91] – Wink describes the destruction of Jesus as a 'divinely set trap'.[92] His programme for the Church (in relation to the world's powers) is as follows:

> to unmask their idolatrous pretensions, to identify their de-humanizing values, to strip from them the mantle of respectability, and to disenthrall their victims ... What the church can do best, though it does so all too seldom, is to delegitimate an unjust system and to create a spiritual counterclimate.[93]

It is not the task here to explore or extend the work of people like Page and Wink, and many others like them, in the field of 'exousiology'. However, the narrative of the following chapters will trace a historical path through periods when the domination model was prominent in the engagement of Church with state, but it will arrive at the kind of questions these new theologies have asked about the Church and will try to imagine diakonal sovereignty as informing the future of church–state relations in Scotland.

Sovereignty in Covenant Relation

The exercise of this divine sovereignty among the human subjects of God is, for Reformed theology, the function of covenant between God and people. Retaining sovereignty at all times, God has from time to time delivered a promise and a command together, as received by Noah, Abraham and Moses. In the language of jurisprudence, these were not contracts because there were not two negotiating parties. Covenant is the medium of the sovereignty of God. To a covenanted people is delegated[94] responsibility, authority and God's Word, and through them God's ministry is delivered to the world. Sovereignty is inherent only in the divine; its exercise is delegated to humans and delegated variously for temporal or spiritual functions.

Reformed Christianity, especially in Scotland, acknowledges the idea of this special kind of compact in which God is one of the parties. A 'covenanted nation' was one conscious of such a relationship and guided by its implications; this provided substantive direction for political leadership, and it had the capacity to impose the values of the gospel on secular decision making, in what is known as 'confessional politics'.[95] In the years immediately preceding the Scottish Reformation, Knox believed that England was a covenanted nation but Scotland was not yet covenanted. He believed that Scotland could be won for the Reformation cause only by gradual change, beginning with the people's self-reformation spiritually and culminating in national change. The same principle appears in Rutherford's *Lex, Rex*, which describes the bilateral political relationship of king and people against a background of the relationship each has spiritually with God.[96]

Christians, especially Reformed ones, talk about 'covenant' to express the belief that God's will is sovereign. The language of covenant often conveys the sense that its human parties are subjects of an initiating Providence, so that the covenant is not of people's choosing but imposed upon them as an aspect of their Christian belonging. One implication of this is that God does not relate to people through negotiated contracts but sets the terms of his providence. Another implication is that God declares a covenant without waiting for the people to decide whether they will enter it too; he is prevenient with his grace and not constrained by the need for his initiative to be accepted by his human creation. The sovereignty of God so expressed puts into question other, lesser, secular sovereignty, and all constitutional explanations that are insistently humanistic.[97]

The theological development of the concept of the covenant after the Reformation is discussed in Chapter 2, as is its use as a philosophical basis for the banding together of like-minded protagonists in the struggles in Church and politics that followed the Scottish Reformation. In any conflict, religion is unlikely to reduce the intensity of the hostility, because all parties earnestly believe God is on their side. The concept of covenant made things worse in some episodes of Scottish history, because it gave certain parties the sense that they enjoyed an especially close relationship with God, and so it fuelled their fanaticism. It is important, however, not to dismiss the importance of the covenant relationship with God because of its abuse by some people or because their belief may have led to disastrous outcomes in the past.

Sovereignty in Church and State

The Historical Background, before the Reformation

The development of a relationship of Church and state as two separate sovereign entities contrasted with the very different understanding of the ancients. The early Roman Empire and the Jewish world had no clear and developed concept of a distinction between civil and religious functions.[98] The view of society as a single whole was the self-understanding of the later Eastern Empire throughout its history and engagement with the post-Constantinian Church.[99] Belief in the single sovereignty of God predated any dichotomy between the civil order and the Church, so ecclesiology and political theory were virtually a single subject.[100] The group of theories that connect the Church and the civil order inherently or logically together are known as the concept of 'Christendom'. A society that is governed by the same authorities for religious and non-religious purposes displays a very pure form of Christendom theory.

Almost as pure was the medieval era of the Holy Roman Empire, where there were separate secular authorities, but they organised temporal affairs in the interests of the greater whole and on behalf of the Church. Using an image of spiritual and secular swords,[101] the Church claimed to hold both, *utrumque gladium habitu*, but to wield only the spiritual one *actu*.[102] Whoever enjoyed the secular power could hardly be described as a sovereign in any absolute sense: that power was being exercised only in the interests of the Church and, ultimately, for its sovereign God. In the early Middle Ages, therefore, single-sovereign Christendom remained the prevailing model, but here with non-spiritual powers delegated to a civil ruler.

In about 1100, Justinian's *Corpus Iuris Civilis* had been rediscovered and the medieval civil law tradition centred in Bologna extended the distinctiveness of civil law from the *Corpus Iuris Canonici* of the Church.[103] The same Scholasticism that received and used the *Corpus Iuris Civilis* rediscovered also the teachings of Aristotle, and encountered the pre-Christian idea that the inherent nature of the human individual includes the ability to understand and regulate one's own affairs. Rationalism was a presumption of the quality of the individual mind; it contrasted with the prevailing doctrine of the external authority of the Church delivering truth and law. This encouraged the idea that secular rule could be independent of the spiritual authority of the Church, even if it was still answerable to the sovereign God. The new alternative to the 'two swords' theory was a theory of 'two regimes', which recognised that there was still a single society, but now maintained that it had two equal earthly heads, one of which did not need to be the Church.[104]

Marsilius of Padua's doctrine of popular sovereignty has been described earlier. In the same work, *Defensor Pacis*, he articulated also the dismantling of any coercive power of the leaders of the Church because, he argued, the clergy cannot be responsible for the use of force.[105] Only Christ can punish spiritual offences,[106] and so the punishment of this world can only relate to matters of human law.

Christ himself came into the world not to dominate men, nor to judge them by judgement ... nor to wield temporal rule; but rather to be subject as regards the status of the present life; and moreover, that he wanted to and did exclude himself, his apostles and disciples, and their successors, the bishops and priests, from all such coercive authority or worldly rule, both by his example and by his words of counsel or command.[107]

This was a further advance in the church–state debate, because now the nature of the authority exercised by the two regimes was different. Not only is the Church's lack of coercive force significant for the Church itself but also it has implications for the relationship between the two sorts of authority. If the Church needs to compel someone's behaviour, either it must exercise a force Marsilius argued it does not have or it must apply for help to the civil regime. The question of whether and how the civil regime should support the life of the Church was one the early European Reformers tried to address.

The Reformers' View

In the political thinking of Martin Luther there is another development in the distinguishing of spiritual and temporal authority. For Luther the human individual was not a member of a single society with two heads, but of two distinct communities. The Church as the society of the elect was distinct from the secular society of the world, so the Christian belonged both to the kingdom of God (and in this life to the Church) and to the jurisdiction of the civil powers. Those powers had no spiritual remit and existed to keep order and suppress the worst of worldly evils, *propter peccatum*. The civil sphere was, as Aquinas and others had discovered, subject to the power of reason, and for Luther this meant that in it God could appear only behind a mask.[108] This was faithful to Augustine of Hippo's notion of the state as a necessary evil, which Gilby describes as believing:

> almost that a thief should be set to catch a thief, that evil should be treated homeopathically.[109]

Both kinds of government belonged to God,[110] because the work of civil government had the potential to create the conditions for the preaching and advance of the gospel. If the civil ruler were a Christian, he was a vice-regent of God's and his task of governing was a Christian duty. In his hands was the only sword, that is, the only power to coerce.[111] Indeed, for Luther, the Church was so removed from earthly power that he denied the validity of the *Corpus Iuris Canonici*;[112] human law was not a fitting tool for Christ's Church because the Church was not the bearer of a sword.

This is known as Two Kingdoms thinking, where the ecclesiastical and secular authorities remain separately defined, but so now are the communities they rule, albeit with overlaps and close connections inevitable between the two. It is slightly different from St Augustine of Hippo's 'two cities' idea, contained in his *De Civitate Dei*, which described the city of God and the earthly city as fundamentally opposing communities.[113] For Luther, in contrast, the secular authority may or may not be in sympathy with the ends of the Church; and, if it is sympathetic, the civil regime can only help to create conducive conditions for the Church's own, entirely separate, work.

John Calvin's understanding of the civil powers developed differently from Luther's. In the Reformed view, the civil magistrate wielded his sword for the positive and direct benefit of the Church, not just against the world's sins, and so civil law became a constructive means of religious reformation.[114] In the 1543 edition of his *Institutes of the Christian Religion*, he spoke of the ecclesiastical and civil powers working together in issues of discipline, but in different jurisdictions. However, by the 1559 edition he regarded the civil magistrate as having a responsibility to protect worship, *pietas*, and the Church's status, and a duty extending to both tables of the law.[115]

> For, seeing the Church has not, and ought not to wish to have, the power of compulsion (I speak of civil coercion), it is the part of pious kings and princes to maintain religion by laws, edicts, and sentences.[116]

So where a Calvinist theology prevailed throughout a community, for example Geneva in Calvin's lifetime and Scotland in parts of the later sixteenth century, there was achieved a return to a model of two regimes over a single kingdom, very much like Marsilius' position of two hundred years earlier.

Metaphors of two cities, two swords, two regimes and two kingdoms are all different from each other; but they are all structures in which at different times churches have tried to locate God's sovereignty over the whole world, and to distinguish within it the regulation of matters of particular spiritual concern.

The Conceptual Background of the Church as Community

A great deal can be learned about the conceptual framework of the Church as a legal institution by turning to the Roman Catholic Church and observing whether and how its canon lawyers balance ecclesiological considerations with juridical ones. In the course of the twentieth century, the *Codex Iuris Canonici* has undergone a dramatic transformation in its undergirding legal philosophy, and this has been charted by the Church's constitutional experts. The rest of this book examines the Church of Scotland experience in similar terms, so it is useful to borrow the language and pattern already analysed by others in respect of the older and larger Church.

The last hundred years have seen two versions of the *Codex*, one published in 1917 and the next in 1983, with the Vatican Council of the 1960s between the two. According to James Provost and Knut Walf, editors of a number of editions of the *Concilium* journal dedicated to Church law,[117] the two versions contained different ecclesiologies.[118]

The 1917 code assumed the Church was a *societas perfecta* (a perfect legal institution), whereas the 1983 code is based much more on a sense of *communio* (the Church as a communion). The *societas* model originally arose out of the Catholic Church's confrontation with the churches of the Reformation, and later with the modern secular state. The Church had to assert its autonomy, and defend a self-contained system to ensure its stability and legal integrity.[119] The flaw was that the argument claimed for the Church exactly what it resisted in secular society, so it exalted the operation and effectiveness of the institutional Church and emphasised its juridical functions above its ecclesiological or sacramental life. It developed a view of the Church structured by its hierarchical power of jurisdiction, and identified Christ with a legislator.[120]

The 1983 code was constructed in the light of Vatican II's shift back to a communion-based ecclesiology,[121] and it better balances the necessary elements of *societas perfecta* with the insights of the new understanding of the whole Church. *Communio* acknowledges the inseparability of all the constitutive elements that make up the Church when defining it, and is open to the possibility of change and development.[122] It emphasises Church order rather than canon law: in other words, it calls for the de-juridicising of theology and the de-theologising of the law.[123]

One example of the way in which the new model had immediate practical outcomes was a new emphasis on human rights under the Church law. Pope John Paul II gave to canon lawyers the task of defining for the first time the basic Christian rights within the wider context of general human rights.[124] This was clearly a change of philosophy, away from a concentration on what power the Church was able to exercise over the faithful and towards the entitlements of the individual believer, even against the institution of the Church. The Roman Catholic experience has been touched on to provide useful linguistic tools for later chapters. It demonstrates that the ecclesial body must be spiritual, but there are different ways in which it may be a legal entity.

Presbyterianism and the Civil Magistrate

The next chapter begins to apply all these concepts and arguments to the history of Scottish Presbyterianism. Presbyterianism is a form of political philosophy that has often been troublesome for the civil magistrate. Writing before the passing of the 1921 Church of Scotland Act, the constitutional historian J. N. Figgis pointed out what he believed were the inherent dangers of this form of Church polity.[125] Taken to its logical conclusion, he thought, Presbyterianism would subordinate all state actions to ecclesiastical considerations,[126] ending logically in the return to a Two-Swords theory.[127] The early English Presbyterianism he was familiar with as a scholar was in some ways worse than the medieval papal claims mentioned earlier; and so the purpose of the English version of the Divine Right of Kings was in part to resist Papacy and Presbyterianism alike.[128] There is in the Reformed tradition an attitude towards authority that anti-Calvinists like Figgis (and others long before him) have found simply alarming. Figgis thoroughly approved of the seventeenth-century complaint of the Royalist John Nalson, who said:

No person whatsoever, let him pretend never so much religion, sanctity, or innocence, can possibly be a good subject, so long as he continues a true Presbyterian or of their offspring; in regard they always carry about with them as the main of their religion such principles, as are directly contrary to monarchy and destructive of loyalty; to which he can never be a firm, true and assured friend who owns a power superior to that of his prince within his dominions; and that such a power may of right depose him, and take away his crown and life, which has been proved to be the avowed doctrine of the consistorians of Geneva, Scotland, and England, both in point and practice.[129]

James Smith, a contemporary proponent of the theology known as 'radical orthodoxy', echoes this but in an approving way, in his striking statement:

The church, then, is not an organization that can fit within the civil society of the nation state or regnant *polis* because it is an alternative *polis* that calls into question the aims of the state – whether ancient or modern.[130]

Conclusion

This chapter has demonstrated how profoundly different is God's sovereignty from the legal sovereignty of the world's political institutions. Observed phenomenologically, sovereignty appears to be a property of human political relationships, though within that definition it may be regarded in different ways or identified in different places. According to some definitions sovereignty is for all practical purposes unlimited by any higher claims; and according to others it is subject to religious or moral limitations. According to some emphases, sovereignty is exercised primarily over subordinates; and according to others it is mainly used to define an area of jurisdiction against competing power claims. According to some articulations sovereignty is the natural property of the natural ruler; according to others it is the legitimacy given to rule by those who subject themselves to it; according to another viewpoint it is first and foremost the moral authority of the individual; and finally some identify it belonging to the whole people as a collective institution.

A theologically motivated analysis of sovereignty surely cannot regard it entirely as a human property, but must begin by remembering that sovereignty belongs to God as a divine characteristic, and so it can belong to any human institution only derivatively. Because of this premise, the tradition of Reformed theology has always concluded that the sovereignty of God extends over all earthly institutions of authority whether they recognise it or not; and that profoundly affects the view of church–state relations that can be maintained.

This chapter has further observed that the qualities of the divine sovereignty – and of the Church community in obedience to that sovereignty – are understood today in ways that are very different from conventional political theories of sovereignty and power. Models of power, force and compulsion, for example, are spurned by much contemporary theology. So using the language of 'sovereignty' is risky for the Church, because it is all too easy to slip from it into the language and secular concepts of overwhelming power and legal coercion. Instead, the Reformed ideal should be to claim words like Nalson's[131] (even though they were meant as an insult), and maintain a rigorous and faithful distinction between temporal and spiritual duties of obedience.

The next two chapters follow, in chronological order and in outline, the post-Reformation Church history of Scotland, using the tools of analysis employed in this chapter to explore the constitutional science of each major event or period. Three questions will be relevant:

1. Did the Church of Scotland appear to aspire to be a legally sovereign body: was it ever right to do so and did it succeed?

2. Did the Church heed the proper limits of sovereign power described above?

3. Did it observe the distinction between the sacred and the secular, or overstep that distinction to exercise a kind of authority that did not inherently belong to it?

The overall contention of the argument will be that the Church has too readily adopted a human style of legal sovereignty where it ought to have pursued a divinely inspired style. The survey of possible locations of human sovereignty has been set out above to show the different patterns the Church has variously borrowed and adopted from secular thought in its search for a form of institutional authority that can coexist alongside the rule of the civil magistrate.

Notes

1 J. Bodin, *On Sovereignty; Four Chapters from 'The Six Books of the Commonwealth'*, ed. and trans. Julian H. Franklin (Cambridge: Cambridge University Press, 1992), editor's introduction, p. xvi.

2 C. Schmitt, *Political Theology: Four Chapters on the Concept of Sovereignty*, 2nd edn 1934, trans. George Schwab (Cambridge, MA: MIT, 1985), p. 10. The dangers of acknowledging that sovereignty exists in a power that goes beyond any other authority become sobering when it is remembered that Schmitt became an admirer of the Third Reich, and eventually lost much of his academic respectability as a result.

3 W. J. Rees, 'The Theory of Sovereignty Restated', in P. Laslett (ed.), *Philosophy, Politics and Society* (Oxford: Basil Blackwell, 1963), pp. 67–8.

4 B. de Jouvenel, *On Power: Its Nature and the History of Its Growth*, with preface by D. W. Brogan, trans. J. F. Huntington (from 1945 edn) (Boston, MA: Beacon, 1962), pp. 4–11.

5 H. Kelsen, *General Theory of Law and State*, trans. Anders Wedberg (Cambridge, MA: Harvard University Press, 1945), p. 370.

6 St Thomas Aquinas, *Summa Theologiae* 1a2ae, ed. Thomas Gilby (London: Eyre & Spottiswoode, 1966), pp. xxi–xxv.

7 Ibid., Question 96.

8 Ibid., Question 91.3.

9 Ibid., Question 94.1.

10 Ibid., Question 95, and see editor's introduction generally.

11 Ibid., Question 94.3.

12 O. Gierke, *Natural Law and the Theory of Society 1500–1800*, trans. with introduction by Ernest Barker (Cambridge: Cambridge University Press, 1958), p. 37.

13 B. de Jouvenel, *Sovereignty: An Inquiry into the Political Good*, trans. J. F. Huntington (Cambridge: Cambridge University Press, 1957), p. 200. By convention, the phrase is singular in Latin and plural in English.

14 G. Buchanan, *De Iure Regni Apud Scotos, Dialogus* (Edinburgh, 1579, facsimile edn Amsterdam: Theatrum Orbis Terrarum, 1969); for a translation see *De Iure Regni Apud Scotos: A Dialogue Concerning the Rights of the Crown in Scotland* (Edinburgh, 1799).

15 J. Ellul, *The Theological Foundation of Law* (London: SCM Press, 1961), preliminary ch. (point 1).

16 J. H. Burns, 'Conciliarism, Papalism, and Power, 1511–1518', in D. Wood (ed.), *The Church and Sovereignty c. 590–1918: Essays in Honour of Michael Wilks* (Oxford: Basil Blackwell, 1991), p. 420.

17 J. H. Burns, *Lordship, Kingship and Empire: The Idea of Monarchy, 1400–1525* (Oxford: Clarendon Press, 1992), p. 140.

18 M. Wilks, *The Problem of Sovereignty in the Later Middle Ages: The Papal Monarchy with Augustinus Triumphus and the Publicists* (Cambridge: Cambridge University Press, 1963), pp. 463–88.

19 Summarised in Wilks, *Problem of Sovereignty in the Later Middle Ages*, Part Three.

20 Marsilius of Padua, *Defensor Pacis*, trans. and Introduction by A. Gewirth (Toronto: University of Toronto Press, 1980), Introduction, pp. xxxii, lii and lv. The matter of the Church's exercise of coercive power is addressed towards the end of this chapter.

21 Some might be persuaded by the increasing distinction between the sacred and the secular, while others' objection would stem from their governing territories where the Reformation movement was strong.

[22] This is the statement of the theory given in J. N. Figgis, *The Theory of the Divine Right of Kings* (Cambridge: Cambridge University Press, 1896), ch. 1.

[23] C. Dawson, *Religion and Culture*, Gifford Lectures 1947 (London: Sheed & Ward, 1948), VI(3); and Figgis, *Theory of the Divine Right of Kings*, ch. 1.

[24] J. H. Burns, *The True Law of Kingship: Concepts of Monarchy in Early-Modern Scotland* (Oxford: Clarendon Press, 1996), p. 226.

[25] Bodin, *On Sovereignty*, Franklin's Introduction, p. xii.

[26] Ibid., p. 2.

[27] Ibid., p. 2.

[28] Ibid., p. 49.

[29] Ibid., pp. 13 and 31.

[30] Ibid., p. 43.

[31] R. A. Mason, *Kingship and Commonweal: Political Thought in Renaissance and Reformation Scotland* (East Linton: Tuckwell Press, 1998), p. 216.

[32] G. Burgess, *Absolute Monarchy and the Stuart Constitution* (New Haven and London: Yale University Press, 1996), p. 21.

[33] H. J. Laski, *Political Thought in England: Locke to Bentham* (London: Oxford University Press, 1920), p. 20.

[34] J. C. D. Clark, *English Society 1688–1832: Ideology, Social Structure and Political Practice during the Ancien Regime* (Cambridge: Cambridge University Press, 1985), chs 3 and 4.

[35] R. M. MacIver, *The Modern State* (London: Oxford University Press, 1926), p. 438.

[36] It was a claim to power based on a genuine belief in divine choice and appointment.

[37] William Croft Dickinson, Introduction, in John Knox, *John Knox's History of the Reformation in Scotland*, ed. William Croft Dickinson, 2 vols (Edinburgh: Thomas Nelson, 1949), vol. 1, p. liv.

[38] Wilks, *Problem of Sovereignty in the Later Middle Ages*, p. 488.

[39] R. W. Mansbach and J. A. Vasquez, 'Reassessing the Past: Global History from a Changed Perspective', *In Search of Theory: A New Paradigm for Global Politics* (New York, NY: Columbia University Press, 1981), p. 337.

[40] *Social Contract: Essays by Locke, Hume and Rousseau*, with Introduction by Sir Ernest Barker (London: Oxford University Press, 1947), p. viii.

41 W. C. Dickinson, G. Donaldson and I. A. Milne, *A Source Book of Scottish History*, 3 vols (Edinburgh: Thomas Nelson, 1958–61), vol. I, p. 153.

42 W. Bagehot, *The English Constitution*, with Introduction by R. H. S. Crossman (London: Collins, 1963).

43 Bagehot, *English Constitution*, pp. 219–20.

44 S. Rutherford, *Lex, Rex: A Dispute for the Just Prerogative of King and People* (Edinburgh: Ogle & Boyd, 1843), Question II.

45 Ibid., Question IV.

46 Ibid., Question VII.

47 Ibid., Question XIX, p. 86.

48 Ibid., Question XVI.

49 Ibid., Question VIII.

50 O. Gierke, *Political Theories of the Middle Age*, trans. with an Introduction by F. W. Maitland (Cambridge: Cambridge University Press, 1900; repr. Key Texts series [Bristol: Thoemmes, 1996]), p. 150, nn. 158, 159.

51 Romans 13:1–7 discusses worldly authority. The pericope begins: 'Let every person be subject to the governing authorities; for there is no authority except from God, and those authorities that exist have been instituted by God. Therefore whoever resists authority resists what God has appointed, and those who resist will incur judgement' (NRSV).

52 Q. Skinner, *The Foundations of Modern Political Thought* (Cambridge: Cambridge University Press, 1978), vol. 2, p. 230.

53 Bodin, *On Sovereignty*, Book II, ch. V, p. 120.

54 Dickinson, Introduction, in Knox, *History*, p. xl.

55 Jouvenel, *On Power*, p. 256, explains that such individual liberties must always be in conflict with a theory of sovereignty, even when that is located in the people.

56 H. J. Berman, *Faith and Order: The Reconciliation of Law and Religion*, Emory University Studies in Law and Religion (Atlanta, GA: Scholars Press, 1993), ch. 11.

57 B. Tierney, *The Idea of Natural Rights: Studies on Natural Rights, Natural Law and Church Law 1550–1625*, Emory University Studies in Law and Religion (Atlanta, GA: Scholars Press, 1997), I.II.

58 Ibid., ch. I.II.

59 Jouvenel, *Sovereignty*, p. 258.

[60] N. MacCormick, *H. L. A. Hart*, Jurists: Profiles in Legal Theory Series (London: Edward Arnold, 1981), p. 89.

[61] Jouvenel, *Sovereignty*, p. 276; MacIver, *Modern State*, p. 10.

[62] T. F. Torrance, *Juridical Law and Physical Law: Towards a Realist Foundation for Human Law* (Edinburgh: Scottish Academic Press, 1982), p. 13.

[63] Troeltsch, 'The Idea of Natural Law and Humanity in World Politics', in Gierke, *Natural Law and the Theory of Society*, Appendix 1, p. 206.

[64] Using the description by M. van Creveld, *The Rise and Decline of the State* (Cambridge: Cambridge University Press, 1999), p. 416.

[65] Jouvenel, *Sovereignty*, p. 77.

[66] Marsilius of Padua, *Defensor Pacis*, I.xv.7.

[67] T. Hobbes, *Leviathan: or the Matter, Forme and Power of a Commonwealth Ecclesiasticall and Civil* (Oxford: Basil Blackwell, 1946), Introduction, p. 5.

[68] MacIver, *Modern State*, pp. 431–2.

[69] J. N. Figgis, *From Gerson to Grotius 1414–1625* (Cambridge: Cambridge University Press, 1916), Lecture 1.

[70] This time using the description by H. L. A. Hart, *The Concept of Law* (Oxford: Clarendon Press, 1961), p. 216.

[71] Kelsen, *General Theory of Law and State*, pp. 182–5.

[72] B. Bosanquet, *The Philosophical Theory of the State* (London: Macmillan, 1958), pp. 140–1.

[73] E. Brunner, *Justice and the Social Order* (London: Lutterworth, 1945), ch. 1 (Introduction).

[74] Ibid., ch. 10.

[75] S. P. Huntington, *The Clash of Civilizations and the Remaking of World Order* (London: Touchstone, 1998), p. 36.

[76] Ibid., p. 54.

[77] Ibid., p. 111.

[78] Berman, *Faith and Order*, ch. 20.

[79] MacIver, *Modern State*, p. 469.

[80] S. Sassen, *Losing Control?: Sovereignty in an Age of Globalization* (New York, NY: Columbia University Press, 1996), p. 14.

[81] K. Barth, *The Knowledge of God and the Service of God according to the Teaching of the Reformation: Recalling the Scottish Confession of 1560*, The Gifford Lectures 1937 and 1938; trans. J. L. M. Haire and I. Henderson (London: Hodder & Stoughton, 1938), p. 115.

[82] Brunner, *Justice and the Social Order*, p. 189.

[83] Jouvenel, *Sovereignty*, p. 210.

[84] A technical term is devised here, to carry understood distinctions and criteria from this chapter into the analysis contained in the following ones. It reflects the contrast between *diakonia* and *arche*, which the canon lawyer Josef Blank describes as characterising the New Testament understanding of power. Josef Blank, 'The Concept of "Power" in the Church: New Testament Perspectives', in J. Provost and K. Walf (eds), *Power in the Church*, Concilium 197 (Edinburgh: T&T Clark, 1988), pp. 3–12, p. 8. 'Diakonal' is here spelled with a 'k', to avoid confusion with 'diaconal', relating to an order of ministry.

[85] Huntington, *Clash of Civilizations*, p. 92.

[86] O. O'Donovan, *The Desire of the Nations: Rediscovering the Roots of Political Theology* (Cambridge: Cambridge University Press, 1996), p. 30.

[87] R. Page, *God with Us: Synergy in the Church* (London: SCM Press, 2000).

[88] Ibid., p. 24. Ruth Page's contention goes further than the argument of this book, because she criticises the use of conventional 'sovereignty' language applied to *God*, and so by extension to the Church. Without necessarily disagreeing with that conclusion of her theology, this argument does not go so far, and borrows her thought only to the extent that it puts into sharp question the use of conventional sovereignty-language in application to the *Church*, because it is problematic to use it as the foundation of Christian freedoms.

[89] Ibid., pp. 52–4.

[90] W. Wink, *Engaging the Powers: Discernment and Resistance in a World of Domination* (Minneapolis, MN: Fortress Press, 1992); *Naming the Powers: The Language of Power in the New Testament* (Philadelphia, PA: Fortress Press, 1984); *Unmasking the Powers: The Invisible Forces That Determine Human Existence* (Philadelphia, PA: Fortress Press, 1986).

[91] Wink, *Engaging the Powers*, ch. 6.

[92] Ibid., p. 140.

[93] Ibid., pp. 164–6.

[94] D. B. Forrester, 'The Political Teaching of Luther, Calvin, and Hooker', in L. Strauss and J. Cropsey (eds), *History of Political Philosophy* (Chicago, IL: Rand, McNally, 1963), D.1.

[95] D. B. Forrester, 'Radical Reformed Orthodoxy: Can It Be Retrieved?', *Truthful Action: Explorations in Practical Theology* (Edinburgh: T&T Clark, 2000), pp. 161–84.

[96] Rutherford, *Lex, Rex*, Question XIV.

[97] The language of covenant is not a religious monopoly, and is useful for describing other, similar relationships in human society. In his version of social contract theory, Thomas Hobbes used the religious terminology of 'covenant' rather than the more neutral language of 'contract'. He regarded the parties as the people on the one hand and the ruler (not God) on the other. In the act of mutual covenant the people surrender not only the exercise of their natural rights but also the very rights themselves. Hobbes in his view of the state of nature did not see it constrained, as John Locke thought, by any element of Natural Law. For Hobbes, therefore, the raw state was one where each individual lived in a desperate and horrible sovereign (i.e. unruled) state. Consequently, the sovereignty of the society created by the covenanting of those individuals would be equal to the measure of that individual sovereignty each gave away. In the historical narrative that follows, the language of covenant usually appears where God is regarded as a party to a relationship; this theological application of the term is its most common use.

[98] A. Cunningham and M. di Maio (trans.), *The Early Church and the State*, Sources of Early Christian Thought Series (Philadelphia, PA: Fortress Press, 1982), p. 2.

[99] Ibid., p. 13.

[100] J. N. Figgis, *Churches in the Modern State* (London: Longmans Green, 1914), Lecture II; Wilks, *Problem of Sovereignty in the Later Middle Ages*, p. 42.

[101] The image was first used by the fifth-century Pope Gelasius in a letter to Anastasius II, cited in S. Z. Ehler and J. B. Morrall, *Church and State through the Centuries: A Collection of Historic Documents with Commentaries* (London: Burns & Oates, 1954), p. 11. The biblical reference is to the two swords mentioned in the narrative of the Garden of Gethsemane (p. 91), and it was used by Henry IV in the letter summoning the German bishops to the Diet of Worms in 1076.

[102] Gierke, *Political Theories of the Middle Age*, p. 14.

[103] Berman, *Faith and Order*, ch. 2; and H. J. Berman, *The Interaction of Law and Religion* (London: SCM Press, 1974), ch. 3.

[104] Wilks, *Problem of Sovereignty*, p. 75.

[105] Marsilius of Padua, *Defensor Pacis*, II.v.7.

[106] Ibid., II.x.

[107] Ibid., II.iv.3.

[108] F. E. Cranz, *An Essay on the Development of Luther's Thought on Justice, Law, and Society*, Harvard Theological Studies XIX (Cambridge, MA: Harvard Theological Press, 1959), IV.1.

[109] T. Gilby, *Between Community and Society: A Philosophy and Theology of the State* (London: Longmans, Green, 1953), p. 137.

[110] Marsilius of Padua, *Defensor Pacis*, IV.3.

[111] Forrester, 'Political Teaching of Luther, Calvin and Hooker', B.3. Ellul, *Theological Foundation of Law*, ch. III.3.a, remarks that the content of the law is secular; all it can do in respect of religion is maintain a condition of openness.

[112] Berman, *Faith and Order*, ch. 5(i).

[113] J. K. A. Smith, *Introducing Radical Orthodoxy: Mapping a Post-secular Theology* (Grand Rapids, MI: Baker Academic Press, 2004), p. 132, claims that Augustine saw the notion of a state as a parody of that of *ecclesia*.

[114] Figgis, *From Gerson to Grotius*. In Lecture IV he regards this as a near-medieval wielding of the temporal sword for the good of the Church.

[115] H. Hopfl, *The Christian Polity of John Calvin* (Cambridge: Cambridge University Press, 1982), pp. 119–22 and 172; and see Calvin, *Institutes of the Christian Religion*, IV.XI.16.

[116] Calvin, *Institutes of the Christian Religion*, IV.XI.16.

[117] J. Provost and K. Walf (eds), *Canon Law – Church Reality*, Concilium 185 (Edinburgh: T&T Clark, 1986); *From Life to Law*, Concilium 1996/5 (London: SCM Press, 1996); *Power in the Church*.

[118] Provost and Walf, *Canon Law – Church Reality*, p. xi of the editorial.

[119] R. Potz, 'The Concept and Development of Law according to the 1983 CIC', in Provost and Walf, *Canon Law – Church Reality*, pp. 14–22, p. 16.

[120] K.-C. Kuhn, 'Church Order instead of Church Law?', in Provost and Walf, *From Life to Law*, pp. 29–39, p. 30.

[121] This is not a novel concept; but the Catholic Church was recovering a *communio* ecclesiology. According to Potz, *communio* could be traced back to 'koinonia' teaching in Aristotle and it featured in high Scholasticism and Humanism.

[122] E. Corecco, 'Ecclesiological Bases of the Code', in Provost and Walf, *From Life to Law*, pp. 3–13.

[123] Provost and Walf, *From Life to Law*, p. viii of the editorial.

[124] See Kuhn, 'Church Order instead of Church Law?', p. 33.

[125] Figgis, *Theory of the Divine Right of Kings*.

[126] Ibid., p. 187.

[127] Ibid., p. 198.

[128] Ibid., p. 197.

[129] Figgis, *Divine Right of Kings*, pp. 283–4, quoting John Nalson, *Common Interest of King and People: shewing the original antiquity and excellency of Monarchy, compared with Aristocracy and Democracy, and particularly of our English Monarchy, and that absolute, papal, and presbyterian popular supremacy are utterly inconsistent with prerogative, property and liberty* (1677). Nalson was a staunch Royalist and defender of the Church of England during the revolutionary period in mid-seventeenth-century England.

See also D. Fergusson, *Church, State and Civil Society* (Cambridge: Cambridge University Press, 2004), p. 10, pointing out that the possibility of conflict always exists for those whose highest allegiance is to God.

[130] Smith, *Introducing Radical Orthodoxy*, p. 237.

[131] See n. 129 and the Nalson quotation to which it refers.

Chapter 2

The Church of the Reformation: The Battle for Covenanted Sovereignty

The historical exploration that begins in this chapter demonstrates the belief that the Scottish Reformation was a constitutional and political sequence of events as much as it was a theological turning-point, and that the Church of Scotland and the civil order ever since have struggled to resolve questions of authority and sovereignty between them. In the sixteenth and seventeenth centuries especially, before Presbyterian Church government was affirmed at the Union of 1707, it was difficult to consider separately the legal structure of the Church and civil government because of their entanglement. Inevitably therefore, many of the contributions to political science and constitutional thought came from intellectuals who were protagonists in the religious conflicts of that age.

In the immediate post-Reformation period, the same period in which many of the secular theories of sovereignty described in Chapter 1 were being developed, the Church too was developing and constantly working out how best it should relate to those human institutions of political authority. The analysis of the 1921 church–state settlement that is the focus of the next chapter will require the understanding of the Church's previous record in relations with the state.

The Protestant Reformation

The point of entry of the narrative that follows is the era of the Scottish Reformation of the sixteenth century. In order to describe the major changes in the Church's polity effected by those events, five elements need to be described: (1) the sort of social interaction ('banding') in which it was traditional in Scotland to acquire or convey power and press for change; (2) the ideas inherited by Knox and others from earlier, Continental Reformers about God's gift of authority and those to whom he conveyed it; (3) the possible effects of the Reformation upon civil rule; (4) the thinking of Knox on issues of Church and secular power; and (5) the elements of Scottish life which the Reformation succeeded in changing.

Banding

> [W]hile bonding or banding for various causes, or the achieve-
> ment of a desired end, was not new, the religious connotation
> was an innovation and one which was to be extended as time
> went on.[1]

The 'band' was a traditional agreement that defined relation-ships between individuals, often those of equal status or, in the feudal system, persons of different social rank.[2] The original Reformation use of the band appeared in the Godly Band of 1557, involving 'the Lords of the Congregation' (Argyll, Glencairn, Morton, Erskine of Dun and others)[3] who undertook together to work for a religious purpose that they knew was against the prevailing Catholic customs of Scotland. The Lords were motivated in part by theological conviction, but in part also by the sense of political threat from France,[4] and so their agreement had both civil and religious aims.[5]

The ensuing events of the Scottish Reformation comprised a series of alliances that changed structures and people, sometimes against their will. Banding was the way to achieve dynamic change in an era whose political institutions, for example the Estates,[6] were limited and rather stagnant and whose monarch did not share the point of view of those who were banding against her.

The Godly Prince and the Godly Magistrate

The monarch had a key role in determining the religious shape of society in the Reformation period. The maxim *cuius regio, eius religio* emerged from the Peace of Augsburg in 1555. It was the principle whereby the sovereign prince of each realm within the Holy Roman Empire had the power to determine the polity of the official Church of the realm. This was necessary because some territories had remained Roman Catholic whereas other parts of the Empire had become Lutheran. Luther was somewhat inconsistent in determining what would be the area of the prince's sacred jurisdiction: it 'expanded and contracted in direct proportion to the godliness or lack of it of the rulers in question'.[7] Where the *Landesherren* did not meet Luther's spiritual standards, Luther tended to place more emphasis on the role of the Church's own leaders to bring about the Reformation. The idea of a 'godly prince' nevertheless dominated the planning of some early Reformers, entering the language of Protestant parties attempting to establish Protestant religion in their own countries, even countries beyond the Empire. Scotland was one such country outside the Empire, but learned this theological principle through the influence on the Scottish Reformers of Continental Reformation thought.

John Calvin had not discussed the term 'godly prince', and his pupil John Knox was forced by circumstance to look to the influence of the Estates of Scotland, not its monarch, to achieve Reformation there. In 1560 Scotland had in the Lords of the Congregation a powerful group of the nobility who were determined to reform the country, but in Mary

Stuart the country had a Catholic monarch who resisted.[8] The monarch had been regarded as the sovereign of the nation for both spiritual and temporal purposes. He or she had power through national legislation and power of influence through his or her symbolic representation of the life of the country. The lower nobility had local power over dependents, tenants, feudal inferiors and so on, and could influence the many communities that made up a nation as a whole. The prince, therefore, was not the only 'magistrate', and the prince and nobility were not always in agreement. Some reforming initiatives involved the exercise of sovereign authority, and others constituted revolutionary struggles for spiritual power in the nation. Where the 'prince' was regarded as not 'godly' in the Reformers' meaning of the term (i.e. sympathetic to the Protestant cause), there were other, lesser magistrates who were enthusiasts for the new movement. It was possible to identify a godly magistrate in the absence of a godly prince, but it meant that the Church was relating to a new body of influence in the nation and not to the existing sovereign.

Magisterial Reformation and Radical Reformation

Alister McGrath in his discussion of Reformation thought explains the distinction between a 'magisterial' Reformation and a 'radical' one. In a magisterial Reformation the existing civil magistrate achieves the religious change, applying the *cuius regio, eius religio* principle to the territory over which he rules; a radical Reformation takes place in spite of the magistrate's resistance and so it has equally dramatic social implications.[9] The Scottish Reformation appears to have been a hybrid in its earlier stages, because the Lords of the Congregation were Protestant while Mary Queen of Scots insisted on remaining Roman Catholic. Later in the century, debate continued inside the Protestant Church and centred on questions about the best form of Church government and church–state relations; but even then, the king was often at odds with other influential spiritual and civil leaders.

> Normally, where the reformed church obtained recognition from the sovereign, authority over the church would lie with the Crown, as happened in the Lutheran countries and in England; but exceptionally such authority might lie with the estates of the realm or with lesser magistrates, and that is what happened in Scotland.[10]

In respect of the Estates the Reformation was both magisterial (to the extent that influential figures in Scottish society, who for some purposes constituted the civil magistrate, were committed to reform and introduced it in their own local situations)[11] and radical (because those same figures tried to make it a national reform, in the teeth of Mary's resistance). The Reformers did not initially adopt Luther's device of regarding sovereignty as divided between the Church and the civil order for different purposes, so it mattered very much to them that the civil sovereign should be a Protestant. The monarch as sovereign was subject to the Divine Law, but the Reformers and the monarch had different interpretations of God's commands. The Protestant party, therefore, resorted to popular resistance and the rhetoric of covenant in pursuit of their theological motives, which amounted *in extremis* to obedience to their idea of the sovereign will of God in face of the queen's failure to behave as they thought she should. The overlapping of secular and sacred authority meant that there was no clear horizontal articulation of two separate jurisdictions. It was therefore not possible for the Reformers to ignore the Crown and proceed with religious reformation as if it were an entirely private matter. What there was, however, was an involvement of the nobility and even the commons in the transformation of society, and an assertion against the monarch of the authority of those who had hitherto simply been ruled by a Catholic Crown.

The Reformation under John Knox

Lutheran theories of resistance against the magistrate were adopted by Calvinists and applied in the 1550s in Scotland and elsewhere. Two developments facilitated the Scottish Reformation as a social, as well as a religious, change. One was Calvin's extension of the right of resistance *of* the sovereign *by* the magistrate, to become a right of resistance *of* the magistrate *by* the people. He believed that those elected to rule the people could be resisted when the circumstances demanded it, and they included not only the highest, most distant secular powers; and he thus made the right of resistance part of the exercise of popular sovereignty.[12] The other development was the belief adopted by Knox and other radical Calvinists that the 'powers that be' are not necessarily ordained by God in the first place,[13] so do not necessarily enjoy the protection of Romans 13. These arguments allowed Reformers of every social standing to stand up against their Catholic rulers, and with a clear conscience.

These developments are visible in the Scottish experience of the Reformation. The Church and the civil order were aspects of a single society. In the days of Knox's religious revolution it was not a foregone conclusion that the sacred and secular realms would need to be disentangled, and a clear theory of two distinct kingdoms had not emerged. Indeed, Knox believed that the Church and the civil order both stood in need of a single process of reform.[14]

> [Knox] justified the wide jurisdiction over ecclesiastical matters enjoyed by the temporal ruler through the use of biblical examples ... Knox came close to the full Lutheran position that the secular magistrate had jurisdiction over all aspects of temporal life including ecclesiastical ones.[15]

John Knox used explicitly religious language, that of 'covenant', to describe the spiritual state of a Protestant nation. Before the Scottish Reformation he regarded England as a 'covenanted' nation, because it had officially accepted the Protestant gospel, but he regarded Catholic Scotland as being as yet 'uncovenanted'.[16] It became in Knox's opinion the duty of the godly magistrates, the covenanted nobility, to resort to civil disobedience if need be to gain salvation in the face of a hostile Crown.[17] He visualised a secular ruler so much at odds with the people that armed resistance could be appropriate; so the political debates of the era of the Reformation centred on the unwillingness of the Protestants to be subject to the Crown in matters of religion, a principle expressed in the Articles of Leith of 1559.[18] In short, the Reformers persuaded themselves that the monarch forfeited part of his or her authority when resisting the new Church order.

Knox extended this principle to the whole people in his *Letter to the Commons of Scotland* of 1558, and in the draft outline of his second *Blast of the Trumpet* of the same year.[19] In the latter he asserted that, since the monarch should not be an idolater in a nation subjecting itself to God, he or she could be deposed by the whole people because they all shared the responsibility for establishing the new religion. So in the Articles of Leith of 1559, the Reformers promised obedience to the Crown in all matters except religion, for which they demanded freedom to follow their own personal opinions.[20]

By the year from which the Scottish Reformation is conventionally dated, 1560, these concepts were enshrined in the systematic doctrinal expression of the Church. In the *Scots Confession* prepared in just a few days by Knox and others, the demands of 'good works' include obedience towards rulers and superior powers provided the orders are not contrary to the commands of God and their givers are not exceeding the bounds of their office.[21] In the chapter devoted to the civil magistrate,[22] conspiracy against civil powers is regarded as rebellion against God, but always with the qualification that the civil magistrate should be acting within its own 'sphere'.

The concept of a covenanted nation is significant because it introduces already to Reformed thought the idea of a corporate spiritual personality belonging to the whole nation. The nation might therefore constitute a party to religious agreements, express an intention, compromise a principle or enforce a theological point of view on others. A covenanted nation was a living political entity, a spiritual being to be striven over. The danger of this kind of rhetoric is that individual freedom of conscience is subordinated to the personality of the corporate body. A device designed to serve people's interests comes to replace their individual expression.

The governance of the civil and ecclesiastical realms overlapped; and since the first leaders of the Reformation of 1560 were among the magnates (i.e. the wealthy and powerful), burghers and senior nobility, their first General Assemblies were, naturally, gatherings of members of the same Estates that made up parliament. The Assembly was a 'generall assemblie of this haill realme',[23] suggesting that a single decision-making mechanism was separately, but only slightly differently, constituted for its spiritual and for its secular tasks. The Assembly had a particular problem between the arrival of Mary from France and the attaining of majority by her son James VI in 1578. Scotland in those years did not have someone that its Protestant lords could regard as a 'godly prince', and so the first General Assemblies related to the 'godly magistrate' to be found in the Privy Council and not to the queen.[24]

When John Knox intended that the inferior but godly magistrates of Scotland would effect Reformation in spite of the Queen's opposition,[25] he meant them to establish the Protestant religion first by founding it locally and protecting it against the legal and financial might of the Roman Church. The Reformers did not countenance religious pluralism, that is, the establishment of one Church but the toleration of others. The person who suggested this solution was the queen herself, who in 1565 refused the Estates' request for her to establish *and* adopt the Protestant form of religion. She was quite willing to establish it, but she refused to adopt it for herself and she wished to have her own faith tolerated.[26] Centuries later, during the nineteenth-century debate over Establishment, writers like Thomas Chalmers pointed out the compatibility of Establishment and toleration; this first, royal attempt came to nothing.

The Early Effects of the Reformation

The new Protestant Church worked out, in the Scots Confession and *Books of Discipline*, its own doctrinal standards and constitution, doing so under the authority of the Estates but in freedom from royal supervision or interference.[27] *The First Book of Discipline*[28] was compiled by the Reformers in haste and probably discussed at the first General Assembly, in December 1560, but it was never formally ratified by Parliament. It tentatively began the process of teasing out ecclesiastical and non-ecclesiastical functions, assuming the civil order had responsibility for bringing its law into conformity with Divine Law and making provision for the maintenance of the ministry, poor-support and education. The jurisdictions began to be separated in the Reformers' thought: for example the seventh head of the book allotted the response to capital crime to the civil magistrate, while the eighth left the discipline of ministers to the Church. Duncan Shaw, in his study of all the sixteenth-century General Assemblies,[29] points out that there was no appeal from the Assembly to Parliament, so the two must have had equal authority.

Yet neither was there any complete separation of these two spheres of authority. Just as the membership of the Estates and the Assembly largely overlapped, so also in the parishes civil magistrates often served as elders, manning both jurisdictions and ruling the same body of people.[30] It was not difficult, therefore, to transfer functions from one jurisdiction into the other. For example, when in 1560 the courts of the Catholic Church were abolished, an awkward vacuum was left in relation to the matters such courts had regulated, including consistory matters (marriage, executries, etc.). Until Kirk Sessions were sufficiently established to take up this responsibility, civil courts had to fill the gap, which was why Scotland had for centuries after the Reformation the curiosity of Commissary Courts. At the same time, the consistories (the Church courts) that exercised the ecclesiastical jurisdiction not only made judgements within their sphere of jurisdiction but also judged what that sphere included.[31] In time, especially in the strongly Protestant areas of the south and east of Scotland, a great deal of individual behaviour was scrutinised by the Kirk Session.

> The disciplinary efforts of the consistories represented an early example of an attempt at social engineering on a societal scale.[32]

In a legal system like Scotland's that has grown rather than been invented, anomalies and uncertainties characterise the edges of jurisdictions. In the legal reality of early Protestant Scotland the areas of overlap were not merely marginal or trivial. Parallel jurisdictions, civil and ecclesiastical, regulated the same people and situations, often without controversy or challenge. There was, however, a growing sense of the distinctiveness of each authority, and so in some instances the uncertainty or overlap was seen as unjustified encroachment by the officers of one jurisdiction on the privileges of the other. This could happen in either direction. It was not in order for the Church to interfere with non-spiritual affairs, and Calvin's disciple Beza advised the Scottish Reformers that the king would be entitled to send someone to interpone his authority if he suspected that the Assembly or a synod was overstepping its authority in that way.[33] In contrast, the Church was wary lest the king should attempt to usurp the sovereignty of Christ over his Church: for instance as early as the December Assembly of 1561 it was not clear (and for many decades to come it would remain in doubt) whether the General Assembly could meet without the permission of the Crown.[34]

The Consolidation of Reformation Thought

George Buchanan's De Iure Regni apud Scotos

George Buchanan, Moderator of the General Assembly of 1567, had been a member of the Reformed Church from 1561, even while working for the queen in St Andrews: he remained on friendly terms with her until the birth of Prince James and the murder of Darnley, and later became tutor to James.[35] In the first few years after the Reformation he helped to revise the *First Book of Discipline* and worked with Knox on questions relating to the jurisdiction of the Church. His unique contribution to Scottish thought, however, was not primarily a theological one but lay in the realm of constitutional theory, as mentioned in the previous chapter. Brought up in the humanist tradition,[36] he was an admirer of the Roman civil polity and his writing is more inspired by that kind of influence than it is directly by Scripture. He continued the strand of thought of his natural precursors John Ireland (the confessor of James III, who worked also for James IV) and John Major or Mair (Buchanan's teacher and also tutor to James V), both of whom understood political authority as dependent on the consent of the subjects.[37]

De Iure Regni Apud Scotos is Buchanan's most celebrated work, written in 1567 (the year in which papal authority was finally removed from the Church of Scotland by Act of Parliament) though not published until 1579 (the year in which another parliamentary Act recognised the ecclesiastical jurisdiction as belonging only to the Church itself). Buchanan believed that a king receives his rights and power from the people, who prescribe the boundaries of those privileges.[38] The most substantial parameter of the king's power is the fact that, for Buchanan, the people is the routine legislator, through their representatives:[39] this thinking points forward to the idea of representative democracy and the sovereignty of an institution other than the monarchy. In *De Iure Regni* society as a whole is described as deriving from God, not from utility;[40] so to this extent it is not legitimate to describe Buchanan as an early social contract theorist, but fairer to identify an element of divinely covenanted social order.

Buchanan's theory is not compatible with the claims to the Divine Right of Kings that were being articulated by Bodin and others.[41] Instead, Buchanan posits an arrangement between people and monarch by which the latter acquires a right of heredity; but that means that any succeeding king might not be the best possible candidate for the job, which is why his powers must be rather constrained.[42] Those powers traditionally exist to promote the common weal of the whole nation ('*Populi salus suprema lex esta*'):[43] the basic elements were the defence of the realm and the administration of justice.[44]

De Iure Regni is not directly concerned with the spiritual jurisdiction and does not give explicit answers to questions about the relationship between civil power and spiritual authority. The historian J. H. Burns points out that *De Iure Regni* fails to make clear what precisely the remaining powers of the king are beyond those described in detail by Buchanan,[45] and concludes that they probably involved being a moral exemplar. That is clearly a much weaker spiritual role than one of ecclesiastical government, but Buchanan was writing in 1567 and so he would not easily have attributed such power to a monarch. His theories did not include royal sovereign power extending over the life of the Church, because for him the sovereign power consisted only of what the people were able to confer upon the monarch, that is, civil power. One key effect of the Scottish Reformation was that after Mary the monarch could not presume the Church would recognise his attempts to regulate it, but he would have to contend for that spiritual part of his authority.

Had it not been for theories like Buchanan's, the kings and queens of Scotland might have enjoyed wider acceptance of the idea of total sovereignty over their subjects for both secular and spiritual purposes, once the authority of the pope was removed. If the theory of Divine Right of Kings had flourished unchallenged as it did in England, an undifferentiated jurisdiction could have continued; and a very simple model of ruler sovereignty, constrained only by Divine and possibly Natural Law, would be easy to identify.

The Second Book of Discipline

In 1572 Knox died and in the same year Morton became regent of Scotland. This decade marked the end of the struggle, throughout society, between Catholic and Protestant, and marked the beginning of the political struggle within the Reformed Church between the Crown's integrating view of church–state relations and the developing Two-Kingdoms view that eventually matured as Presbyterianism. Banding and contracting began to take place inside the original Reformation party, between elements whose personal and political interests differed.

For some time after the Reformation the Crown tried to continue the existence of bishops and to use them as the mechanism for royal influence over Church affairs. In 1571, following a Crown appointment to the vacant bishopric of St Andrews,[46] many in the Church concluded that they were unable to tolerate this kind of subjection to the secular regime. The Concordat of Leith of 1571/2 was a compromise that allowed the creation of bishops who exercised the powers of the Reformed Church's superintendents and who were entirely subject to the Church for spiritual purposes (*in spiritualibus*) and subject to the Crown only for secular and property purposes (*in temporalibus*).[47] By the time the *Second Book of Discipline*[48] was drafted in 1576, received by the 1578 General Assembly and formally adopted at the Assembly of 1581,[49] this belief in the distinctness of the two realms became common, a belief in the mutual exclusion of two powers albeit serving the same ultimate ends and acknowledging a practical responsibility towards each other.[50] The book was written under the auspices of the Assembly and was probably influenced by Andrew Melville, Moderator of the 1578 General Assembly. Melville is normally credited with being the first doctor of the Church to use an explicit Two-Kingdoms theory to advance the purposes of the Reformation.[51]

The Church asserted its own God-given internal jurisdiction, and the civil magistrate was told that his religious responsibility was limited to the external peace of the Church.[52] His spiritual task was to exercise sovereignty in the service of the Church, not over it. The perceived failure of godliness in Scottish society, especially in the Crown, had forced the development of this Two-Kingdoms model of Church and state. James Kirk, the modern editor of the *Second Book of Discipline*, uses a phrase common later in the history of the Church of Scotland, 'co-ordinated but distinctive jurisdictions':[53] but, for the first three hundred years after the Reformation, the two were imperfectly co-ordinated and only patchily distinctive.

Duncan Shaw points out[54] that the outcome was more like 'two regiments' (what in the previous chapter was termed 'two regimes') than two kingdoms, because both powers ruled over coterminous jurisdictions (since everyone was deemed to be subject to the spiritual as much as to the secular authorities). It is safer in the longer run to use the 'kingdoms' language, because once this differentiation had been affirmed the way was open for the boundaries of the jurisdictions under the two authorities to differentiate as well. This happened, for example, as soon as plurality of religion developed in the latter part of the next century, leaving the whole population subject to the civil jurisdiction but not quite all of it subject to the spiritual jurisdiction of the Church of Scotland. At the end of the sixteenth century, however, there were now two legal powers seeking to influence the same population but sometimes in conflict with each other.

As Kirk observed in his introduction to the *Second Book of Discipline*, '[T]he assistance of the civil power in reforming the Church was never allowed to obscure the separate identities of civil and ecclesiastical councils'.[55] The authority of the civil magistrate was required to purge and conserve religion, though this did not imply that he had any ecclesiastical jurisdiction. This involved, for example, the parallel secular punishment of those convicted of a religious offence, for example, by putting to the horn anyone who had been excommunicated.[56] A single offence would produce a response in each jurisdiction. The *Second Book of Discipline* therefore articulates a system in which the civil authority fulfils the Genevan requirements of providing the ordinances of religion and remains involved in the system of Church finance, but loses control over spiritual matters entirely to the Church authorities.

This brings the discussion to the concept of Establishment in the experience of the Reformers. Genevan Establishment expected two things, according to McGrath: (1) the maintenance of political and ecclesiastical order; and (2) the provision of doctrinal teaching (provision in this case not to be confused with the defining of its content).[57] Scholarly discussion about Church Establishment is based on a distinction between the state's control of a Church (a form of vertical sovereignty) and the state's support and protection of a Church (which might be regarded as a form of servant sovereignty). Though the former definition is popularly and loosely used, it is the latter definition that constitutes Establishment in historical and legal literature[58] and is therefore relevant to the present discussion. Proponents of Establishment regard the state as having an obligation to maintain, defend and promote the Church. While this responsibility is in theory unconnected with the question of spiritual independence, it has proved difficult to keep the two from becoming entangled, because religious Establishment has often appeared to come with a political price. Much later in this book, this discussion will reappear, as the established status of the Church in modern Scotland is debated.

Andrew Melville and James VI

The *Second Book of Discipline* described the Church's ideal of a spiritual independence from the Crown: however, the Crown (the young James VI) did not accept the constitutional theory of his tutor George Buchanan, nor the theological contention of people like Melville. When James VI reached his majority and personal rule, he expected as sovereign to enjoy an extensive authority over many aspects of the Church's life. As the theory of Two Kingdoms put into question his sovereignty over one realm, he adopted a view firmly opposed to that of the Church. In his pamphlet *The True Lawe of Free Monarchies*[59] his high view of the Divine Right of Kings – not quite an absolute view but not much limited – clearly took issue with Buchanan's *De Iure Regni*. He had a strong sense that his was a unitary sovereignty over all the affairs of the nation, including the ecclesiastical, and so he regarded the ideas of Melville as articulated in the *Second Book of Discipline* as challenging his sovereign authority. For example, in his *Basilikon Doron*[60] James wrote that the king should give reverence to his spiritual office-bearers but should reject even the advice of spiritual leaders if in his own opinion it went beyond the Word of God; and this raised again the question of where the demarcation lay between the secular and the spiritual.[61] For the Church's leaders, it was one thing for the state to claim that the Church did not have a secular jurisdiction, but unacceptable for the king to try to determine what the spiritual jurisdiction included.

The Church pressed the distinction of jurisdictions. In 1579, it achieved the passing of the Act anent the Jurisdiction of the Kirk,[62] which recognised that there was no ecclesiastical jurisdiction except what was contained in the Church or came from it. In 1581 the voting membership of the General Assembly was restricted to ecclesiastical figures to facilitate the sovereignty of the Church in the spiritual sphere.[63] And in 1582 the Assembly felt morally compelled to complain to the Crown that it had assumed an authority that was not proper to it,[64] when the so-called 'Black Acts' of that year granted supreme ecclesiastical jurisdiction to the king,[65] and Andrew Melville found himself on trial.

The confrontation between James and Melville over several years crystallises the dispute. At his trial after the 1582 General Assembly,[66] Melville demanded to be tried by the competent (i.e. Church) authority, on the ground that he was not calling into question the jurisdiction of the king but merely distinguishing it as purely temporal. At the same time, says Melville's sympathetic early nineteenth-century biographer Thomas McCrie, James was seeking sovereign authority over all causes, including ecclesiastical ones.[67] This, in a nutshell, is the dispute of that time:

> Knox and his colleagues asserted the claim of Christ's prophetic and priestly offices; those who came after them contended mainly for his kingly prerogatives.[68]

The famous encounter at Falkland in 1594 saw Melville summarise the significance of the Two-Kingdoms theory to the king.[69] James's difference of opinion with the Melvillian party about the nature of his relationship with the Church meant that they did not regard him as a godly prince, try

as he might to support the Church as he thought right.[70]
King James believed that covenants were contractual (in
the sense of being negotiated) and concluded that they were
possible only in respect of mutable things, not in respect of
universal unchangeable principles – there were some things
that could not be compromised for any purpose.[71] So his
differences with people like Melville could not be resolved
by negotiation, when irreducible principles (like the Divine
Right of Kings) were at stake. James's problem lay in his
attempt to be a godly prince over the Church but on his
own terms. When James's dependence on and attachment
to the suspected Catholic Esme Stewart, Duke of Lennox,
became intolerable to the Church, it retaliated in 1581
by insisting the king should sign a document called the
King's Covenant (which came to form part of the text of
the National Covenant in 1638). The Church also insisted
that the covenant be signed by Lennox, though there was
scepticism at the time about whether he was genuine in his
subscription.[72] This early example of covenanting under
pressure illustrates the potential of this religious tool to have
a corrupting effect.

The complex history of relations between the Crown and
the Church between the Black Acts of 1582 and the Golden
Acts of 1592[73] adds nothing to the stalemate in the thinking
of the two sides, and therefore is passed over here. The
Golden Acts of 1592 did not loosen the king's power over
the Church and did not remove clerics from Parliament. If
Melville's version of the Two-Kingdoms theory could be
said to oppose the Divine Right of Kings with something
approaching a divine right of presbyters, in his lifetime
he did not succeed.[74] The nineteenth-century Free Church
lawyer Lord Moncrieff described the question of spiritual
jurisdiction in terms of the two regimes thus:

In times when the Royal Supremacy was denied, and the divine
origin of the spiritual jurisdiction of the Church admitted, the

appeal lay to the General Assembly. When the Royal Supremacy was asserted, as it was by James in 1606, the appeal lay to the temporal Court of the Privy Council.[75]

In the 1590s the Church settlement involved a measure of the civil control that is known as 'Erastianism',[76] in three ways: (1) the reservation to the Crown of the right to choose the date and place of the General Assembly – a right struggled over especially in the later years of James's personal Scottish rule;[77] (2) the ratification by Parliament of the form of Church government; and (3) the failure to annul the 1584 Act that gave royal supremacy.[78] The Melvillian era produced the theory of two separate kingdoms but could not overcome a monarch determined to claim an undifferentiated, divinely granted personal sovereignty.

The Reformed analysis of authority maintains that the ultimate sovereign in any jurisdiction is God, so to the Protestant eye both kingdoms belong to the reign of God. This means that the distinction between the theory of Two Kingdoms and the older theory of One Kingdom is at times a fine one, having as they do a single ultimate sovereign, and much of the analysis of one theory can fit the other. The twentieth-century Scottish historian Gordon Donaldson, for example, defined the One-Kingdom theory as follows:

> [It] sanctifies the state as well as the church, seeing them as both alike subject to the Kingship of Christ.[79]

The same might equally be said of the Two-Kingdoms theory, except that there the manner of subjection to the sovereignty of God differs between the two realms. The structures of authority are not intrinsically connected, and the relationship between the two is open to debate. In the medieval One-Kingdom theory the same sword-bearer (ultimately the pope) has two weapons, civil and spiritual, and lends one to the secular authority: in Reformed Two-

Kingdoms theory there ought to be only one sword, and it is in the hand of a secular authority answerable only to God, but not to the Church, for its exercise of power. The decades that followed saw this pure version of the theory lost in a tremendous struggle.

Before the Union of the Crowns in 1603, the Church in Scotland had arrived at a position that recognised that Church and state had two kinds of relationship simultaneously. There was an element of independence between the two, visible in the separate Church courts that pressed a separate jurisdiction in matters the Church believed were primarily spiritual. There was an element of connection between the two, expressing the Genevan model of the state's Establishment of the Protestant religion. In other countries quite different models of church–state relations developed that did not have this particular balance of the two elements. The tension of independence and dependence continued in the following century, and has always existed in some form, even to the present day.

The Seventeenth-Century Struggle for Sovereignty

Federal Theology and the Doctrine of Covenant

In the later years of the sixteenth century, a new theological theory supported the religious interpretation of covenant. Reformers like Bullinger developed a system of thought known as Federal Theology, which qualified slightly Calvin's assumption of the impenetrable sovereignty (*voluntas*) of God. Bullinger spoke of a covenant between God and humankind that was a kind of agreement, and emphasised the human responsibility to fulfil its terms. It was bilateral, but its terms were determined by God: it was a form of dynamic compact,[80] but without an element of negotiation.[81] Federal Theologians strenuously denied that a religious covenant was a contract, in the sense of a negotiation, but insisted that it was part of the exercise by God of his sovereignty over the world.

Federal Theology is controversial because of the tension it produced between covenant and predestination. God's covenant with the human race placed men and women in a living relationship with God (*confoederatio mutuis obligationis*). Meanwhile God's unconditional will (*voluntas*) placed upon those same men and women both an unconditional demand of pure faith alone (*sola fides*) and the judgement that is the most recognisable and contentious element of this theological system.[82] The important aspect for a study of church–state relations is the application of this type of theology to the whole nation together. When Robert Rollock, a doctor of the Church and Principal of the University of Edinburgh, developed his Federal Theology to include the covenanted nation concept,[83] political and religious covenanting were identified in a way that was to set the theme for the political exchanges of the next century. The attitude behind this theme was summarised by Rosalind Mitchison:

> Banding and covenanting gradually merged into a practice which, by associating the civil preceders of the Scottish people with God, encouraged a belief in a peculiarly close relationship between the Scots and their God.[84]

It was an explosive combination; the fledgling state, an artificial corporate personality with the power to negotiate on spiritual affairs, engaging with a Church that was characterised by internal disagreement and free (in its self-understanding) of the regulation of an external human sovereign authority. The double application of the theory of covenant to both the civil and religious spheres was a uniquely Scottish phenomenon[85] responsible for some of the peculiarities of Scottish history.

In the early seventeenth century, the covenant concept featured in Christian political theory, but sometimes the pressures put on people to subscribe to a particular religious view meant they had not truly covenanted in freedom of conscience. The Scottish theologian J. B. Torrance pointed out the damage done to doctrine by the confusion of covenant with contract, which has the effect of rendering divine grace conditional. Torrance had a doctrinal concern because the contractual and therefore highly conditional expression of divine covenant tended to the impoverishment of the concept of grace.[86]

> ... it seems to me that we find a situation emerging in the 17th century, not only in Scotland, but also in France, England and New England, where the political struggles for religious and civil liberty (which were the birth pangs of modern democracy) too often led to contractual ways of thinking about God's relation to men ...[87]

The Church was certain it represented God in his relations with the state. The relationship between the two authorities during the early seventeenth century could hardly be said to exemplify the notion of a covenant, because each tried to exercise the power of compulsion over the behaviour of the other. When they engaged with each other it was more like a relationship of contract than of grace, as James Torrance indicates.

Jacobean Sovereignty over the Scottish Church

At the beginning of the seventeenth century and with the Union of the Crowns, the royal court was no longer present in Edinburgh, and so new kinds of distance appeared between the rule of the Church (through the General Assembly) and the secular order (through the royal court). The Stuart monarchs, however, continued to try to blur the demarcation between the civil protection of the Church and the exercise of royal sovereignty over it. The years immediately surrounding the removal of James VI to his new English kingdom on the death of Elizabeth I were effectively a period of civil episcopacy, in which the General Assembly exercised little effective authority in resistance to the king.[88] The period after 1610, when Assemblies scarcely met at all, was a time of increasing Anglicisation of Church polity and worship, culminating in the display of royal authority at the General Assembly of 1618 in Perth at which the so-called Five Articles of Perth[89] were approved, probably against the will of most parish ministers present.[90] The Articles imposed kneeling at communion, private administration of both sacraments, the observance of major feast days and episcopal confirmation. The remainder of James's reign saw rather futile attempts to implement the Articles, and the beginning of Charles I's reign saw energetic efforts to speed up the change. These were very busy and significant years, but it took until the mid-1630s before the Church succeeded in pressing its own theory of polity to dramatic effect, and so this account passes straight to that point.

When Charles introduced Canons upholding the royal supremacy in ecclesiastical affairs in 1636,[91] and then produced his Scottish liturgy ('Laud's Liturgy') in 1637, he did so as an expression of his belief that the Church lay under the protection of a single, sovereign prince.[92] When the Church responded with the sequence of events that led up to the signing of the National Covenant, they did so because they had learned to regard the civil magistrate (i.e. the King) as properly being as remote from ecclesiastical affairs as if he were not Christian.[93] The leaders of the covenanting movement found themselves facing Calvin's original question, whether the secular law must support the spiritual kingdom. They answered it in a new way in late 1637, when the non-ministerial members of the movement took over the governing of the realm through a committee meeting in Parliament House – initially to await the response of the king but eventually taking over the authority of government

– which was known as the 'Tables'. It was the point at which political feelings gave way to treasonous activity.[94]

A perceived breach by the king of the distinction between the two kingdoms was thus met with a breach of the same divide by the Church's party, which shows how hard it was to find the proper demarcation between the two.[95] It demonstrated also the temptation to the Church of wielding a civil sword, contrary to the reliance claimed by the first Reformers on the non-coercive Word.

> In the seventeenth century the preaching of Presbyterian ministers had on occasion persuaded men to ignore their duties to their social superiors, and instead to give first priority to their obligations to God under the Covenants, but when this happened the unquestioned authority of the minister had been substituted for that of the landlord.[96]

The distinction between secular and ecclesiastical regimes held, only just, even here. The movement that was to become the Covenanting party in 1638 consisted of noblemen (who were members of the Estates) and Churchmen, and the former played the political and military roles in the years of upheaval that followed. D. H. Worthington, in his thesis on the political thought of the Covenanters, observes the distinction:

> The Kirk required the co-operation of the political, lay Covenanters to control the radical shift ... Recognizing some overlap of responsibilities, the Kirk accepted a limited employment of civil instruments in their campaign.[97]

The radical element in the Church tried to observe the difference between ecclesiastical and secular politics, while expecting the state to support the true Church as they understood it. Though the General Assembly in this period took an interest in many civil matters that were not strictly its internal business,[98] it did not directly govern civil society.

However, the leaders of the Assembly exercised so much influence over the identity of the civil authorities from year to year in this period that the support of the civil magistrate was guaranteed. The fears of the political scientist Figgis mentioned at the end of Chapter 1, that Presbyterianism had the potential for theocracy and domination over the civil order, had been realised even before the National Covenant was signed.

The National Covenant and the General Assembly of 1638

Archibald Johnston of Wariston, a drafter of the National Covenant and Clerk of the General Assembly of 1638, was a reader of Althusian political theory, which said that society was made up of a complex pattern of compacts, including everything from the family and economic relationships to local and national politics.[99] Wariston therefore believed in the covenanted nation, 'bound under God to uphold a Presbyterian church polity'[100] and his intentions were for the whole Church and nation.[101] The National Covenant[102] consisted of a transcription of the King's Covenant of 1581 followed by a long list of Acts establishing the new, Reformed religion and denying the older. Together they narrated the current legislative position of the Church, which the Covenant's promoters claimed to be defending. The other element of the document was drafted by Alexander Henderson, Moderator of the 1638 Glasgow Assembly, and consisted of the 'General Band', the declaration appearing above the space for the subscription of the Covenant. This part expressed loyalty to the king, but also set out objections to the recent innovations that the Covenanters believed were contrary to the Word of God: the support promised to the Crown was conditional on the Crown taking the right attitude to religion. This effectively compromised the royal prerogative even in civil matters by making obedience to it contingent on the religious behaviour of the Crown,[103] so it went further than any previous contention by the Church. Though the Band was attached to facilitate individual subscription, the intention was that the National Covenant was a covenant of the whole nation and not just of those who signed it. In these ways particularly, the National Covenant moved towards replacing the theory of the Divine Right of Kings with a kind of social contract theory,[104] which was religious because it was based on theological argument, secular because it went beyond strictly theological issues, and contractual because it imposed conditions to be fulfilled by the king.

The anomaly of the idea of national covenanting could not have been lost on the royalist side. The nation consisted of individuals not all of whom shared the beliefs of Wariston, Henderson, Rutherford, etc. The covenanted nature of society must therefore have been an external aspect of its *corporate* personality, not a spiritual quality of every one of its *individual* members: it was possible to be personally hostile to the Covenant but remain a member of the nation that was politically committed to it in Parliament and government.[105]

This mattered a great deal in the case of Charles I. For the king remained uncommitted and, throughout all the negotiations between him and the Covenanting leadership, Charles did not sign the Covenant,[106] fatal as that ultimately proved for him. Like his father, Charles believed some issues of principle could not be negotiated away for any gain, but he was willing to negotiate about issues of expediency and entered the 'Engagement' in 1647. This was an agreement with elements of the Scottish nobility (not with the Church itself) in which he promised royal confirmation of Presbyterian polity at the end of the armed struggle, in exchange for Scottish support in the English campaign. Neither part of the agreement succeeded, and after its failure the more hard-line leaders of the Covenanting movement turned against the

Engagers, passing the Act of Classes in 1649 which excluded them from public office and prevented their subscribing the Covenant.[107] This represented a new corruption of the original intention of covenanting. A document that had been designed to represent the spiritual status of the whole nation was now a symbol of inclusion or exclusion, a tool of classification and discrimination. Within a generation, religious covenant had been used, first, to attribute a particular religious sentiment against the consciences of a social minority (the king's supporters) and, second, to deny to individuals the expression of personal belief. At its most corrupted, the Covenant separated Christians' private opinions from their public profession of belief.

The National Covenant was not itself a Melvillian document because it did not try to effect complete separation between two kingdoms. After all, the long list of legislation it contained was civil legislation establishing religion, and it presumed the supremacy of the king in Parliament (albeit an ideal, covenanted king) over the Church.[108] More Melvillian was the General Assembly of 1638 in Glasgow, at which the Duke of Hamilton was the Lord High Commissioner. Failing to control the Assembly as the King intended, Hamilton left; but the commissioners continued with their business,[109] demonstrating their belief that the Assembly did not meet under the mandate of the Crown. They repealed all the unacceptable ecclesiastical laws of the period since 1610, denying the legitimacy of those General Assemblies that had operated under the influence of the monarch's Anglicising preferences.[110] It abolished the clerical estate in Parliament, on the one hand, and insisted that the Assembly should determine the dates of its own meetings, a principle still observed today by Act of the Assembly, on the other. The experience of civil government at the time means that the Church cannot be regarded as separating from the state completely at this stage, but the Assembly had taken the step of separating the Church from the control of the Crown.[111]

Something of the royalists' intellectual response to this situation can be seen in the *Letter about Soveraigne and Supreme Power*.[112] It was attributed at the time to Montrose (whose moderate attitude to the Covenant eventually saw him fighting against the more extreme covenanting leaders including the Duke of Argyll) but it was probably drafted by his colleague Napier, and it appears to concede a position akin to Buchanan's *De Iure Regni*. Sovereignty, no matter who bears it, is bounded by natural and fundamental law, and has the tasks of enforcing obedience to the law and uniting the body politic. It is in the people's hands to secure religion and justice, and the power of the sovereign is compromised either when it extends beyond its proper limit or, more disastrously, when it is too constrained to carry out its task. The letter resists the idea that the people appoint the king, or might have an interest different from his, or enjoy power divided between him and them. The understanding of those who were finally to be so loyal to the king was a long way beyond James VI's view of kingship. It was a long way short, however, of the next intellectual voice of the Church, Samuel Rutherford.

Rutherford's Lex, Rex

Samuel Rutherford, who was a leading member of the anti-Engagement Protesters' party and represented the Scottish Church at the Westminster Assembly from 1643, subscribed to Melvillian Two-Kingdoms theory.[113] In 1645 he wrote the populist work *Lex, Rex*, based on the idea of the sovereignty of the whole people, and again went much further than, say, Buchanan by assuming a single corporate political and spiritual personality for the population as the Covenant had done.[114] *Lex, Rex* is much less a work of Natural Law than Buchanan's and much more a work about theonomy, the sovereignty of God: so it does not discuss the location or content of fundamental law, but is concerned much more with the conferring of sovereign authority.

According to Rutherford, since the sovereignty of the monarch is derived from God through the people, the immediate divine covenant is with the people and not solely with the king.[115] Rutherford talked of the calling of a king to office through the agency of the whole people, constituting a system of *temporal* monarchy within a philosophy of popular sovereignty. All forms of jurisdiction by one man over another, he said, were artificial and, in legal-philosophical terms, 'positive'[116] – a contention at odds with Divine Right of Kings theory. For Rutherford, that 'positing' was the granting of fiduciary dominion, the collected sovereignty of all the people, described in Chapter 1 above. In exercising that dominion the king was accountable because of his covenant relationship both with God and with the people,[117] and the people had an ultimate responsibility to enforce the king's obligations if he did not fulfil them.[118] What Rutherford did allow the monarch was the kind of emergency power that Schmitt believed was the essence of sovereignty, in Rutherford's terms a prerogative of equity to guarantee the *salus populi* when all else failed, provided the king did not act arbitrarily to achieve this.[119]

As early as Question V of *Lex, Rex*, Rutherford stressed that callings to *spiritual* office are immediately of God without human settlement.[120] W. M. Campbell, in his doctoral thesis on Samuel Rutherford, summarises the argument thus:

> Secular power of government he admits vests in the people who conveyed by election, but ecclesiastical power is supernatural from Christ and cannot be conveyed by them.[121]

The implication of this distinction is this: civil and ecclesiastical rulers are not created by the same processes, and so they need not be necessarily the same people. This challenged the tenacious Jacobean view that secular sovereignty must imply the simultaneous ecclesiastical sovereignty of the monarch. But, in common with his predecessors, Rutherford never suggested that spiritual independence was inconsistent with the Establishment principle: the king could not make spiritual laws, but he had a responsibility to help to enforce them. According to Campbell, Rutherford was in this respect a radical pupil of Knox,[122] in that he held to the principle of civil Establishment of Christian religion. Campbell appears to use 'radical' to refer to Rutherford's strong sense of spiritual independence of the Church from state interference or sovereignty, which goes beyond the understanding of Knox's generation.

The Covenanters' final position may be summarised simply, thus:

> The Redeemer had Crown rights which were expressed in the freedom of His Church to rule itself in His Name without permission of a lesser monarchy.[123]

The Later Seventeenth and Eighteenth Centuries

The Westminster Standards that Rutherford helped to formulate were approved by the General Assembly of 1647. Chapter XXX of the *Westminster Confession of Faith* contains the proposition that Christ has an ecclesiastical government distinct from civil government, though it is an illustration of the variation from country to country of church–state relations that other denominations involved in the Westminster Assembly did not all use this section of the text.[124]

The problem of the age was less and less the question of whether there were two different jurisdictions, but more and more the interference in the civil jurisdiction by the Church as it implemented the extremes of its theory of covenant. The more powerful the religious leaders were, the more able they were to use covenant as the kind of compact where other people's wills were either changed or overridden. For example, the last symbolic use of the contractual model was at the crowning of Charles II (who did agree to the National Covenant before his coronation), during which the sermon explicitly described a contractual interpretation of the covenants of the Old Testament.[125] The weaker the Church party became, the less able were they to impose any covenant on others. So, for example, at the height of the persecution of the later Covenanters, when all their political power had gone, the Rutherglen Declaration of 1679[126] was an expression of the common intent of like-minded rebels, like the original 'banding' of the Reformation; this time opposed to prelacy but devoid of the power to change the position of other people. In contrast, the Test Act of 1681 expressed the intention of the restored monarchy that office-holders in both Church and state would pledge their allegiance – whether they really felt it or not – both to the Protestant faith and also to the monarch as governor in all causes, ecclesiastical as well as civil.[127] The *Claim of Right* of 1689, too, was at first an expression only of desire and determination,[128] before the support of constitutional forces brought the Protestant William of Orange to the throne. The covenanting period had illustrated the corrupt use of covenants to force the unwilling, and the pure use to express deep-felt religious passion.

At the end of the seventeenth century the civil and spiritual realms established an arrangement of their authority that has provided the basis of constitutional law ever since. The sacred and secular kingdoms were geographically divided from each other in 1707 when there occurred the Union of Parliaments between Scotland and England without any corresponding union of churches. Secular government moved from Edinburgh to London, leaving behind the Church's continuing Scottish governance protected by the provisions of the Act of Security of November 1706.[129] The British sovereign remains obliged to preserve Presbyterian Church government in Scotland and the Church enjoyed exemption from civil oversight in matters of worship, doctrine, discipline and Church government. There was no difficulty treating

the Church differently from the temporal authority, and
this was illustrated in the period after 1707, when a single
secular Parliament existed alongside two different established
Churches in England and Scotland.

There have been some unusual ways of understanding
these events. Looking back to 1707 from his post-Disruption
vantage point, James Ferrier, a respected Established Church
moral philosopher, believed that the Scottish Parliament
and the General Assembly formed together the complete
Parliament of Scotland, which accordingly had been
abolished in 1707 only *quoad civilia* but continued *quoad
sacra*.[130] This illustrates the survival beyond the Union of
a One-Kingdom theory, contending for the inseparability
of sacred and secular affairs in national government. If
Ferrier's curious understanding were right, there must have
been a respect in which everyone subject to the jurisdiction
of Parliament was also subject to the jurisdiction of the
General Assembly, which was more true in 1707 (before the
toleration of other denominations) than in 1848 when he
wrote. This is reminiscent of Hooker's theory of the Church
in England, centuries earlier.[131] It is difficult to see how such a
One-Kingdom theory could be compatible with the toleration
of religious pluralism.[132]

More conventional is the view that the authority of the
Scottish Parliament was absorbed entirely by the Westminster
Parliament after 1707, but that the Church of Scotland
retained the tasks of spiritual jurisdiction as a separate body.
However, there were areas in which both jurisdictions had
an interest, and those were the areas with the potential for
dispute within the Church, as people took different views
about the function of civil support of national religion.

This discussion passes over the remainder of the eighteenth
century. It was a significant time in the life of the national
Church, when religious pluralism extended to the Reformed
family of churches because of the various Secession move-
ments of that century. None of those events, however,

had any direct and immediate effect on the constitutional relationship between the Church and the civil magistrate, a relationship undoubtedly tested to breaking point in the 1830s and 1840s.

Conclusion

One hundred and fifty years of Protestant religious development in Scotland brought Church and state to the point of a separation of jurisdictions. Such a separation means and achieves nothing until history has decided what should be the content of each area of authority, and where the boundary should lie between them. That problem has never been fully solved, and remains essentially the challenge of today. It was brought most sharply into political focus in the mid-nineteenth century, and resolved as far as it possibly could have been in the early twentieth; and the next chapter describes those periods and the settlement that was ultimately produced.

Notes

[1] I. B. Cowan, 'Church and Society in Post-Reformation Scotland', *Records of the Scottish Church History Society* xvii (1971), pp. 185–201, p. 198.

[2] D. Stevenson, *The Covenanters: The National Covenant and Scotland* (Edinburgh: Saltire Society, 1988), p. 28.

[3] J. Lumsden, *The Covenants of Scotland* (Paisley: Alexander Gardner, 1914), pp. 21–7.

[4] I. B. Cowan, *The Scottish Reformation: Church and Society in Sixteenth-century Scotland* (London: Weidenfeld & Nicolson, 1982), p. 118.

[5] E. J. Cowan, 'The Making of the National Covenant', in J. Morrill (ed.), *The Scottish National Covenant in Its British Context* (Edinburgh: Edinburgh University Press, 1990), p. 70.

[6] G. Poggi, *The Development of the Modern State: A Sociological Introduction* (London: Hutchinson, 1978), ch. 3, describes the Estates as the form of polity linking the feudal era to the era when kings sought to exercise absolute rule. The Estates were not, however,

a parliamentary form recognisable in a modern liberal democracy and were not designed to facilitate the kind of political project the Lords of the Congregation were pursuing.

7 Hopfl, *Christian Polity of John Calvin*, p. 30.

8 The debate is found in Knox, *John Knox's History of the Reformation*, Book 4.

9 A. E. McGrath, *Reformation Thought: An Introduction* (Oxford: Basil Blackwell, 1999), pp. 5–6.

10 G. Donaldson, *The Scottish Reformation* (Cambridge: Cambridge University Press, 1960), p. 131.

11 The Reformation proceeded at different speeds in different counties and burghs of Scotland. For a detailed account of the method of reform pursued in St Andrews, for example, see L. J. Dunbar, *Reforming the Scottish Church: John Winram (c. 1492–1582) and the Example of Fife* (Aldershot: Ashgate, 2002).

12 Skinner, *Foundations of Modern Political Thought*, p. 230.

13 Ibid., p. 227.

14 J. Knox, *On Rebellion*, ed. R. A. Mason (Cambridge: Cambridge University Press, 1994), *Appellation*, p. 87; D. Shaw, *The General Assemblies of the Church of Scotland 1560–1600: Their Origins and Development* (Edinburgh: Saint Andrew Press, 1964), p. 21.

15 J. Dawson, 'The Two John Knoxes: England, Scotland and the 1558 Tracts', *Journal of Ecclesiastical History* 42 (1991), pp. 555–76, p. 575.

16 Ibid., p. 571.

17 Mason, *Kingship and Commonweal*, pp. 144–5. This invoked the medieval political doctrine of *necessitas*: Shaw, *General Assemblies*, p. 14.

18 Knox, *John Knox's History of the Reformation*, Book II, pp. 202–3.

19 Knox, *On Rebellion*, pp. 128–9; Dawson, 'Two John Knoxes', regards the 1558 tracts as the core of Knox's political writings.

20 Knox, *John Knox's History of the Reformation*, pp. 202–3.

21 *Scots Confession*, in *The Book of Confessions* (Louisville, KY: Office of the General Assembly of the Presbyterian Church [USA], 1999), pp. 9–25, see ch. XIV.

22 *Scots Confession*, ch. XXIV.

23 Shaw, *General Assemblies*, p. 18; T. McCrie, *Life of Andrew Melville* (Edinburgh: Wm Blackwood & Sons, 1856; John Menzies & Co., 1902), pp. 174–5.

[24] Shaw, *General Assemblies*, p. 25.

[25] Dawson, 'Two John Knoxes', p. 568.

[26] *The Booke of the Universall Kirk of Scotland*, ed. Alexander Peterkin (Edinburgh: Edinburgh Printing & Publishing Company, 1839), pp. 25–35.

[27] J. Kirk, *Patterns of Reform: Continuity and Change in the Reformation Kirk* (Edinburgh: T&T Clark, 1989), p. 337.

[28] *The First Book of Discipline*, with introduction and commentary by J. K. Cameron (Edinburgh: Saint Andrew Press, 1972), and recently reprinted by Covenanters Press (Glasgow).

[29] Shaw, *General Assemblies*, p. 20.

[30] McCrie, *Life of Andrew Melville*, p. 155.

[31] A. Herron, *Kirk by Divine Right: Church and State: Peaceful Coexistence*, The Baird Lectures 1985 (Edinburgh: Saint Andrew Press, 1985), ch. 1.

[32] M. F. Graham, *The Uses of Reform: 'Godly Discipline' and Popular Behaviour in Scotland and Beyond, 1560–1610*, Studies in Medieval and Reformation Thought LVIII (Leiden: E. J. Brill, 1996), p. 2.

[33] G. Donaldson, *Scottish Church History* (Edinburgh: Scottish Academic Press, 1985), ch. 11.

[34] S. Mechie, *The Office of Lord High Commissioner* (Edinburgh: Saint Andrew Press, 1957), p. 3.

[35] P. H. Brown, *George Buchanan, Humanist and Reformer: A Biography* (Edinburgh: David Douglas, 1890), pp. 183–95.

[36] Mason, *Kingship and Commonweal*, p. 182.

[37] Burns, *True Law of Kingship*, see ch. 1.

[38] Buchanan, *De Iure Regni Apud Scotos*, p. 32.

[39] Ibid., p. 33.

[40] Ibid., p. 11.

[41] I. D. McFarlane, *Buchanan* (London: Duckworth, 1981), p. 399.

[42] Buchanan, *De Iure Regni Apud Scotos*, p. 63.

[43] Ibid., p. 34.

[44] R. Mason, 'Covenant and Commonweal: The Language of Politics in Reformation Scotland', in N. MacDougall (ed.), *Church, Politics and Society: Scotland 1408–1929* (Edinburgh: John Donald, 1983), see section III of ch. 16.

[45] J. H. Burns, 'The Political Ideas of George Buchanan', *Scottish Historical Review* 30 (1951), pp. 60–8, p. 65.

[46] G. Donaldson, *Scottish Historical Documents* (Glasgow: Neil Wilson, 1997), p. 137.

47 Donaldson, *Scottish Reformation*, p. 164.

48 *The Second Book of Discipline*, with introduction and commentary by J. Kirk (Edinburgh: Saint Andrew Press, 1980), also recently reprinted by Covenanters Press (Edinburgh and Glasgow).

49 A. R. MacDonald, *The Jacobean Kirk 1567–1625: Sovereignty, Polity and Liturgy* (Aldershot: Ashgate, 1998), p. 21.

50 See below for the content of the nation's responsibility to the Church exercised through the model of Establishment. See Burns, *True Law of Kingship*, p. 181.

51 Burns, *True Law of Kingship*, pp. 222–5, discusses the disagreement between James VI and Melville.

52 *Second Book of Discipline*, Book 1.

53 Ibid., Introduction, pp. 1–158, p. 12.

54 Shaw, *General Assemblies*, p. 52.

55 *Second Book of Discipline*, Introduction, p. 12.

56 See Graham, *Uses of Reform*. By the blowing of a horn an individual was made an outlaw, normally at the same time as having been excommunicated by the Church.

57 McGrath, *Reformation Thought*, p. 232.

58 Lord Murray, 'Church and State', *Stair Memorial Encyclopaedia* (London: Butterworth 1987), vol. 5, paras 679–705, paras 684–91.

59 James VI, True Law of Free Monarchies, *and* Basilikon Doron: *A Modernized Edition* (Toronto: Centre for Reformation and Renaissance Studies, 1996). Burns, *True Law of Kingship*, ch. 7, discusses James's political beliefs and writings.

60 James VI, *Basilikon Doron*, ed. James Craigie; 2 vols (Scottish Text Society, 1944 and 1950), vol. 1, p. 49.

61 Before the Reformation, for example, contract law was partly administered by the Church because so much of it was based on oaths, which were regarded as spiritual acts.

62 Act anent the Jurisdiction of the Kirk 1579 ch. 69.

63 J. G. MacGregor, *The Scottish Presbyterian Polity: A Study of Its Origins in the Sixteenth Century* (Edinburgh: Oliver & Boyd, 1926), pp. 119–20.

64 *Booke of the Universall Kirk*, p. 256.

65 MacDonald, *Jacobean Kirk*, p. 26.

66 McCrie, *Andrew Melville*, pp. 84–96.

67 James's biographer (D. H. Willson, *King James VI and I* [London: Jonathan Cape, 1956], p. 70) points out that the only use James made

of the Two-Kingdoms theory was to complain when he believed the Church was too much involved in secular affairs.

[68] J. D. Douglas, *Light in the North: The Story of the Scottish Covenanters* (Exeter: Paternoster Press, 1964), p. 13.

[69] McCrie, *Andrew Melville*, pp. 174–5. This was the oft-quoted occasion when Melville described the king, in the spiritual kingdom, as no more than 'God's sillie vassall'.

[70] K. M. Brown, 'In Search of the Godly Magistrate in Reformation Scotland', *Journal of Ecclesiastical History* 40 (1989), pp. 553–81, p. 581.

[71] A. H. Williamson, *Scottish National Consciousness in the Age of James VI: The Apocalypse, the Union and the Shaping of Scotland's Public Culture* (Edinburgh: John Donald, 1979), pp. 50, 66.

[72] Lumsden, *Covenants of Scotland*, pp. 111–13.

[73] Ratification of the Liberty of the Trew Kirk; of General and Synodal Assemblies; of Presbyteries; of Discipline; all Lawes of Idolatrie are abrogate; of Presentation to Benefices (Act 1592 c. 116).

[74] Donaldson, *Scottish Reformation*, p. 219.

[75] Lord Moncrieff, 'Church and State from the Reformation to 1843', in R. Rainy, Lord Moncrieff and A. Taylor Innes, *Church and State Chiefly in Relation to the Law of Scotland* (Edinburgh: Thomas Nelson, 1878), p. 130.

[76] After the Swiss Reformation theologian Thomas Erastus, who believed that, where there was only one religion in a country, the civil authority had the responsibility of exercising a spiritual jurisdiction.

[77] M. Lee, Jr., 'James VI and the Revival of Episcopacy in Scotland 1596–1600', *Church History* 43 (1974), pp. 50–64.

[78] MacDonald, *Jacobean Kirk*, p. 48.

[79] Donaldson, *Scottish Church History*, p. 235.

[80] T. F. Torrance, *Kingdom and Church: A Study in the Theology of the Reformation* (Edinburgh: Oliver & Boyd, 1956), p. 2.

[81] See E. H. Emerson, 'Calvin and Covenant Theology', *Church History* 25 (1956), pp. 136–42, pp. 137–8; and S. Strehle, *Calvinism, Federalism and Scholasticism: A Study of the Reformed Doctrine of the Covenant* (Bern: Peter Lang, 1988), p. 135.

[82] Kirk, *Patterns of Reform*, p. 72.

[83] M. Steele, 'The "Politick Christian": The Theological Background to the National Covenant', in J. Morrill (ed.), *The Scottish National Covenant in Its British Context* (Edinburgh: Edinburgh University Press, 1990), p. 47.

[84] R. Mitchison, *Lordship to Patronage: Scotland 1603–1745* (London: Edward Arnold, 1983), p. 28.

[85] Cowan, 'Making of the National Covenant', p. 70.

[86] J. B. Torrance, 'Covenant or Contract? A Study of the Theological Background of Worship in Seventeenth-century Scotland', *Scottish Journal of Theology* 23 (1970), pp. 51–76.

[87] J. B. Torrance, 'The Covenant Concept in Scottish Theology and Politics and Its Legacy', *Scottish Journal of Theology* 34 (1981), pp. 225–43, p. 231.

[88] W. R. Foster, *The Church before the Covenants: The Church of Scotland 1596–1638* (Edinburgh: Scottish Academic Press, 1975), pp. 12–19.

[89] P. Donald, *An Uncounselled King: Charles I and the Scottish Troubles, 1637–1641* (Cambridge: Cambridge University Press, 1990), p. 13.

[90] MacDonald, *Jacobean Kirk*, p. 163.

[91] A. I. MacInnes, *Charles I and the Making of the Covenanting Movement 1625–1641* (Edinburgh: John Donald, 1991), p. 147.

[92] G. Donaldson, *The Making of the Scottish Prayer Book* (Edinburgh: Edinburgh University Press, 1954), p. 101.

[93] Douglas, *Light in the North*, p. 46, quoting the Covenanter Gillespie.

[94] D. H. Worthington, 'Anti-Erastian Aspects of Scottish Covenanter Political Thought 1637 to 1647', PhD thesis (University of Akron, 1978), p. 143.

[95] D. Stevenson, *Revolution and Counter-Revolution in Scotland, 1644–1651* (London: Royal Historical Society, 1977), p. 106; J. Buckroyd, *Church and State in Scotland: 1660–1681* (Edinburgh: John Donald, 1980), p. 9.

[96] Stevenson, *Covenanters*, p. 71.

[97] Worthington, 'Anti-Erastian Aspects of Scottish Covenanter Political Thought 1637 to 1647', p. 157.

[98] Ibid., pp. 160–7.

[99] Cowan, 'Making of the National Covenant', p. 78.

[100] D. Reid, *The Party-Coloured Mind: Prose relating to the Conflict of Church and State in Seventeenth Century Scotland* (Edinburgh: Scottish Academic Press, 1982), p. 38.

[101] See Donaldson, *Scottish Church History*, ch. 16.

[102] The texts of the King's Covenant (also known as the 'Negative Confession') may be found in Donaldson, *Scottish Historical*

Documents, pp. 150–3. It forms part of the National Covenant, which is set out in full in Appendix 1 of this book.

[103] Morrill, *Scottish National Covenant*, p. 42.

[104] H. MacPherson, 'The Political Ideas of the Covenanters', *Records of the Scottish Church History Society* i (1926), pp. 224–32, p. 229.

[105] J. Coffey, *Politics, Religion and the British Revolution: The Mind of Samuel Rutherford* (Cambridge: Cambridge University Press, 1997), p. 167.

[106] Donald, *Uncounselled King*, p. 310.

[107] Stevenson, *Revolution and Counter-Revolution*, p. 229.

[108] W. Makey, *The Church of the Covenant 1637–1651: Revolution and Social Change in Scotland* (Edinburgh: John Donald, 1979), p. 29.

[109] Donald, *Uncounselled King*, pp. 105–15.

[110] See the Reports of the 1638 General Assembly, bound together with those of subsequent Assemblies and available in the Scottish Divinity Libraries.

[111] Makey, *Church of the Covenant 1637–1651*, p. 53.

[112] Reid, *Party-Coloured Mind*, pp. 71–8.

[113] Ibid., p. 31.

[114] Douglas, *Light in the North*, p. 54.

[115] J. F. McLear, 'Samuel Rutherford: The Law and the King', in G. L. Hunt (ed.), *Calvinism and the Political Order* (Philadelphia, PA: Westminster Press, 1965), p. 78.

[116] Rutherford, *Lex, Rex*, Question II.

[117] Ibid., Question XIV.

[118] Ibid., Question XL.

[119] Ibid., Questions XXII–XXVI.

[120] Ibid., Question V; I. M. Smart, 'The Political Ideas of the Scottish Covenanters: 1638–88', *History of Political Thought* i (1980), pp. 167–93, p. 169, says people were encouraged to believe they had the right to enforce their direct relationship with God.

[121] W. M. Campbell, 'Samuel Rutherfurd: Propagandist and Exponent of Scottish Presbyterianism: An Exposition of His Position and Influence in the Doctrine and Politics of the Scottish Church', PhD thesis (Edinburgh University, 1937), p. 139.

[122] Campbell, 'Samuel Rutherfurd', p. 150.

[123] A. I. Dunlop, *William Carstares and the Kirk by Law Established*, Chalmers Lectures 1964 (Edinburgh: Saint Andrew Press, 1967), p. 26.

[124] A. F. Mitchell, *The Westminster Assembly: Its History and Standards*, Baird Lecture 1882 (London: James Nisbet, 1883), pp. 321–3.

[125] Torrance, 'Covenant Concept', p. 238.

[126] Lumsden, *Covenants of Scotland*, p. 325.

[127] A. C. Cheyne, *Studies in Scottish Church History* (Edinburgh: T&T Clark, 1999), p. 55.

[128] As were those of the nineteenth and twentieth centuries; and they too led, some years later in each case, to constitutional change.

[129] Donaldson, *Scottish Historical Documents*, p. 275.

[130] J. Ferrier, *Observations on Church and State* (Edinburgh: William Blackwood, 1848), p. 23.

[131] R. Hooker, *Ecclesiastical Polity*, ed. Arthur Pollard (Fyfield, 1990): Hooker believed the citizens of England to be members of the Church of England by virtue of their citizenship, so his theory had conclusions for Church polity that were similar to those of Erastus.

[132] C. G. Brown, 'The Myth of the Established Church of Scotland', in J. S. Kirk (ed.), *The Scottish Churches and the Union Parliament 1707–1999* (Edinburgh: Scottish Church History Society, 2001), p. 52, resists any claim that the 1707 provisions created any kind of state-church.

Chapter 3

The Church of the Disruption Era and a Settlement of Sovereignty

In the centuries following the Scottish Reformation a great legal and political struggle eventually resolved the question of sovereignty over spiritual and temporal affairs. The nation state and the national Church each recognised in the other an authority and power over ... what? What sorts of subjects, and what sorts of cases belonged to the jurisdiction of the Church, and what ones belonged to the secular courts? How were causes to be classified and distributed between the two legal systems? And, when all else truly failed, who would make those decisions?

In modern times, the difficulties have been most vividly visible whenever the dispute has surrounded the ministry of the Church, the professional class whose interests and rights would in any other organisation be secured by civil law, but whose lives and doctrine have always been subject to the scrutiny and regulation of the Church's own laws. The most controversial situation of all emerged in the early nineteenth century, and was eventually to force Church and state to attempt to reach a once-and-for-all accommodation with each other.

The Ten Years' Conflict

The Veto Act of 1834 and the Position of Thomas Chalmers

In the early nineteenth century, there was in the Scottish Church a small but growing movement of what was known as Non-Intrusionism, which was an objection to the intrusion of secular authority into matters pertaining to the call of ministers to charges and, by implied extension, to the Church's whole spiritual jurisdiction. As far as patronage itself was concerned, the situation was complex:[1] it was recognised that the power of patronage was a civil property right that could not simply be expropriated by the Church from the current holders, some of whom were perfectly unobjectionable in the way they exercised it.[2] The social reformer and later leader of the Evangelical Party, Thomas Chalmers, recognised this tension and did not join the calls for the repeal of the 1712 Patronage Act which regulated the system, believing instead that it was possible to introduce the philosophy of non-Intrusion into the existing system.[3] The General Assembly of 1834, influenced by Chalmers and the Evangelical Party, passed a Veto Act giving the congregational electors not only the task of calling the nominated minister but also a new power to veto him against the will of the nominating patron. The opponents of the Veto Act believed it was creating a strange new ecclesiastical process, when adequate safeguards already existed. This, some felt, was an illegitimate encroachment by the General Assembly into the jurisdiction of the civil law, because it gave to the congregation an element of discretion that it had not had when its task was only the symbolic one of signing a formal Call.

In 1838, just before the beginning of the series of legal cases that was to force the issue five years later, Thomas Chalmers gave a celebrated series of lectures in London in which he set out his position.[4] It was certainly not a Melvillian, radically Two-Kingdoms type of theory, because Chalmers clearly thought in terms of a single godly commonwealth in which the Church and state, in separate spheres of jurisdiction, complemented one another for a common end. The political theologian Duncan Forrester observes that this position is closer to the vision of the *First* than of the *Second Book of Discipline*.[5] Chalmers believed that the legislature had to decide a question of religious truth only in choosing which denomination was its partner, but should never have cause to consider questions of theological detail beyond that.[6] From the Church's point of view, Chalmers stated, 'We have no other communication with the State than that of being maintained by it ...'[7] This is the most vivid illustration in Scottish history of the difference between Establishment (which we have seen originated in the Genevan model of the protection and provision of religion) and civil involvement in the governance of the Church. Grasping the fact that Chalmers was not anti-Establishment is the key to avoiding confusion over the remainder of the historical story.

The Pre-Disruption Cases

A series of actions in the civil courts resulted from the Veto Act, and the first of them was the Auchterarder case,[8] which ran from 1838 to 1843. The Earl of Kinnoull, a patron thwarted by the local congregation's veto, resorted to civil law. In the first of a series of judgements, the Court of Session instructed the induction of the presentee, Mr Young, on the basis that statute law had not sanctioned the passing of the Veto Act by the General Assembly. The second case was a claim for damages by the presentee; this constituted a claim that the civil courts, in instructing a spiritual act by the Church courts, created a quantifiable interest for the individual. The third case in the series ordained that the minority of the Presbytery of Auchterarder (those who were willing to obey the earlier civil judgement) could ordain and induct the presentee. This effectively defined the authority of the Church's courts according to their obedience to the civil courts, circumventing any stand-off between the courts of two jurisdictions but treating the Church as if its authority was a privilege conferred, not a power of its own. This last judgement was never fulfilled, as the Disruption occurred just after the final judgement was delivered.

The Auchterarder case involved both spiritual and temporal questions, because the issues of the induction of the appointee and his patrimonial interest were both raised. The case would have been unexceptional if it had dealt only with the patrimonial elements, since there would have been nothing unusual in its being appealed through the civil appeals process.[9] But Dean Hope of the Faculty of Advocates had voted in the 1834 General Assembly against the Veto Act, and he raised in the civil courts the question of its general validity, encouraging a grave act of intrusion in the eyes of the Evangelical party.

Stewart Brown, biographer of Thomas Chalmers,[10] and the late Alex Cheyne, historian of the Disruption,[11] have both made the comment that by appealing the Auchterarder case to the House of Lords the Church inadvertently conceded the very jurisdiction they were seeking to preserve for themselves. Ferrier, the philosopher mentioned in the previous chapter, made a similar comment in respect of the Disruption, which he thought was a tactical blunder in resigning the very authority claimed by its supporters.[12] These commentators are, strictly speaking, right, but one or two distinctions from the discussion so far may help to explain this apparent error by the Church. Since the patrimonial interest of Mr Young was entangled in the larger question of the congregation's veto, it was reasonable for the Church to appeal the civil element of the problem through the civil courts, conscious no doubt that the effect would be that the House of Lords would have to take a view on the whole issue. But the majority of the Presbytery expected the House of Lords to support them, by respecting their independent spiritual jurisdiction and the right of congregational veto. In other words, the Church probably expected the House of Lords to decline jurisdiction on the greater issue of principle and adhere to the decision of the Presbytery. This would not have been a concession of jurisdiction by the Church, but an affirmation of the Church's spiritual authority by the civil court. What mattered to the Presbytery was that the exercise of the veto was a legitimate exercise of legal independence; it mattered less which jurisdiction declared it so. The principle of Establishment involves the state protecting and supporting the Church: there is no reason why the religious freedoms of a congregation, Presbytery or a whole Church may not be protected by that civil jurisdiction. While the Presbytery did not analyse these distinctions, it is probably important to point out that their interest was in religious freedom and the headship of Christ, and they were less concerned how or from whom those freedoms were conveyed. They probably did not regard themselves as having made a mistake; for them the error was on the part of the Lords, with disastrous constitutional implications.

Amid several related legal actions, the most interesting and significant was the *Marnoch* case[13] where the question at issue was substantially the same as in *Auchterarder*. However, in *Marnoch* the majority of the Presbytery of Strathbogie distinguished this case from the others by obeying the judgement of the civil court and disobeying that of the General Assembly.[14] Part of the significance of the 'Reel of Bogie', as this complex series of connected cases was known, lay in the way the Moderate majority was treated immediately after the Disruption. They were suspended from the exercise of their ministries by the Commission of Assembly in 1839 and deposed by the 1841 Assembly. The Established Church General Assembly of 1843 saw no need to take any positive steps to reverse those depositions, because it was simply assumed that the last pre-Disruption Assembly's sentence of deposition had been invalid. The Presbytery had properly obeyed the civil court, there had never been anything requiring punishment, and so the Presbyters were effectively restored by default.[15]

There was a second strand of cases running concurrently with the ones related to the Veto Act. The 1834 Assembly had passed another contentious measure, the Chapels Act, giving seats in Presbytery, Synod and General Assembly to the ministers of new *quoad sacra* parishes that had been created in various parts of the country to meet the demands of population growth and movement. In the *Stewarton* case,[16] the local heritors resorted to civil action to prevent the subdivision of their historical *quoad omnia* parishes into new parishes. The judgement in the case declared the Chapels Act to be illegal because it was the creation of a jurisdiction the Church did not possess; but the effect of the judgement would be to prevent the ministers of those parishes, who helped to provide the strength of non-Intrusionist influence, from sitting in the higher courts of the Church. The Free Church apologist Thomas Brown, in his 1892 *Annals of the Disruption*, remarked that a parish *quoad sacra* had by definition fewer civil law interests than a parish *quoad omnia*, which made the interference of the civil courts even less warranted than in the Veto Act cases.[17] In all these cases, the civil courts asserted a power of direction in matters which the non-Intrusionists believed lay on the Church's side of the temporal-spiritual divide between the two regimes.

The Disruption

Chalmers was the convener of the Church's Non-Intrusion Committee, which was formed to negotiate with the government during the period of these cases. By 1839, he had begun to use the term 'Disruption' to refer to a reluctant severing of the traditional alliance of Church and state, reluctant because it was likely to involve the loss of many of the benefits of Establishment. Compared with the apparent reality of increasing 'Erastian' control by the state, and the strong allegiance of some people to the principle of complete Voluntarism (which would involve no state support for religion at all),[18] Chalmers tried to find a way to avoid both.[19] After the *Strathbogie* judgement of 1840 Chalmers hoped that Parliament would pass an Act which would affirm the Church's sovereign power in passing the Veto Act. In a complex political scene and following a sharp disagreement between Chalmers and Lord Aberdeen (on whose lack of hostility in Parliament the Church had been relying), Chalmers resigned his convenership and the parliamentary measure fell.[20]

An Overture presented to the General Assembly of 1842 by 150 of its members came to be known as the Claim of Right of that year:[21] it set out the objections of the non-Intrusionists to the results of the legal cases, even before the last of the judgements had been delivered. Its legal claim was that the Court of Session had acted with powers that had never been conferred upon it by the British constitution, and its theological conclusion was that the Church's natural powers had been usurped.

When the members of that same party walked out of the General Assembly of 1843 in St Andrew's Church Edinburgh, and proceeded to the Tanfield Hall to begin their own Assembly, they signed and delivered to the government a document of Protest that reiterated their objections. The moment of Disruption was the sending of this Protest, not the walk-out from the Established Church's Assembly, because the point of Disruption related to the problem between Church and state, not the division between the Churches. The outgoing minority instantly created a Church that was certainly not the ecclesiastical arm of the state, nor a beneficiary of Establishment, and so in those senses it was 'free': time would tell what degree of genuine spiritual freedom would be acknowledged in it by the civil law.

The Post-Disruption Division

The Debate Immediately after the Disruption

All the protagonists and interest groups tried to interpret what had just occurred, and very different explanations were offered.[22] At one extreme was the position adopted by Lord President Hope in the Court of Session, and by some who remained in the Establishment after the Disruption: they regarded the Church, in terms of its legal constitution, as the creation of the state and so the judicial activity of the Church as properly subject to the civil courts. Less extreme was the position of some Moderates in the Established Church, who did not regard the Church as the creation of the state. They thought that the Church had an implicit contract with secular power, acquired the position and privilege of being the national Church, and in return accepted the secular definition of its legal powers. The feeling that there was no action required to reinstate the Strathbogie Seven after the Disruption, because they had behaved properly in terms of civil and church law, illustrates these first two positions. Thomas Chalmers occupied a third position, favouring the purest balance of Establishment and spiritual independence: he saw the state as accepting its duty of religious provision for the nation, but trusting the delivery of that to a national Church that enjoyed self-determination and internal controls. The fourth position is that of complete separation without Establishment or any other kind of spiritual relationship between Church and state. Included in this approach would be the admirers of Samuel Rutherford, who regarded the Church as maintaining its own life despite state hostility, along with those who had observed other countries where the prevailing philosophy was 'the notion of states as secular entities and ... of churches as voluntary associations within them'.[23] Most modern discussions of the relationship of Church and state argue for some version of one or other of these last positions.

On the issues of Establishment and spiritual independence the radical 'state-Church' view was shared by Ferrier[24] and Lee (an Established Church theologian). They both started with the premise that the nation has a corporate spiritual identity and responsibility, and from this contention[25] Ferrier derived his belief (alluded to earlier) that Church and state are equally spiritual organs, which was a form of One-Kingdom theory. For Ferrier, the General Assembly was the junior chamber of Parliament, and held its authority as an integral part of the state, not from a (separate) state; hence his distinctive interpretation of the events of 1707, mentioned already. He doubted whether the Assembly held its authority direct from God, arguing that would be a denial of the divine authority shared by the whole Christian community.[26]

Lee, writing in the year after the Disruption,[27] had taken the same train of thought to radical conclusions, questioning by what inherent right the General Assembly claimed to be a supreme legal authority of the Church. He denied the claim of the Church during the Ten Years' Conflict to judge what was the content of the ecclesiastical jurisdiction because he saw no legal basis for its power to allocate sovereignty. His conclusion was that the idea of spiritual independence was an arbitrary principle, since the state was a fully spiritual entity: no such independence for the Church was appropriate or necessary. It should be noted that this philosophy treated the nation as a corporate spiritual entity capable of development and self-definition, but did not accord any self-defining sovereignty to the institutional Church.

Ferrier and Lee are significant because they refused to accept that either the Church or its General Assembly were sovereign bodies for legal purposes. The later history of the Church's constitutional development was premised on the notion of some kind of legal sovereignty in the Church, and it is important to recognise that such a presumption was not self-evident or non-contentious even after the Disruption.

In similar vein but much more moderately, the Establishment constitutionalist William Balfour, writing in opposition to the disestablishment movement in the 1870s, began with the concept of the state as a moral entity, which he derived from the belief that:

> [T]he obligations of religion lie upon men in their relative and social capacity, as well as individually and personally.[28]

He alluded to the tradition of the Covenanters and the idea of the covenanted nation, saying that any presumption that only individuals could subscribe a creed was disloyal to their tradition.[29] Voluntarism, therefore, was tantamount to 'national atheism'.[30] Yet Balfour did not subscribe to a One-Kingdom theory: he was clear that Establishment defined the relationship between two entities, which guaranteed independence in alliance provided that the Church remained true to its credal identity.[31]

The Established Church's thinkers took a view of the maintenance of the Church that involved some elements of authority and control over it, but they were convinced that the Church had the freedoms it needed to fulfil its function. The Free Church's writers believed their practical experience led to a different conclusion, and that the Established Church was fatally compromised in its relation with the state. By the 1870s the Free Church was moving to the Voluntarist position long held by the United Presbyterians (former Seceders): having lost the benefit and protection of Establishment and the financial support of patronage, the Free Church was forced to rely entirely on the voluntary contributions of its members. Voluntarism is the belief that this form of Church funding is desirable in its own right, and it became a strong principle of the United Free Church in due course. The resourcing of the Church was not the most important issue, however. The Disruption had separated the Free Church from the benefits of Establishment, not because of a philosophical objection to the Establishment principle but as the price of the greater principle of ecclesiastical freedom. The same state provided the support of Establishment and the threat to spiritual independence. Chalmers' party reluctantly concluded that to preserve the sovereignty of Christ over his Church it was necessary to break the compact with the state.[32] The loss of the benefits of Establishment was incidental, albeit very important. Cheyne summarised the intensity of their predicament:

> [W]hat kind of freedoms are so essential to a Church that to get them you must risk even the destruction of that Church? A great theme – are there moments in history when you have to kill a Church in order that it may live?[33]

During the debate that followed the Disruption, Free Church writers took the view that the loss of independence was the inevitable price of state support of religion, so their eventual arrival at the Voluntarist position was the natural outcome of their constitutional position. Principal Rainy of the Free Church College taught that the privileges enjoyed by the Church in relationship with the state must always be paid for with the state's right to inspect and remonstrate with the Church's internal decisions.[34] His biographer quotes him as saying, 'our controversy is with the constitution of their Church [i.e. the Established Church], not as fixed by them, but fixed for them'.[35] Taylor Innes, the leading ecclesiastical lawyer of the Free Church, also believed that Establishment was impossible except on a principle of legal subordination.[36] He and other Free Church writers of the late nineteenth century could think of Establishment only in the context of the struggle for spiritual independence, and they regarded the latter as the superior principle. By leaving the Establishment, the Free Church showed that they believed it was necessary to sacrifice privilege to secure freedom: meanwhile the belief of those who stayed behind was that the privilege enjoyed need not necessarily be inconsistent with the freedoms the Church needed. In 1872 the (Voluntarist) United Presbyterian Church issued a statement expressing concern about the civic control of religion, damage to the divine prerogative and the violation of individual conscience. Their point was that only the Church could promote 'a culture of religious willingness' and that the interference by the state could not produce a genuine, individual commitment to faith.[37]

Reviewing these debates in 1917, Harold Laski[38] discussed what he believed were the only two possible ways of regarding the radical separation of the sovereignties of Church and state. One view (essentially the 'Two-Kingdoms' view) regarded the Church as having a sphere of sovereignty uniquely separate from that of the state; and Laski believed that the passage of the Church Patronage (Scotland) Act of 1874 (the abolition of patronage) constituted the state's concession of exactly such a separate jurisdiction to those Presbyterians who had been fighting against the notion of a unitary state. The opposite view (Laski's own, and essentially the 'One-Kingdom' view) stemmed from his belief that sovereignty is essentially indivisible and therefore inalienable; so he concluded that there was no sovereign authority apart from the state, and so no coherent political theory that made sense of this pretended 'alienation' of state sovereignty to the Church.[39]

In Chapter 1 the distinction was made between two understandings of the legal state. One regards it as being a single legal entity and the bearer of the sovereignty of the community; the other regards it as a network of the social geometry of the community, with legal sovereignty lying elsewhere (with the ruler, or the people as a whole, or the individual citizen). The thinkers of the nineteenth century were unwittingly locked into a problematic mindset about spiritual independence because they all presumed the first of these views. They regarded the state as a monolithic authority, and so they struggled to understand how it was possible or meaningful for the Church to have a parallel authority (a 'co-ordinate jurisdiction') that was not just a devolved power conferred by 'the state'. Modern sociology adopts the second way of regarding the two institutions: the Church can fit into society in many more ways than as a legal institution within a legal state. Lindsay Paterson, a sociologist of modern Scotland, describes the level of autonomy achieved by Scotland even though it has not been a self-contained independent state since 1707.[40] A network of distinctive and peculiar institutions has dominated Scotland since the Union (including the Church, the education system and the legal establishment), and these have supplied part of the social framework alongside the British legal state during the last 300 years. Scottish society has had its own social geometry and effective systems of governance without being a nation state; and the Church has been a constituent part of that structure, not a body in competition with it, or subordinate to it, or in a relation of legal contract with it.

> In having retained their church and legal system, the Scots showed a wise appreciation that there are multiple sources of social authority, and that the existence of the nation does not depend on any single one of them.[41]

This provides an understanding of the relationship of Church and society that gets away from the problem of church–state co-ordination altogether; but it was not a thought pattern available to nineteenth-century thinkers at the height of the idea of the nation state. Three hundred years earlier, the Reformation had been driven forwards by the Lords of the Congregation acting subversively against a resistant Crown, and the civil support for the Church did not come from the nation's sovereign power. But, by the Victorian era, the normal understanding of the state had developed to the point that it seemed the natural partner for the Church's national and legal engagement.

The Problems of the Free Church

This kind of thinking had disastrous implications for the legal identity of the Free Church, and it is necessary to mention it briefly because of the significance of the Free Church Case. The courts could not recognise the power of the Free Church to have any element of ecclesiastical jurisdiction, because they believed that this belonged exclusively to the Established Church, granted to it by the state. A trust-law view of the situation regarded the Free Church as a body defined entirely by its original contractual basis (principally the Claim of Right and the papers of the 1843 Disruption Assembly, the latter of which had been recorded at the very beginning of all the Presbytery minute books throughout the Free Church). It was, in law, a denomination incapable of self-definition or development because it was entirely subject to the direction of the civil courts. This mattered when there was a patrimonial dispute to be settled in the civil courts, which arose in 1900 when the United Presbyterians and the Free Church came to unite.

To sum up the case of *Bannatyne* v. *Overtoun*[42] in a couple of sentences: a minority of the Free Church stayed out of the Union and successfully claimed the property of the new Church, essentially arguing that only they (the minority) adhered to the original trust purposes of the Free Church begun in 1843. They persuaded the House of Lords that the Free Church could not change its fundamental principles and keep its identity, and that this was precisely what the majority was attempting to do by uniting with the United Presbyterians: the case was not about the nature of the union, but about the original and current nature of the Free Church. The United Free Church could not accept this 'trust-deed' view, believing the Church was always living and progressing without permanently binding formularies.[43]

After the case was over and the minority of the Free Church had won, their own arguments left them prevented from changing and constitutionally bound to conservatism from then on. The United Free Church was left to find legislative means to overcome the practical effects of its loss, but at least maintained its power of spiritual and legal development and change. The lesson for the Established Church, watching the case unfold, was that without an adequate degree of spiritual independence and power of self-determination a Church might forfeit its original corporate identity in the eyes of the civil law. That realisation would inform both the Church of Scotland and the United Free Church in the discussions of the following years.

Father Noel Figgis, whose deep fear of Presbyterian abuse of church–state relations was quoted in Chapter 1, nevertheless sympathised with the problem, and identified the absolute necessity for a Church of having the possibility of growth and change. Otherwise every Church must be regarded either as the creature of the state, or examined on the trust-deed view used in *Bannatyne* v. *Overtoun*. Such a body would be 'enslaved to the dead',[44] unable to have any supernatural life beyond that of its individual members; and this, Figgis concluded, denied the reality of the Church's meaningful social existence. It was left to the churchmen of the early twentieth century to acknowledge doctrinal freedom by legislation, to allow space for the independent spiritual jurisdiction and to find a new intellectual basis for the spiritual independence from the civil magistrate. The model they opted for was one that defended spiritual freedom by asserting ecclesiastical sovereignty, that recovered a form of Two-Kingdoms thinking by devising virtually a Two-States model.

The Settlement of the Church's Jurisdiction
1907–21

Following the Free Church case in 1904, both the Established Church and the United Free Church benefited from legislation to assert their powers of theological self-determination. In 1905 there was passed in Parliament the Churches (Scotland) Act, which was primarily designed to unscramble the property mess left by the 1904 decision but also gave statutory recognition of the Established Church General Assembly's powers to change the Formula subscribed at ordinations. In 1906 the United Free Church General Assembly passed an Act anent Spiritual Independence, claiming independent jurisdiction over the four traditional areas of spiritual life: worship, government, doctrine and discipline.

By these steps the Churches that were eventually to unite in 1929 took steps towards self-determination and drew a new boundary between the ecclesiastical and civil orders. Within the Reformed understanding of the relationship between the Church and the civil magistrate, a distinction was clarified and an area of exclusion was marked. The claim to a power of self-determination outwith the framework of civil Establishment implied that the Church enjoyed status as a legal person, at least for spiritual purposes. Unquestioned by politicians and untested by case law, the main weakness of this assertion of legal personality was never pressed. Who or what exactly was the legal personality that had these rights of spiritual determination with no involvement from any other institution? As the Churches acted then as now mainly through smaller agencies or courts, how could it be the denomination as a whole? Was it the General Assembly of each denomination, which met for ten days each year and by occasional commissions between? These questions were and are important:[45] it is rarely the case that the Church as a whole is the relevant party; but it is more likely to be an Assembly committee, a Presbytery or a Kirk Session. Scottish civil society did not have a single source of authority and influence, but rather a network of interrelated social institutions: one might say that the Church, equally, is a complex organism whose legal competence is not located in a single authority. The contracting parties to the union negotiations set out with important questions of legal identity unasked and unanswered, but were at least armed with the resources to engage constructively with each other.

Searching for a Constitutional Settlement of the Church of Scotland

The initiative for union began in 1907, when Archibald Scott, minister of St George's Edinburgh, raised the question of inter-Church discussions at the Established Church's Presbytery of Edinburgh.[46] The United Free Church Assembly of the following year responded to this approach; they advanced the timetabling of their Church and State Committee's debate before the Established Church had held their equivalent debate, in order to call for the disestablishment and disendowment of the Church of Scotland.[47] Again, when the Church of Scotland formally asked in 1908 for discussion with the United Free Church, the latter replied the following year with a request for unrestricted conference on union.[48] At each stage the United Free Church had taken the initiative in challenging the Church of Scotland to go further on the problem of Establishment that stood in the way of the reunion of the two.

Each Church set up a 100-strong committee to conduct the negotiations, and the leading officials of the 'Hundreds' were to be the key historical figures in the long process of reunion. Most influential of all were the two clerks. The Church of

Scotland appointed John White, who was the minister of the Barony Church in Glasgow: he was, in due course, to provide solutions to the problems relating to Article I of the Articles Declaratory (on doctrine) and to the problems of disendowment during the 1920s. The United Free Church's secretary was an academic, Professor Alexander Martin of New College. The most important figure in relation to the legal and constitutional problems was Christopher Johnston, the Church of Scotland's Procurator who became Lord Sands in 1917. The complex story of the process leading towards reunion, and the human stories of these men of leadership, may be found in Douglas Murray's *Rebuilding the Kirk: Presbyterian Reunion in Scotland 1909–1929*.[49] The story of the process falls into three main phases: (1) overcoming the impasse on the question of Establishment (this was addressed in the years before the First World War); (2) agreeing the wording and status of the statement of faith in the Church of Scotland's Articles, which followed an internal debate between the high and low Church parties in that Church (around the end of the War); and (3) effecting the disestablishment and, especially, the disendowment of the national Church before union could proceed (after the 1921 Act). The first of these three, and part of the third, are the subject matter of the present discussion.

We have seen that Establishment does not necessarily equate with lack of independent jurisdiction, but in the pre-union negotiations the two had to be disentangled in order to guarantee the Church's spiritual freedom. Establishment involved the use of the power of the civil order to promote or defend Presbyterian government in the national Church.[50] The nineteenth-century arguments had always centred on the source of the Established status, and whether or not the state conveyed it to the national Church. Impasse seemed inescapable between the negotiating parties, because both Churches were committed to the Reformed idea of the religious duty of the civil magistrate, but the United Free

Church retained the fear of lack of spiritual independence that their constituent denominations had complained of in the nineteenth century. So any model that implied the continuing subordination of the Church to the state was unacceptable, but any transfer of those powers from the state to the Church, even irrevocably, still implied that the powers had originally belonged to the state, which was philosophically offensive. The Established Church side could imagine change coming only through legislative authorisation, but the United Free Church side wanted to achieve it through autonomous action: each for reasons of ecclesiological principle. What was needed was the *removal* of the state's control of the Church of Scotland, but without any implication of the *conveyance* by the state of the Church's power, all the while retaining some spiritual function in the civil magistrate short of sovereign authority over the Church.[51]

At the 1911 Assembly of the Church of Scotland John White articulated the idea that the powers at issue could not have been originally conferred by Parliament on the Church, since they were inherent within the Church, and all that the state could possibly give was protection of them.[52] They were not new rights, but they had effectively been submerged throughout the long period since the superiority of Church over state had been lost, and had been removed altogether by the decisions in the pre-Disruption cases.[53] This argument was another step in distinguishing the Church as a self-contained constitutional body, and it was therefore another stage in imputing to the Church characteristics of legal personhood. By November 1912, Professor Martin of the United Free committee recognised that progress had been made away from the old Established Church position that saw the Church as an institution of the state.[54]

This conceptual trick was bolstered by a linguistic device offered by Christopher Johnston.[55] He distinguished two meanings of the word 'grant', one expressing the sense of conveyance or transfer, the other expressing the sense of acknowledging a truth or proposition (as when one speaker agrees with the other by saying 'I'll grant you that'). He suggested that the latter meaning was intended in the Act of 1567 recognising the Scottish Reformation. That Act responded to a petition of the General Assembly craving 'that too this our Kirk be grantit and by the present parliament conformit sic freedom, privilege, jurisdiction and authority as justly appertain to the true Kirk and immaculate spouse of Jesus Christ'.[56] He suggested that the function of Parliament in the process that was now unfolding was to grant the Church of Scotland her powers in the latter sense only, that is, to acknowledge that they were already properly the Church's. This implicitly meant that the civil power was to concede all that the non-Intrusionists had claimed in the pre-Disruption cases and all that had been argued over in the lengthy and fruitless attempts in the late nineteenth century to dismantle Church Establishment legislatively. At a stroke, the ever-mutating theories of one or two kingdoms was replaced by what can only be described as an embryonic theory of Two States. The Church implicitly abandoned its claim to any of the temporal elements of the jurisdiction of the civil magistrate, claimed only what inherently belonged to its own, spiritual nature, and finally declined those elements of its established past that relied on the substantive, 'efficient' elements of Establishment to empower the Church's authority. Instead, the Church acquired a self-understanding as an entirely independent, sufficient authority in the wholly spiritual matters of doctrine, worship, etc.: it was thinking of itself as a separate but equal authority alongside the nation state, as if it were a little state in its own small dominion.[57]

It is important to recognise the difference between the constitutional position of the Church of Scotland and that of other denominations.[58] In terms of the 1921 Act, the Church of Scotland has the power to make determination of its doctrines and purposes from time to time; in other words, it has the power of a developing self-determination within its constitution. So if it properly decides to make a conscious shift in its doctrinal position (as the General Assembly did in Act V 1986, when it dissociated itself from parts of the Westminster Confession of Faith) it does not lose essential continuity with its own constitution, and so does not risk civil action by a dissenting minority. Other Churches (with the possible exception of the small United Free Church, whose roots lie in the United Free history from 1900 to 1929 just described) have only the precedent set by the *Overtoun* case (the 'Free Church case'), which was decided on the basis of civil trust law. The effect is that where there is an internal dispute with a patrimonial claim or interest the courts must determine whether either party has strayed beyond the purposes of the foundational documents or events that determine in law what may be said to be the purpose of the organisation. They will then award the property of the organisation to the side that has remained within the purpose that has been so determined by the court. Most religious organisations do not have anywhere in their constitutional documents the power to change, because most religious organisations at the time of their first institution have a high view of a single revelation, and that makes doctrinal change anathema. A wily group could so constitute themselves in law as to provide such power of change within their trust purposes (thus arranging for themselves substantially the benefits of the 1921 Act), but it would be a most unlikely event for reasons of theological conservatism. It is for the Church of Scotland under the 1921 settlement to adjust from time to time its theological self-understanding; and it differs from most other Presbyterian Churches in Scotland in this respect. To this extent, the Church of Scotland was to exercise a 'sovereignty' that was quite different from the authority of the other denominations.

The clever thinking of White and Johnston was used in the preparation of a Memorandum, which comprised a collection of propositions and an early draft preamble for the Bill that was to become the Church of Scotland Act 1921. The Memorandum was presented successfully to both Churches' Assemblies in 1912, and the resolution of the constitutional hurdle was within sight.[59] Most of the remaining years before 1921 were spent wrestling over the doctrinal issues that were eventually to be expressed in Article I, which does not concern this study.

The Articles Declaratory

The 1921 settlement of the Church of Scotland's constitution made possible the negotiation of the 1929 union with the United Free Church. The settlement was expressed in the Articles Declaratory[60] prepared by the Established Church between 1914 and 1919 in a number of drafts and it was effected by the very brief Church of Scotland Act 1921 to which the Articles were appended. It was regarded by historians of the period as a triumph.

> A charter of spiritual freedom had been won which seemed to meet all requirements. Parliament with hearty goodwill loosened its grip on the Church, and agreed to undo the consequences of its old Erastian policy.[61]

The constitutional independence of the Church is articulated in the Fourth and Sixth Articles. In the Fourth Article the Church claims powers of legislation and adjudication in the areas of worship, government, doctrine and discipline (the areas articulated in the 1906 United Free Church Act), powers that are derived directly from Christ, and the Church declares her spiritual independence from the civil magistrate. In the Sixth Article the civil magistrate is deemed to have a separate spiritual duty under God, which does not touch the sphere of the Church's life except in the promotion of her welfare, and the Article retains for both parties the continuing right and responsibility of reviewing its implications.

The cumulative effect of the Articles, the Act and all that led to their formation was a move in the direction of the theory that emphasises the separation of Church and state as much as their relation. The problem of spiritual freedom had been answered by placing the Church of Scotland in a new constitutional situation, by recovering the Melvillian version of the theory of separate kingdoms,[62] expressing it in the modern, state-like language of spheres and realms, and leaving the legal implications of it to unfold in due course. The chief of those implications was the recognition that the Act represented the first breach in the sovereignty of the United Kingdom Parliament.[63] Professor Sir Neil MacCormick, the legal philosopher and Nationalist politician, described the settlement as a strong doctrine of divided sovereignty, and not one that allows that the Church is ultimately subject to state sovereignty.[64] He concluded that this is a perfectly legitimate view of the kind of sovereignty that exists in federal systems of rule, and implied that the British constitution became federal to this limited extent even as early as 1921.[65] MacCormick applauded this outcome, but the overall argument of this book questions its legitimacy in a spiritual organisation that is the Body of Christ.

Twentieth-century Scottish Church history has not been extensively studied, compared with the many treatments that exist of the seventeenth and nineteenth centuries in particular; and those studies that do exist include sociological works that trace the decline of the Church especially over the last forty years of the twentieth century.[66] It would be easy therefore to imagine that any decline in the efficacy of the 1921 settlement was owing only to factors such as secularisation or religious pluralism; but the aim of this study is to approach the era from a legal, not sociological perspective. Using only the latter would miss the inherent weaknesses of the Act and Articles, which meant from the outset that the settlement would be unable to withstand legal pressures against it from future case law and constitutional change.

The Legacy of the Settlement

Problems inherent in the Church of Scotland Act 1921

The 1921 Act declared the lawfulness of the Articles, dealing with the corpus of existing civil legislation as follows:

> [N]o limitation of the liberty, rights, and powers in matters spiritual therein set forth shall be derived from any statute or law affecting the Church of Scotland in matters spiritual at present in force, it being hereby declared that in all questions of construction the Declaratory Articles shall prevail, and that all such statutes and laws shall be construed in conformity therewith and in subordination thereto, and all such statutes and laws in so far as they are inconsistent with the Declaratory Articles are hereby repealed and declared to be of no effect.[67]

There are two problems inherent in the text of the Act. First, it contains no exhaustive list of the repeals to which it refers. Second, it gave to the Church the sole right to interpret the Articles and, as Johnston (now elevated to the bench as Lord Sands) pointed out, a genuine right of interpretation must include the right to reach conclusions different from those of the civil courts.[68]

The main problem with the 1921 Act is interpretative: lack of specification of Acts in the repeals section leaves open to judicial interpretation or academic speculation the extent of the survival of pre-1921 legislation. The following Acts arguably survive in whole or in part, so far as they are consistent with the 1921 Act:[69] the Act anent the Abolishing of the Pape, and his usurped Authoritie 1567 c. 2 (being the post-Marian re-enactment of the Act of 1560); the Act Ratifying the Presbyterian Order of the Church 1592 c. 116; the Claim of Right of 1689 c. 28; and the Act Ratifying the Confession of Faith, and Settling the Presbyterian Church Government 1690 c. 5, which the historian A. I. Dunlop described as 'Erastian, but necessarily so in the age it was passed'.[70] Explicitly constitutional provisions affecting the nature of the monarchy include the Act of Settlement 1700 c. 2 and the Union Agreement of 1707 (which includes the Act for Securing the Protestant Religion and Presbyterian Church Government).

However, problems have been identified with the phenomenon of lack of specification of unrepealed legislation. The constitutional lawyer Francis Lyall refers with approval to the judgement of the Lord Ordinary, Lord Pitman, in the case of *Ballantyne and Others* v. *Presbytery of Wigtown and Others*[71] (see below), that it was a pity that the drafters of the Act had not specified which old Acts, or parts of them, should be repealed. Lyall says:

> To base such repeal simply on inconsistency with what expressly purports to be a declaratory Act may have been politically useful, but it results in legal uncertainty.[72]

The legal uncertainties are several. The judge Lord Murray,[73] for example, feared that the Westminster Confession was enshrined in the 1707 Act but that there was no power in the 1921 settlement to replace it and so the Church was trapped inside one particular doctrinal position. As it happened, a more flexible view was taken of the status of the Confession during the confessional controversy of the 1970s, when the Church came close to replacing its subordinate standard of doctrine with a modern statement of faith.[74] However, such removal of a doctrinal standard would render the relevant parts of the 1707 Act incompatible with the Articles and thus automatically obsolete in terms of the

1921 Act. Where would that leave the 1707 provision? The problem, then, is not that the Church lacks the freedom of doctrinal development – the Articles Declaratory guarantee it – but rather that if the Church exercises those powers of development it may bring its standards into conflict with ancient statutes that have not clearly been repealed. The implication of the 1921 Act's repeal provision is that those ancient civil laws would have to be regarded as having been repealed, quite unintentionally, by actions of some future General Assembly, long, long after 1921. It must be unparalleled in the British constitution (and, frankly, inconceivable in practice) that an institution other than Parliament could have this power, by its internal actions, to alter the corpus of extant parliamentary legislation from time to time. Yet that is what the 1921 Act appears to presume. Lord Murray was forced believed that the solution to this mess was that the General Assembly would have to rely on Parliament to adjust the civil law in the event that the Church were to do anything inconsistent with the recognised civil law – an interpretation that necessarily ran counter to the letter and spirit of the Act. If Murray was right, what would happen if Parliament declined or failed to make the necessary adjustment? The problem of self-development, key to the 1904 Free Church case, emerges here in quite a different form in respect of the post-Union Church.

The obverse of this problem is the question of what would happen to these ecclesiastical provisions of the civil law in the event of the repeal of the 1921 Act, rather an important question in a book considering the fundamental merits of the Act. According to legislative convention, repeals are not reversed by the repeal of the repealing measure itself, because if they were there would be a nightmarish thread to be followed, working out which former measures must spring back into life. To use Lord Murray's example of the Westminster Confession: if the 1921 Act were repealed first, and thereafter the General Assembly sought to replace its current subordinate standard in the second Article with a modern statement of faith, the Assembly could utilise the provisions of Article VIII to amend Article II. But without the provisions of the 1921 Act, the 1690 and 1707 Acts would not consequently be repealed to that new extent, and it would be more difficult in the absence of the 1921 Act to seek the amendment of the now-inconsistent civil legislation. It is confusing enough to imagine the General Assembly inadvertently repealing civil laws by changing its standards, as envisaged in the previous paragraph. In the absence of the 1921 provisions, however, the Church would be dependent on Parliament to remove the resulting anomaly, because the problem would be caused not by the enactment of the more modern legislation but by the non-repeal of the more ancient.

If the 1921 settlement were to be dismantled, by what authority would the privileges of the Church that were declared by that legislation be safeguarded? An example should illustrate this problem. In the next chapter there appears a discussion of the *Ballantyne* case, but one aspect of it may be anticipated here. The debate in that case concerned the 1874 Act of Parliament abolishing patronage, and its significance after 1929. The right of a congregation to call a minister without imposition by a patron was regulated by the Church's courts with the passing of the 1921 Act, but the declaration of the congregation's rights lay in the Act, the civil law, and were never translated into the body of Church law. If the 1921 settlement were to be repealed or become obsolete, would the extant portions of the 1874 Act be once again the responsibility of the civil authority to implement? (Would the secular authority be remotely interested in fulfilling such a spiritual duty?)

One obvious circumstance in which such a profound constitutional change might be anticipated would be the alteration of the Church's structure through a process of further union with a non-Presbyterian Church. In terms of this line of argumentation, to have the necessary effect in civil law, the Church need do nothing more than make the necessary alterations to the Articles Declaratory, especially the Second (Presbyterianism was deliberately left out of the first Article, which is more problematic to change).[75] The present argument implies that the effect would be the automatic repeal of the Act of Settlement by the removal of its main provision, the guarantee of Presbyterian Church government. While much political debate surrounds the desirability of repealing that Act on grounds of religious and anti-discriminatory sensitivity, it would appear that future denominational union may, bizarrely, have the same effect without the assistance of Parliament.[76]

These arguments demonstrate that the Melvillian ideal of separate Church and state jurisdictions apparently achieved in 1921 falls short of the actuality. The legislative basis of the Church of Scotland's constitution is not simply the 1921 Act, but includes many civilian Acts. The extent of these is unclear and the status of them compromised by a repeal provision so peculiar and flexible that, far from separating Church and state in Scotland, it gave the power to the Church, even unwittingly, to compromise constitutional law. And yet, conversely, the whole weight of spiritual independence hangs on the fragile thread of a single Act of Parliament, the only place where the underlying theological principle is authoritatively articulated, while the legislative machinery of civil control remains only disabled by qualification but not eradicated by proper repeal. All the imagined developments used above as illustrations would clearly have bizarre and chaotic implications. Who knows how far away is a real legal development with just such implications?

The Problem of Establishment

A further objection to the state of civil law repeal came from the United Free Church minority led by James Barr, who complained that the ancient statutes appeared to have been repealed to the extent necessary to render them consistent with the Articles, but were not repealed to the extent necessary to remove the privileged and Established nature of the Church.[77]

> For many Established churchmen, untying the knot with the state weakened the presbyterian character of Scotland, and the various measures enacted by parliament were carefully formulated to maintain the appearance of a church still protected by the state.[78]

The forms of covenant between Church and state described in Chapter 2 were one way of ensuring that national allegiance to the Christian faith took the form of the promotion and defence of Presbyterian Church government. Establishment in the Reformed sense is simply one way of achieving that promotion, by use of the resources of the nation, legal, cultural and/or financial. As the Union approached, one of the partners still had the burden of Establishment to shed.

Within the Church of Scotland and Gladstone's Liberal Party there had been a long-running debate about disestablishing the Church, but without success. In 1880, an attempt by pro-disestablishment activists to dominate the organisation of that party failed. In 1882, a Bill (known from the identity of its proposer as the Peddie Bill) to effect secularisation of Church revenue and separation of Church and state did not make it as far as the House of Commons. It was recognised by people like the young John White that this measure would have deprived the Church of revenues and the benefits of endowments, and there was significant Established Church opposition to it.[79] In 1886, a different kind of Bill (Finlay's Bill) was intended to facilitate the return of the Free Church to the Establishment, and was based on the 1842 Claim of Right. According to Christopher Johnston, the Established Church grudgingly tolerated it because it declared a spiritual independence they had never doubted sufficiently existed; but it was unacceptable to the Free Church because it did nothing about Establishment, so the freedoms it declared appeared to them to be conferred on the Church by the state.[80] Gladstone remained neutral in the debate, waiting to see what the majority opinion was on the issue, and for this Johnston criticised him for his apparent lack of decisiveness.[81] The matter was finally dropped by Parliament in 1895, to be dealt with in quite a different way by the Church itself.

As early as the 1890s Professor Flint, an Established Church academic delivering a public lecture, suggested the idea of removing Establishment as it was an obstacle to Church union.[82] He pointed out that Establishment was not itself a necessary principle, but one form of the application of the wider principle of national allegiance.[83] William Mair, the principal jurisprudential thinker of the Church of Scotland, wrote of Establishment at the time of the Free Church case and said it was 'a term of convenience and may well be dropped'.[84] Looking back on the process and defending it in an article written in 1920, Johnston (now Lord Sands) again offered a linguistic trick. He suggested that the questions facing the negotiating Churches had been translated out of the language of 'Establishment' and into a vocabulary that properly reflected the recent changes to the Church's constitutional position. The new reality of the Church's freedom and territorial responsibility became unambiguous, he believed, but the language used would reassure those who feared continued control by the state.[85] Opponents of Church union, including James Barr of the United Free Church minority, noticed that the process of translation could work in two directions, and after 1921 translated back into the language of Establishment what had been achieved using the more diplomatic, neutral terminology of the negotiations. On the basis of that exercise, the United Free minority complained that the post-settlement Church of Scotland was not disestablished after all. The practice of translating the reality of Establishment out of the traditional language used of it, in order to avoid alarming the United Free negotiators,[86] did not alter the fact of its existence. The point of this part of the discussion is that the process of disestablishment was just as unclear as the process of determining the independent jurisdiction and spiritual independence of the Church, because parts of the settlement could be translated quite readily back into the language of Establishment from which they had so carefully been translated ten years before.

James Barr spotted examples. For instance, of the capitalisation of endowments during the process of preparation for union, he said:

> The public resources of the State are to be turned over permanently to the private possession of the Church. This is not disendowment; it is capitalised, complete, final, and irretrievable endowment. It is not a stroke for national justice; it is a raid on national funds.[87]

This is not a discussion of the accuracy or otherwise of Barr's underlying premise that the funds belonged to the state and should be used for properly national purposes; rather Barr is quoted to show that the contentious concept of a continuing Establishment haunted the debates of pre-union years.

The Remnant of Establishment

Today there is an occasional debate over the question of whether Scotland still has an Established Church. Those who assume that a national Church must be an 'established' Church make a mistake built on two errors: (1) the failure to separate properly the issues of Establishment and spiritual independence, a distinction that both sides of the debate after the Disruption seemed to grasp without difficulty; and (2) the failure to observe what Establishment originally meant in the Scottish context.

For example, in an article addressing the Establishment question,[88] the constitutional lawyer Colin Munro looks in vain to the 1707 settlement for a definition of Establishment, and resorts to what he describes[89] as the ordinary meaning of the word. He proceeds to presume that Establishment involves the granting of a different legal status to one Church compared with others, which makes no sense when looking at the immediate post-Reformation context of monolithic Protestantism – an age of state support but no 'other' religions to compare. There is no need for this: the Calvinist theology of the post-Reformation Scottish Church made quite clear what was the task of the civil magistrate in the Genevan model, as observed in the previous chapter. Beginning with that definition, it is clear that Scottish establishment is about support, not privilege or control or state interference. Worst of all, Munro concludes that Establishment must still exist because, having identified the Church of Scotland immediately before 1921 as Established, he observes that the 1921 Act is clearly not a 'disestablishing' measure, and concludes that Establishment must therefore have survived to date. He is looking at the wrong Act. A proper conceptual distinction between Establishment and state control of the Church would recognise that the 1921 Act dealt with the latter, while most of the elements of civil support and provision of religion were removed either by the Church Patronage (Scotland) Act 1874 or by the Church of Scotland (Property and Endowments) Act 1925. There was a massive exercise of disestablishment in Scotland, but it was not the function of the 1921 Act; and those who misunderstand the Church of Scotland in this way tend to be examining the wrong evidence.

Now more than eighty years later, several elements of Establishment might be detected as continuing remnants from the older constitutional situation.[90] The Acts of

Parliament discussed earlier in this chapter are clearly problematic and are still the subjects of much debate. The other highly visible elements that remain of the old order are what Professor James Mackey called the ceremonial, rather than the substantial Establishment,[91] in an echo of Bagehot's famous distinction between the dignified and efficient parts of the state.

The Lord High Commissioner is a reminder of the age when the Establishment of the Church of Scotland made it vulnerable to the control and interference of the Crown. Today he or she does not contribute to debate *qua* Lord High Commissioner, does not appear on the floor of its chamber in that capacity, does not open or close the Assembly and does not convey the opinions of the Crown on the affairs of the Church. But he or she is part of the royal household, and in Britain's formal Order of Precedence the current Moderator also holds a very high rank. It was another example spotted by Barr of the state's support for the machinery of the Church's life, that the expenses of the Lord High Commissioner to the General Assembly were met from the Consolidated Fund of the United Kingdom.[92]

It is the monarchy, the pinnacle of the ceremonial element of the British constitution, that bears the most obvious element of the substantial or efficient support by the state for the Church and its government.

I, Elizabeth the Second by the Grace of God of Great Britain, Ireland, and the British Dominions beyond the Seas Queen, Defender of the Faith, do faithfully promise and swear that I shall inviolably maintain and preserve the Settlement of the true Protestant Religion as established by the Laws made in Scotland in prosecution of the Claim of Right and particularly by an Act for securing the Protestant Religion and Presbyterian Church Government and by the Acts passed in the Parliament of both Kingdoms for the Union of the two Kingdoms, together with the Government, Worship, Rights and Privileges of the Church of Scotland. So help me God.[93]

The current situation is this: the monarch has taken this oath to implement throughout her reign the terms of the Acts referred to in its text, and this pledge she renews each year in writing or in person to the General Assembly. Meanwhile the Union settlement is the subject of constitutional debate, because the Act of Settlement precludes a Roman Catholic (but not a member of any other religion or of none) from becoming or marrying the monarch. In the spirit of anti-discrimination and anti-sectarianism that informs the debate, the question exists whether the Act of Security and the Oath above should be abandoned. Once again, the Church of Scotland's constitutional position is not entirely clear. There exists the lifelong oath taken more than fifty times now by the current monarch, the Act upon which it is based, the inherent rights and privileges recognised by Parliament upon which the Act is based and, arguably, the claims of the Church itself to its own inherent rights. Is the removal of one of those elements, even the Act, fatal to any or all of the others? If, for example, the Act were repealed in the lifetime of the present Queen, what would become of the status of her oath? Is she obliged to resist any developments in the ecumenical movement that might be deemed to constitute a departure from the form of Presbyterian Church government intended by the oath? Would such an obligation in her survive the repeal of the Act? If the Act is based on inherent rights and privileges (granted originally by Christ, not the secular sovereign) what becomes of them if the Act is repealed? (The same question pertains to the repeal of the 1921 Act.) Does the Church have to face the probability that an increasingly secular society has simply lost its recognition of these inherent privileges? Are the Crown Rights of the Redeemer no longer presumed by the legal and political establishment of Britain and Scotland? The Reformation itself exemplifies the ability of the secular order to realign its religious allegiance and relocate the perceived institutional authority of Christ. Could it happen again in a new way? And what, if all else fails, is the responsibility of the Church itself, the Body of Christ, to assert those rights if it still believes they exist? These questions demonstrate, in yet another way, that the apparently neat settlement of 1921 raises even more questions than it answered, and has survived only because there has been so little practical testing of the implications in politics, legislation or case law.

Is the Church of Scotland established? Opinions vary, because some commentators fail to understand that the question is different from the same question asked in England, some are influenced by the remnants that remain, and others are convinced that the Church is truly, spiritually free. Perhaps it is fairest to conclude that there are building materials of the Establishment lying about undestroyed, but none that seriously impinges on the Church's legal life except when major constitutional change is discussed, and then ancient legal history – especially the 1707 Union – comes curiously to life again. The fragments of Establishment do not add up to the civil provision of religion that Calvin would have recognised: so in *Reformed* terms Scotland does not now have the Establishment of religion, whatever a less theologically-informed legal view might conclude.

Spiritual Independence and Jurisdictional Independence

The reunion of the fragments of the Church was brought about by the recognition, at last, of the inherent spiritual freedoms of Christ's Church. Since the Church had an existing legal structure, complete with powers of legislature, executive and judiciary, the spiritual freedom was presumed to be guaranteed by the legal machinery of the Church, a jurisdiction separate from, but co-ordinated with the remainder of the legal machinery of the state. And since the sceptics around the process could not be persuaded that spiritual freedom was perfectly compatible with Establishment of religion, the latter had to be sacrificed, though the argument of this chapter has been that it was dismantled through force of political circumstance, not the demands of logic.

The account so far has been careful thus to distinguish, as Chalmers did, the Establishment of the Church of Scotland from the question of the location of spiritual jurisdiction. This chapter has indicated another important distinction. Mair's *Digest*, the principal nineteenth-century text book on Church law, distinguishes the independent spiritual jurisdiction of the Church from its spiritual independence[94] (the fourth Article Declaratory mixes them up together). The Church is *spiritually independent* of the state if there is a recognised substantive area of its spiritual affairs that is not regulated by civil law. The Church has an *independent spiritual jurisdiction*, in contrast, if it exercises a juridical authority from which there is procedurally no appeal to civil law. Normally these two areas are coterminous, but not always. In 2007 civil legislation was introduced to outlaw discrimination on grounds of sexual orientation in the provision of goods and services (and this will be discussed at greater length in the next chapter). Some religious people would prefer to have complete spiritual freedom to act according to religious belief. They wish only to be exempt from the civil law; they do not look for Church legislation on the matter. Here is a call for spiritual independence, but it has nothing to do with any independent spiritual jurisdiction. The Church's jurisdiction is a different matter: this refers to the situation where the civil law leaves to the Church's regulation spiritual matters and those secular matters that are ancillary to the spiritual ones.[95] In such an instance the matter need not be inherently part of the Church's area of spiritual independence, but may be allowed to fall into its jurisdiction. The most obvious current example, described in detail in the next chapter, is the extent to which civil government allows the Church's authorities to regulate the terms and conditions of ministers, even including those provisions that are not peculiarly sacred or spiritual. The most fundamental question for this study is whether both elements of the Church's constitutional position are necessary. The next chapter will demonstrate that it is the first of these, the spiritual independence, that is perhaps under greater threat, as employment law and human rights legislation put into question some of the Church's traditional ways. In the rhetoric of the Church it tends to be the second of them, the independent jurisdiction, that is most eloquently defended. It would be admittedly pointless for the Church to have a separate legal jurisdiction if there was no spiritual independence for that to serve. At the same time, it might be possible to protect the spiritual policies of the Church by means other than a legal jurisdiction that is modelled on the judicial sovereignty of the civil law. It is important to be sure of asking the correct questions.

For much of the last two centuries in the constitutional thought of the Church of Scotland, it has been the idea of co-ordination of two different jurisdictions that has prevailed in debate. Co-ordination is the concept used by Sir Neil MacCormick, the Hartian jurisprudent previously quoted, in the context of the diversification of civil jurisdictions.[96] The idea of co-ordination between Church and state was used by Lord Jeffrey in his dissenting judgement in the *Auchterarder* case before the Disruption.[97] The 1921 settlement, especially the language of the Fourth and Sixth Articles Declaratory,[98] enshrined that idea of a constitutional arrangement between sovereign institutions of Church and state, being the two parallel realms of the spiritual and the temporal. The idea that they have a relationship of co-ordination expresses the element of mutual recognition between and mutual restraint by each, as each judicial authority recognises which subjects and cases belong within, and which beyond, its own jurisdiction.[99]

There appear to be difficulties with this model; they concern the sovereign nature of the national state, the sovereign competence of a state-like Church and the management of the co-ordination of the two. The many problems and inconsistencies enumerated in this chapter belong to one or another of these areas.

As indicated before the beginning of this description of the process of pursuing union, the development of a ring-fenced spiritual jurisdiction is only one way to guarantee the preservation of spiritual freedom, but it is not the only way and should not go unquestioned, especially if it displays flaws and weaknesses. The principal weakness of the Two-States-like solution is that the question was never asked whether the Church had the kind of equipment a state needs to carry out its juridical functions. It was observed earlier that the Church is more like the state as social geometry than it is like the state as a sovereign being. It lacks, for example, a police force, a correctional system, and (since Church law is no longer regarded as part of a single Scottish legal system) a professional corps of defence lawyers for Church cases. The nature of the Church simply is not sufficiently the same as the nature of the nation state; and so the 1921 settlement has declared – or required – the Church to act out of its inherent character in order to exercise its real inherent authority.

Conclusion

The Church of Scotland had by 1929 been liberated from the Divine Right of (secular) Kings and the resulting One-Kingdom theology; from federal theology; from patronage and Establishment and from the superior authority of the civil law in spiritual matters. Can we take for granted the legitimacy of the Divine Right of Church courts; a theology of two legal jurisdictions treated for practical purposes as two legal states and a co-ordination of those jurisdictions?

Why, as Lee provocatively asked in 1844, must we locate the freedom of God in a sovereign General Assembly and how do we trace the exercise of God's sovereign will for the Church in Scotland? In other words, if the constitutional self-understanding of the Church has changed so much since the Reformation, why not identify and scrutinise the current constituent elements of that self-understanding as it currently exists?

Notes

1   S. J. Brown, *The National Churches of England, Ireland, and Scotland, 1801–1846* (Oxford: Oxford University Press, 2001), pp. 293–4.
2   S. J. Brown, *Thomas Chalmers and the Godly Commonwealth in Scotland* (Oxford: Oxford University Press, 1982), pp. 225–7.
3   A. C. Cheyne, *The Ten Years' Conflict and the Disruption: An Overview* (Edinburgh: Scottish Academic Press, 1993), p. 3.
4   Brown, *National Churches of England, Ireland, and Scotland, 1801–1846*, p. 226.
5   D. B. Forrester, 'Ecclesia Scoticana – Established, Free or National?', *Theology* CII.806 (March/April 1999), p. 83.
6   O. Chadwick, 'Chalmers and the State', in A. C. Cheyne, *The Practical and the Pious: Essays on Thomas Chalmers (1780–1847)* (Edinburgh: Saint Andrew Press, 1985), p. 73.
7   H. Watt, *Thomas Chalmers and the Disruption* (Edinburgh: Thomas Nelson, 1943), p. 108.
8   *Earl of Kinnoull and Rev R Young* v. *Presbytery of Auchterarder* (1838) 16S 661, (1841) 3D 778, (1843) 5D 1010.
9   F. Lyall, *Of Presbyters and Kings: Church and State in the Law of Scotland* (Aberdeen: Aberdeen University Press, 1980), ch. III.II.
10 Brown, *Thomas Chalmers*, p. 298.
11 Cheyne, *Ten Years' Conflict and the Disruption*, p. 6.
12 G. E. Davie, *The Democratic Intellect: Scotland and Her Universities in the Nineteenth Century* (Edinburgh: Edinburgh University Press, 1964), p. 308.
13 *Presbytery of Strathbogie and Rev J Cruickshank and others, suspenders, and related cases*: (1839) 2D 258, 585, (1840) 2D 1047,

1380, (1840) 3D 282, (1842) 4D 1298, (1843) 5D 909, (1843) 15 Juris 375.

[14] G. D. Henderson, *Heritage: A Study of the Disruption* (Edinburgh: Oliver & Boyd, 1943), p. 83.

[15] P. C. Simpson, *The Life of Principal Rainy* (London: Hodder & Stoughton, 1909), vol. I, p. 70.

[16] *Cuninghame* v. *Presbytery of Irvine* (1843) 3D 427.

[17] T. Brown (ed.), *Annals of the Disruption* (Edinburgh: Macniven & Wallace, 1892), p. 44.

[18] The belief that the provision of the Church should be entirely the product of the voluntary offerings of its people with no support from the state and no Establishment.

[19] Henderson, *Heritage*, p. 73.

[20] I. A. Muirhead, 'Chalmers and the Politicians', in Cheyne, *Practical and the Pious*, p. 98.

[21] Properly the Claim, Declaration, and Protest by the General Assembly of the Church of Scotland of 1842, anent the Encroachments of the Court of Session.

[22] This list is a collation of those offered by Sjolinder, historian of the 1921 settlement, and Watt, historian of the Disruption: see R. Sjolinder, *Presbyterian Reunion in Scotland 1907–1921: Its Background and Development* (Edinburgh: T&T Clark, 1962), ch. I; and Watt, *Thomas Chalmers and the Disruption*, pp. 164–7.

[23] T. M. Parker, *Christianity and the State in the Light of History* (London: A. & C. Black, 1955), p. 170.

[24] See Ferrier, *Observations on Church and State*.

[25] And a leaning towards English concepts of sovereignty and Church polity: see Davie, *Democratic Intellect*, p. 306.

[26] Ferrier, *Observations on Church and State*, p. 34.

[27] R. Lee, *The Popery of Spiritual Independence* (Edinburgh: Myles Macphail, 1844).

[28] W. Balfour, *The Establishment Principle Defended: A Reply to the Statement by the Committee of the United Presbyterian Church on Disestablishment and Disendowment* (Edinburgh: Johnstone, Hunter & Co., 1873), p. 40.

[29] Ibid., p. 44.

[30] Ibid., p. 2.

[31] Ibid., pp. 26 and 158.

[32] Brown, *Thomas Chalmers*, p. 301.

33 Cheyne, *Practical and the Pious*, p. 65.
34 R. Rainy, 'Church and State from Constantine to the Reformation', in Rainy and others, *Church and State*.
35 Simpson, *Rainy*, vol. I, p. 267.
36 A. Taylor Innes, *The Law of Creeds in Scotland* (Edinburgh and London: Blackwood, 1867), ch. V.
37 Balfour, *Establishment Principle Defended*, p. 234.
38 H. Laski, *Studies in the Problem of Sovereignty* (London: Humphrey Milford, 1917), ch. II.
39 Ibid., ch. 2. This conclusion is echoed in N. MacCormick, 'The Kirk and the Theory of Sovereignty', unpublished lecture, para. 13.
40 L. Paterson, *The Autonomy of Modern Scotland* (Edinburgh: Edinburgh University Press, 1994), ch. 2.
41 Ibid., p. 45.
42 *Bannatyne* v. *Lord Overtoun* (1902) 4 F 1083: (1904) AC 515.
43 This description uses the analysis in K. Ross, *Church and Creed in Scotland: The Free Church Case 1900–1904 and Its Origins* (Edinburgh: Rutherford House Books, 1988), chs II and VI.
44 Figgis, *Churches in the Modern State*, p. 39.
45 Their current manifestation is in the area of charity law, as explained in the Introduction. To what extent can the whole Church be a charity in its own right; and to what extent can it be regarded as a charity capable of the superintendence of its smaller component charities (i.e. congregations)?
46 A. Muir, *John White* (London: Hodder & Stoughton, 1958), p. 105.
47 J. R. Fleming, *A History of the Church in Scotland 1875–1929* (Edinburgh: T&T Clark, 1933); see ch. IV for a description of the very early stages of consideration of union.
48 Muir, *John White*, p. 114.
49 The historical treatments of this era are principally: D. M. Murray, *Freedom to Reform: The 'Articles Declaratory' of the Church of Scotland 1921*, The Chalmers Lectures of 1991 (Edinburgh: T&T Clark, 1993); D. M. Murray, *Rebuilding the Kirk: Presbyterian Reunion in Scotland 1909–1929* (Edinburgh: Scottish Academic Press, 2000); Sjolinder, *Presbyterian Reunion in Scotland 1907–1921*; D. M. Thomson, '"Unrestricted Conference?": Myth and Reality in Scottish Ecumenism', in S. J. Brown and G. Newlands (eds), *Scottish Christianity in the Modern World: Essays in Honour of A C Cheyne* (Edinburgh: T&T Clark, 2000).

[50] C. N. Johnston, 'Church Union in Scotland', *Quarterly Review* (1920), pp. 205–25, p. 222.

[51] Ibid., p. 214.

[52] Muir, *John White*, p. 123.

[53] Ibid., p. 153.

[54] Thomson, '"Unrestricted Conference?"', p. 207.

[55] Johnston, 'Church Union in Scotland', generally.

[56] F. A. J. Macdonald, 'Law and Doctrine in the Church of Scotland with Particular Reference to Confessions of Faith', PhD thesis (St Andrews University, 1983), p. 307.

[57] In the interviews that formed part of the research for the PhD thesis on which this book is based, all the legal thinkers interviewed agreed that the 1921 settlement declared the Church's jurisdiction to be outside the scope of the Crown in Parliament, and several of the interviewees quoted the legal maxim *nemo dat quod non habet*, 'no one can grant what he does not possess', as the controlling principle following on from the distinction made by Christopher Johnston (Lord Sands). Sir Neil MacCormick, a professor of jurisprudence at the University of Edinburgh and former Member of the European Parliament, said he applied the maxim not just to the 1921 Act but also to the fact that power over the Scottish Church was clearly excluded from the 1707 Treaty. He believed it was a power the Westminster Parliament should never have exercised (before or after 1921) even if the Scottish Parliament had exercised it – from time to time – before the Union of Parliaments. The 1921-based argument is more attractive because it is built on the notion that these affairs are inherently none of the business of the civil order. The 1707-based argument is founded on the claim that they belong to a civil order that happened no longer to exist, which is a theologically unsatisfactory basis, and rather a risky one since the recent resuscitation of a Scottish Parliament. Parliament did not simply choose to refrain from exercising supremacy over the Church's spiritual affairs, but rather it admitted that it enjoyed no such supremacy, actual or potential, and recognised two separate jurisdictions.

[58] This paragraph reflects the interview conducted with Lord Mackay of Clashfern.

[59] Murray, *Rebuilding the Kirk*, p. 58.

[60] For the early drafts of the Articles, refer to appendices to Murray, *Freedom to Reform*; and for their final text, see Appendix II.

61 Fleming, *History of the Church in Scotland*, p. 107.

62 J. G. Kellas, *Modern Scotland: The Nation since 1870* (London: Pall Mall, 1968), p. 63.

63 A. Marr, *The Battle for Scotland* (London: Penguin, 1995), p. 40; Murray, *Rebuilding the Kirk*, p. 279.

64 See n. 57.

65 MacCormick, 'Kirk and the Theory of Sovereignty', paras 33–6.

66 For example, C. G. Brown, *The Death of Christian Britain: Understanding Secularisation 1800–2000* (London: Routledge, 2001), and his *Religion and Society in Scotland since 1707* (Edinburgh: Edinburgh University Press, 1997).

67 Church of Scotland Act 1921 c. 29 s. 1.

68 Murray, *Freedom to Reform*, ch. IV.4, and *Rebuilding the Kirk*, p. 92.

69 R. K. Murray, 'The Constitutional Position of the Church of Scotland', *Public Law* (1958), pp. 155–62.

70 Dunlop, *William Carstares and the Kirk by Law Established*, p. 73.

71 *Ballantyne and Others* v. *Presbytery of Wigtown and Others*, 1936 SC 625.

72 Lyall, 'Religion and Law', p. 66.

73 Lord Murray, 'Church and State', para. 699.

74 Macdonald, 'Law and Doctrine in the Church of Scotland', ch. XIX, describes the whole controversy.

75 Murray, *Rebuilding the Kirk*, p. 73.

76 The abandonment of the Scottish Church Initiative for Union by the General Assembly of 2003 pushes the prospect of this problem far into the future.

77 Murray, *Rebuilding the Kirk*, p. 214.

78 Brown, *Religion and Society*, p. 145.

79 Muir, *John White*, p. 94; and Kellas, *Modern Scotland*, p. 34.

80 Murray, *Rebuilding the Kirk*, p. 22; and see C. N. Johnston, *Handbook of Scottish Church Defence* (Edinburgh: James G. Hitt, 1892), article on 'Finlay'.

81 Johnston, *Handbook of Scottish Church Defence*, article on 'Gladstone, The Right Hon W E'.

82 Note, for example, the report of the Church and State Committee of the UF Church reporting to their 1901 General Assembly in these terms: 'That we must regard the statutory connection now

maintained by the State in Scotland with the Established Church as objectionable in principle, and that its termination seems to us to be a necessary step towards the relations between the Churches in Scotland, which, we believe, are very widely desired.' Quoted in J. Barr, *The Scottish Church Question* (London: James Clarke, 1920), p. 116.

[83] Sjolinder, *Presbyterian Reunion*, p. 100.

[84] Mair, 'The Scottish Churches: An Appeal', *Blackwood's Magazine*, CLXXX (1906), pp. 728–32, quoted in Sjolinder, *Presbyterian Reunion*, ch. V.

[85] Johnston, 'Church Union in Scotland', p. 220.

[86] Thomson, '"Unrestricted Conference?"', p. 215, points out that the shift away from the traditional language was an attempt to find a *modus vivendi* with people like Principal Martin of the UF Church, because he had dissented from the report of the negotiating committee to their 1910 General Assembly.

[87] Barr, *Scottish Church Question*, p. 37.

[88] C. R. Munro, 'Does Scotland Have an Established Church?', *Ecclesiastical Law Journal* 20, pp. 639–45. Paul Avis, a commentator on Church Establishment from within the Church of England, makes the same kind of mistake about the Church of Scotland wherever it appears in his *Church, State and Establishment* (London: SPCK, 2001).

[89] Munro, 'Does Scotland Have an Established Church?', p. 639.

[90] T. M. Taylor, 'Church and State in Scotland', *Juridical Review* (1957), pp. 121–37. Only part of Taylor's list of elements has been used here, as some of his suggestions, e.g. the territorial ministry, are not elements of the Establishment of the Church in the legal sense used in this discussion; they are elements of the national responsibility fulfilled by the Church referred to in Article III, but are not privileges or forms of secular support.

[91] J. P. Mackey, *Power and Christian Ethics* (Cambridge: Cambridge University Press, 1994), p. 189.

[92] J. Barr, *The United Free Church of Scotland* (London: Allenson, 1934), ch. XI, for examples.

[93] The Oath of Accession.

[94] W. Mair (posthumous), *A Digest of Laws and Decisions Ecclesiastical and Civil relating to the Constitution, Practice, and Affairs of the Church of Scotland* (4th edn, 1912; Edinburgh and London: Blackwood, reprint. with supplement, 1923), ch. I.

95 A modern example was the exemption of church interiors from some planning law, and the regulation of church furnishing instead by the courts of the Church. Burleigh, the Church historian, maintained that the area of ecclesiastical discipline is not confined to purely spiritual matters: see J. H. S. Burleigh, A *Church History of Scotland* (Edinburgh: Hope Trust, 1983), ch. I.

96 N. MacCormick, *Questioning Sovereignty: Law, State and Nation in the European Commonwealth* (Oxford: Oxford University Press, 1999), p. 8.

97 *Earl of Kinnoull and Rev R Young* v. *Presbytery of Auchterarder*, cited in full and discussed in ch. 3, pp. 93–5.

98 The text of these two Articles is discussed in detail in ch. 5, pp. 208–14.

99 J. M. Reid, *Kirk and Nation: The Story of the Reformed Church of Scotland* (London: Skeffington, 1960), p. 164.

Chapter 4

The Church after the Settlement: Sphere Sovereignty under Pressure

I have argued that the content of the ecclesiastical provisions of the civil law was unclear under the terms of the 1921 settlement: what pieces of legislation constituted the Church's legal foundation and how far that foundation could be changed by Church or state. Equally problematic was the relationship between Church and state and the determination of the jurisdictional boundaries between them, and that effectively meant the determination of the limits of the Church's independent powers. This weakness has appeared in the twentieth-century history of Church-related civil litigation.

It is an oddity of the Articles Declaratory that the only reference to the setting of boundaries between Church and state appears not in Article IV (concerning the separate jurisdiction) but in Article VI (concerning the spiritual responsibilities of the state and its relations of mutual wellbeing with the Church).[1] In the absence of any criterion for boundary-setting in Article IV, it has been the habit of the courts to adopt the criterion of Article VI and conclude that both Church and state have a responsibility to determine their own jurisdiction. However, when agreement cannot be reached between them, the state assumes the power to determine the extent to which it concedes a separate sphere of sovereignty to the Church.[2] This gives the lie to Johnston's silky trick of distinguishing two senses of the word 'grant' and arguing that the civil magistrate was denying himself the power to determine or limit the extent of the Church's power.

Twentieth-Century Case Law

Civil Cases

The first major case to test the limitations of the Church's authority was *Ballantyne and Others* v. *Presbytery of Wigtown and Others* in 1936.[3] In the exercise of its authority and responsibility, a local Presbytery had refused to give permission to a vacant charge for an immediate and unrestricted call of a new minister. The congregation (a former Established Church charge) was resisting the Presbytery's attempts to unite it with a congregation nearby (a former United Free Church charge). The recalcitrant vacant congregation resorted to civil law to try to force the Presbytery's hand by invoking the Church Patronage (Scotland) Act 1874, which they believed required the Presbytery to permit the calling of a minister without further ado.[4] The Court of Session judged that the rights under the 1874 Act were now in the competency of the spiritual court and so declined for itself any jurisdiction: the matter accordingly returned to the Church's courts and the congregation's attempt to invoke the civil law failed. The 1921 settlement had proved its worth in preventing a dispute belonging in one jurisdiction from being settled in the other. To this extent the case did no more than fulfil the intention of the original drafters of the legislation, and in all cases raised since *Ballantyne* the Church's lawyers have pursued the same outcome using the same arguments to avoid the civil jurisdiction.

In order to come to its judgement, the Court had to decide what was the content of the spiritual jurisdiction and so, in turn, how a civil court should go about deciding where the distinction lay. In the Second Division, Lord Aitchison referred to the state's recognition of the inherent powers of the Church; and Lord Murray made the point that the cause was indeed relevant in the civil courts, to the extent that they had to decide what was the ambit of the Court of Session and what that of the General Assembly. The innovation in this case was contained in the judgement in the Outer House by Lord Pitman, who addressed the question of what exactly was included in the spiritual jurisdiction and concluded that it was not an easy classification to make. He decided that the Church's authority extended over matters that were not of themselves naturally spiritual in the ordinary meaning, but which so adhered to the matters that were clearly spiritual that they should be included. This inclusion of ancillary matters to the core elements of worship, government, doctrine and discipline, not by exhaustive list – the judge was interested only in the particulars of the case before him – but by what was meant to be common sense, left the spiritual *jurisdiction* less clear than it had been before. It certainly demonstrated that it was more extensive than the Church's area of spiritual *independence*, the point made in the previous chapter. Case by case, the civil courts would have to decide not only what was 'spiritual' in terms of the 1921 Act but also what else might appropriately belong to the Church's courts to decide. That would make it very difficult to set or follow precedent, or to predict the outcome of future cases, or to know when the Church should try to invoke its own, independent authority. For this reason the Church has been lucky that it has so rarely been challenged in the civil courts: when that happens, there is very little case law available to define the Church's area of independence and produce a clear outcome.

Sixty years passed before a second major case reviewed the condition of the 1921 settlement. In *Logan* v. *Presbytery of Dumbarton* in 1995,[5] the pursuer sought a civil remedy in a situation where he believed that the Church's court was not properly exercising its powers; in other words, he requested a judicial review. In the Outer House judgement (which was not appealed) the Lord Ordinary, Lord Osborne, held that judicial review was not possible in respect of an organisation that was not the creature of Parliament. Whether such a judgement could have been reached in the post-Disruption years, when such a relationship of creaturehood was precisely the model argued by the main thinkers of the Established Church, is questionable. However, since the 1921 Act recognised the pre-existing powers of the Church as inherent and uncreated by Parliament or any human authority, the Court of Session disclaimed jurisdiction. Once again, on the face of things, the civil magistrate had acknowledged the distinctive and co-ordinated jurisdictions and the 1921 settlement had worked in favour of the Church. Once again, however, the judgement went further than the basic point, and compromised the settlement a little further. The Court's opinion went on to expand on the duty of the civil court to determine the extent of the spiritual jurisdiction of the Church. It concluded that judicial review would be possible where the Church acted *ultra vires* in its interpretation of the Articles or its use of Article VIII (the stringent process for changing the Articles). The Court suggested that the ultimate sanction in the face of the Church abandoning its constitutional limitations would be the withdrawal of the original recognition (what Johnston had referred to as a 'grant' in the sense of acknowledgement) of the spiritual jurisdiction.

Lord Davidson, a former Procurator of the General Assembly and Court of Session judge, affirms this opinion in a *Stair Encyclopaedia* article[6] to the extent of saying that judicial review should be available if the ecclesiastical courts exceed their jurisdiction. It is easy enough to hypothesise a situation where a Church court might attempt to deal with a matter lying entirely within the civil jurisdiction, though difficult to imagine it happening in practice. If the Church tried to use its own law to deal with a secular employment matter that should have been governed by employment legislation, or in contravening health and safety legislation in the secular use of Church premises, it would be acting *ultra vires*. The Church's courts are not subject to the review of the civil courts when confining their concern to matters judged by those civil courts to fall within their spiritual ambit, but they are subject to the judicial review of a civil magistrate who decides they have exceeded their own jurisdiction and strayed into his or hers.

It is harder, however, to understand the Lord Ordinary's opinion that the misinterpretation of the Articles Declaratory – the overstepping by the Church of its constitutionally recognised powers – could result in the withdrawal by the civil power of recognition of the spiritual jurisdiction. First, in such a circumstance there is bound to be a disagreement, to the point of impasse, as to whether the Church has so overstepped its mark. Christopher Johnston (Lord Sands) made the point that a meaningful right of interpretation of the Articles must include the right to interpret them in a way the civil courts might not have approved. If the Church and the civil judiciary arrived at different interpretations of the same Article, the Church would claim it was entitled to take a controversial view, while the civil magistrate might regard the Church as wrong and therefore as acting *ultra vires*. The Church would refuse to accept that it had acted beyond its power, but the civil magistrate would treat it as if it had. With the substance of the spiritual jurisdiction unclear, because so little case law has emerged to define it, it would be very difficult to determine when the constitutional trigger had been activated and the settlement compromised in this way. Second, the Lord Ordinary's suggested censure in such an eventuality is puzzling. He meant either that the civil court should withdraw recognition of the Church's jurisdiction to the extent of the disputed subject, or that the civil court would have to withdraw recognition of some larger part of the Church's jurisdiction that it believed the Church had abused. If he meant the former he was arguing circularly, because the civil court's belief that the disputed area did not belong to the Church was the origin of the dispute in the first place, so it does not cure the problem just to restate it. If he meant the latter, such a withdrawal of the recognition of jurisdiction seems a curious response: the mischief done is the overstepping of the boundary, so it would seem inappropriate to react by moving the boundary further back and punitively seizing another part of the Church's legitimate responsibility. It is not a true application of Lord Davidson's point about the protection of the different spheres; it is a resort to collapsing the difference whenever it comes under provocation. The function of the civil law should go no further than reinforcing the co-ordinates of jurisdiction and restraining the Church from acting outwith its own *vires*. If these secondary elements of the judgement in the *Logan* case (otherwise won by the Church on the main point about jurisdiction) are to be used as authority in future actions, it leaves the 1921 settlement contingent on the civil courts' opinion of the legal competency of the Church's courts' actings, and therefore leaves it terribly insecure.

The 1921 Act has always been regarded as a fundamental constitutional provision, because it was premised on recognition of the fundamental nature of the Church as an institution that must not compromise its obedience to Christ. The experience of litigation suggests, however, that some compromise is imposed on the Church from beyond it. *Ballantyne* affirmed the civil magistrate's right to determine the contours of the Church's jurisdiction; while *Logan* asserted a civil right of judicial review of the Church when it takes a different view of those contours, and suggests that the continued civil recognition of the independent jurisdiction is contingent on the behaviour of the Church's courts. These arguments, taken to extreme, would return the Church to a position of dependency on the secular political and legal will, which leaves it hardly more free than when it was Established. If the Free Church in 1843 gave up the benefits of Establishment in pursuit of a greater spiritual freedom they ultimately failed to secure, perhaps the Church of Scotland in 1921 did exactly the same thing for exactly the same motivation and with something like the same outcome. The settlement purported to acknowledge or grant the inherent, God-given jurisdiction of Christ's Church, but the civil magistrate quickly claimed the authority to declare the limits of that jurisdiction. The point is not necessarily that the civil magistrate was wrong, but rather that the settlement was unworkable from the outset and this development in case law was inevitable. The settlement had appeared to re-establish the Church as a sovereign authority, but left its external defences extremely weak.

The Church of Scotland Act of 1921 and the Articles Declaratory of the Constitution of the Church of Scotland in Matters Spiritual would have stood for ever if the social and cultural context in which they were set had not changed. In the world of the early twentieth century it did not matter that the Act was woefully deficient in setting out its own implications for the repeal of the corpus of civil legislation relating to the Church's constitutional position, since no one expected that either the new Act or any of the old ones would come radically into question. In the world of the early twentieth century it did not matter that the question of Establishment was fudged and buried, not faced and answered, since no one expected that society would become so religiously plural that the unique position of one Church would become a problem in political life. In the world of the early twentieth century it did not matter in practice that secular judges would determine the contours of the spiritual jurisdiction, since they would do so deferentially to the substantive spiritual independence of the national Church. And even in the world of the late twentieth century, just a few years ago, it did not matter that the civil magistrate would threaten judicial review of a Church acting *ultra vires*, since there was still confidence that both sides knew what those separate legal powers of the Church were, and abided by the limits.

It will take a longer view of recent history to judge whether there has been a substantial turning point ultimately fatal to the Church's independent jurisdiction. Some people believe it came in the form of the *Percy* case.

Helen Percy v. Board of National Mission

In 1997 an Associate Minister, Rev. Helen Percy, was facing a disciplinary charge brought by her Presbytery, which had evidence suggesting that she had had sexual relations with a married Church elder, but the allegations had not yet been fully investigated nor judgement given in a Church court. She resigned ('demitted') her status as a minister with the approval of the Presbytery, and then almost immediately regretted her action; but her demission had removed her from the jurisdiction of that court for the purposes of the case and therefore brought it to an unresolved conclusion. There followed a lengthy series of actions pursued severally in both the Church's courts and at civil law. [7]

The Civil Case 1998–9

In the summer of 1998, Miss Percy brought an action at an Industrial Tribunal, on grounds of unfair dismissal and sex discrimination, against the agency of the Church that had appointed her (importantly, for what followed, she was not an inducted, parish minister). When the tribunal ruled that it had no relevant jurisdiction (for the traditional reasons outlined in e.g. *Ballantyne*), Miss Percy appealed, on the sole ground of sex discrimination (but not unfair dismissal), to an Employment Appeal Tribunal (in autumn 1998) and thereafter to the Inner House (First Division) (in spring 1999). The legislation on which she relied included the Sex Discrimination Act of 1975 and the Equal Treatment Directive of the European Union, and her arguments used themes of human rights based on gender. In the Court of Session and the House of Lords, counsel's arguments focused mainly on the relationship of European Union legislation and the Church's independent spiritual jurisdiction. In both courts, however, the written judgements paid very little attention to questions of European law, and the fascinating question of the relationship of the Church of Scotland to a different civil magistrate, one located beyond British shores, has not been judicially considered.[8]

In the Inner House, the pursuer was relying on the argument that the 1975 Act should be interpreted as covering the case of ministers operating as she had done under a contract, even if that required an implied modification of the 1921 Act, and that to do otherwise was to fail to transpose the Equal Treatment Directive adequately into domestic law. The Church's response was that domestic law is in this peculiar sense limited and the Church is immune from its provisions in certain circumstances. At this, penultimate stage of the possible domestic civil law process, the courts favoured the Church's argument and declined to assert jurisdiction. At this point, Miss Percy followed the logical implication of the civil judgement, and switched jurisdictions.

The Ecclesiastical Cases 1999–2003

The General Assembly of 1999 received from her a Petition, the crave of which asked the Assembly 'to instruct an independent investigation to examine the actions of Angus Presbytery from June 1997, with particular regard to its decision to remove your Petitioner's status in December 1997 ... [and then] ... if fault be found with those actions, to revoke the decision of Angus Presbytery to remove your Petitioner's status'.[9] The

General Assembly felt that Miss Percy was at least stretching the conventional use of Petition in questioning the acceptance of a demission of status that she had herself tendered in the first place. It agreed to hear the Petition, making clear that it was doing so only as an exercise of its *nobile officium* as the supreme court of the Church. However, upon the case being heard the crave was refused *simpliciter*.

Three years later, now using the surname Douglas, the former minister submitted a Petition to the General Assembly of 2002 with the crave: 'to permit the Petitioner to state a claim for damages under and in terms of the Sex Discrimination Act 1975, and to adjudicate upon that claim following due process, and in accordance with the law'.[10] Since the Church's agents had been successfully arguing throughout the civil process that the appropriate jurisdiction was the ecclesiastical, the Petition was clearly competent to that extent. The Assembly's Committee on Bills and Overtures,[11] which gave guidance to the court on questions of competency and relevancy of judicial cases submitted to it, considered other issues relating to the matter. One was the fact that the incidents alluded to had taken place more than five years earlier, raising the question of prescription of the case and therefore of legal relevance; and another was the previous Petition brought to the 1999 General Assembly. Satisfied, however, that the demands of equity and the generosity of the Assembly made it appropriate to receive the Petition, the Committee decided on grounds of the delicate, sexual nature of the facts of the case that it should be heard privately by a small Special Commission. The Committee persuaded the Assembly to remit the case to such a commission of three people, with full powers to dispose of the matter finally as if it were the court itself. The Committee took the opportunity to assert the separation of jurisdictions, an assertion approved by the Assembly and constituting the most recent opinion of the supreme court of the Church on the matter:

The Church being committed to gender equality and the protection of its ministers from discrimination on grounds of sex, the Special Commission should give due consideration to the principles contained in the Sex Discrimination Act 1975, while recognising that because of the exclusive jurisdiction of the courts of the Church to legislate and adjudicate finally in all matters of doctrine, worship, government and discipline in the Church, the Act does not form part of the law of the Church.

It seems to the Committee that in terms of the Church of Scotland Act 1921 the courts of the Church are the only proper jurisdiction to receive any application relating to the events referred to in the Petition of 1999 and the current Petition; and the Committee invites the General Assembly to endorse this view.[12]

The Committee, and it must be assumed the Assembly, believed at the time that it was offering an equivalent remedy to the Petitioner, one that would provide the same quality of justice as if her sex discrimination claim had been competent to be heard in the civil courts. In the light of the Inner House decision (placing the jurisdiction over the case squarely with the Church), the Church did all in its power to allow the Petitioner to benefit from the substance of the terms of the 1975 Act, though it was an Act belonging to another jurisdiction.

The Special Commission, a group of three legally qualified Church members chaired by a sheriff,[13] issued three Opinions between the General Assembly of 2002 that appointed them and October 2003, when the case was dismissed. One of the motions brought before the Special Commission was particularly significant, viewed with hindsight. In December 2002, the Commission heard a motion from the Petitioner seeking a ruling that the Sex Discrimination Act 1975 did apply to the respondents (i.e. the Presbytery of Angus and the Board of National Mission). Though the terms of the Commission's remit, agreed by the Assembly and quoted above, asserted that the Act did not form part of the law of the Church, the motion sought to show that the civil law did apply to Miss Douglas's circumstances after all. As the judgement commented: 'An assertion that the Act does not form part of the law of the Church is not a denial that the Church, may in certain circumstances, such as a relationship of employment, be subject to the provisions of the Act.'[14] This was a different use of the 1975 Act from that made by the Committee on Bills and Overtures. Whereas the Committee and Assembly had instructed the Commission to treat the Act as if the Petitioner could benefit from its terms within the Church's jurisdiction, here the Commission was acknowledging that in certain circumstances the Petitioner could have benefited from it directly, within the civil jurisdiction. As in the civil actions that had preceded this Petition, however, the fact that Miss Percy/Douglas had not been an employee was the main reason why this motion failed before the Special Commission.

It was irksome to the Church at the time, and – as things worked out – very interesting, that Helen Percy/Douglas tried to bring to the Church's courts an argument based entirely in civil law. She appeared oblivious to the fact that as a minister she had subjected herself to a different legal code for these purposes; and throughout her case she tried to have the Church's own legal provisions set aside or ignored. And so perhaps it was predictable that, following her failure in the Church's jurisdiction, she switched back to the civil law to seek her remedy.

The Case in the House of Lords 2005

Commentaries on this case have all been written for lawyers. This account of the outcome of the House of Lords case addresses a wider audience, and so it is worth beginning with two points of clarification.

First, this account does not comment on the substantive merits of the case, which are completely irrelevant here.

Indeed, no one has ever commented with authority on those merits, as they were never tested in any tribunal. The Church, determined to minimise the immense financial costs to it of the case, finally settled the case for an amount that was less than the irrecoverable legal costs would have been in successfully defending the case. And so nothing should be inferred about the actual claim itself from the fact of Miss Percy's having famously won the jurisdictional argument.

Second, there are two types of employment status treated in civil law. One is the narrower, stricter sense of 'employee' as defined in employment legislation, and it gives particular rights and protections, for example against unfair dismissal. After the tribunal stage, Helen Percy abandoned any claim for unfair dismissal, and no longer relied on any argument that she was employed in that narrower, more technical sense. There was nothing about any part of the case that can be taken as authority for the proposition that ministers serving in parishes, without explicit contracts of employment, were now to be regarded as employees in that narrow, technical sense, and none of the pleadings suggested there should be.[15] The other sense of 'employment' is a wider one, in which an individual has a contract to provide work, but does not become the employee of the other party: a contract with a plumber, or for that matter a lawyer, might be regarded in that way. Not for the first time in the Church's history, a huge difference rests on a single letter: the narrower definition is called a 'contract for service' and the wider one is a 'contract for services'. In the Sex Discrimination Act 1975, the Act on which Miss Percy was relying, employment is defined (in section 82[1]) as 'employment under a contract of service or of apprenticeship or a contract personally to execute any work or labour', clearly including both types. Miss Percy's lawyers set a lower bar for themselves in the higher courts by aiming only for the wider definition, with great success.

There were several steps in the rationale of the majority of judges.[16]

First, it was determined that there could be some kind of civil law contract that had to be given weight. Lord Roger of Earlsferry in the Inner House of the Court of Session had found in favour of the Church using a long-held presumption that engagement, even on terms and conditions, to a religious ministry was an act that could not involve an intention by the parties to create legal relations enforceable in the civil courts. He worried the Church rather, by qualifying that by saying the presumption was a rebuttable one.[17] The House of Lords judgement rebutted it, unambiguously innovating as they did so: Lord Nicholls used the phrase 'it is time to recognise …',[18] and so marked a moment of change.

Lord Nicholls observed that in a religious ministry there would be some elements that did constitute such legally enforceable relations, but that there would be other elements that did not.[19] It was not his task in the course of his judgement to list what the latter might be, but it is certainly authority for the proposition that there remains a great deal of room for argument about which parts of a minister's terms and conditions might be reviewable in law.

Second, it was determined that the fact that a minister in a parish is normally regarded as being 'the holder of an office' did not exclude the possibility that a legal contract existed. The majority agreed that it is quite possible to occupy a position generally regarded as an 'office' and still to have a contract for service or services.[20] This was the point on which Lord Hoffmann dissented completely from the majority: he agreed that the presumption against the existence of legal relations had been rebutted, so there was some sort of contract. But he absolutely disagreed that the holding of an office could amount to the same thing as a contract of employment of any kind.[21]

It was also observed that the case would have been resolved very differently if the events had taken place after the enactment of the Employment Equality (Sex Discrimination) Regulations of 2005.[22] These extended the rights under the

Sex Discrimination Act to office-holders, and would have short circuited this part of the debate. It would not have dealt with the whole case, however, as religious exemptions are included in these regulations, so some of the other issues would have remained unresolved.

Third, and building on the previous two points, the majority held that an exchange of correspondence between Miss Percy and the Board of National Mission at the outset of her time as Associate Minister constituted a contract for services, that is, the second and wider understanding of employment.[23] These legal conclusions, put together, placed her squarely in the second half of the definition in s. 82 of the Sex Discrimination Act.

Fourth, Lord Hope, the only Scot on the bench, pointed out that the benefits of the Sex Discrimination Act did not extend to certain activities of certain religious organisations, because of explicit exemptions; but that the Church of Scotland in its own legislation aimed to treat men and women equally, and so this denomination could hardly be assumed to wish to benefit from any exclusion under the Act.[24]

Fifth, and with disappointing brevity, their Lordships dealt with the possible trump card of the Church of Scotland, which was to insist that all these legal arguments were meaningless in the face of the 1921 Act and Articles Declaratory. In an argument that it has to be said seems a little circular, Lords Nicholls and Hope said that because legal obligations did exist therefore the Church must have stepped outside its own jurisdiction.[25] This, of course, is not how the whole thing had felt inside the Church: the General Assembly of 2002 had intended to provide a sufficient remedy within the Church's own legal system, and was trying to argue that that was the correct locus of the case. It hardly seems logically adequate to ask whether the spiritual jurisdiction outranked the civil jurisdiction, thus trumping the existence of a civil contract, and answer that question in the negative because of the existence of the very same legal contract.

The House of Lords decided, too, that the Church's jurisdiction was not up to the task in hand. The General Assembly, when it approved the Report of the Committee on Bills and Overtures (see earlier), was, they said, failing to provide a sex discrimination remedy, despite the fact that the Committee's Report had been careful to assert that the Special Commission was to provide a remedy comparable to that available under the Act. Indeed Baroness Hale believed the Committee, in asserting that the Sex Discrimination Act did not apply, was conceding a lack of internal remedy: one of the drafters of that Committee's Report (i.e. the present writer) can testify that the opposite intention was the case, and the Special Commission was set up precisely because the Church believed it did have an alternative internal remedy, which was the only appropriate one in the situation.[26]

In short, the Church appeared to their Lordships to have done two things that handed the jurisdiction in this case to the civil authorities. First, it had stepped outside the spiritual jurisdiction by entering a legal relationship with Miss Percy in the first place; and second, it had in any case knowingly failed to provide any internal remedy for her problem. This is a problematic pair of arguments. If it is true that the Church's jurisdiction did not apply from the moment (at appointment) when the Church entered legal relations with the Appellant then it is irrelevant whether the internal remedies of that jurisdiction were adequate or inadequate to provide the protections of the 1975 Act. If something is irrelevant, there is no point then in examining its efficacy. This is not simply an effect of five Law Lords writing separate judgements and using conflicting reasoning: Lord Hope used both of these arguments in the course of his judgement. This confusion leaves no clear answer to the question: if Lady Hale were wrong and the Church had been right to think it was able to offer a remedy under the Sex Discrimination Act, would the House of Lords have been able to make the argument that the case belonged in the civil jurisdiction? This illustrates the inadequacy of argument previously mentioned. It is not enough to say that because a matter lies within one jurisdiction it cannot possibly lie in another: there is always the possibility that it might lie in both.

While their Lordships' argument about the jurisdictional boundary bore no relation to the Church's own understanding of the events of the preceding eight years, and may be internally inconsistent, it did at least suggest that – whatever the Church's jurisdiction included – their Lordships did not believe they had shrunk it at all. According to their account, the boundaries of the Church's authority stayed still, and the Church stepped outside them in its legal behaviour. Indeed, in the course of the pleadings of the case, the bench conceded that to change the contours of the spiritual jurisdiction would require legislation, and it could not be done in the course of a court judgement.

Lord Scott, alone among the judges, addressed the Articles Declaratory in a more direct and convincing way. He distinguished between the discipline of the Church (one of the four traditional elements of the spiritual jurisdiction) and the manner of exercise of that discipline. He observed that the latter, the way the Church implemented its disciplinary standards, could trigger the interest of the civil law in the ways this case had demonstrated; and he concluded that the Fourth Article Declaratory did not have in view this element of the Church's activity in referring to 'discipline'.[27] Again, the argument is not that the civil law should step inside the Church's sphere of authority when the Church is doing things badly; rather it is asserting that the Church's sphere of authority does not inherently include matters that are naturally caught by the terms of the civil law. Again: no shrinkage of the Church's jurisdiction is intended, but the Church is probably rather surprised to discover some of the things that, it turns out, lie outside its authority.

Subsequent Response

In the spring of 2007, eighteen months after the Church had lost the case and before the initial round of analysis of the case[28] had appeared in legal and taxation journals, the Church took a step tantamount to abandoning everything it had argued for in the House of Lords – and far more besides.

The Ministries Council of the General Assembly had recently taken over responsibility for all central appointments of parish staff other than inducted parish ministers. Some of these appointments were open only to ministers (e.g. associate ministry posts), while some were open to ministers and others alike. Until that point, ministers occupying either type of post had been given a set of terms and conditions but not a contract. Only a unique administrative error on the part of another Church department (the Board of National Mission) had put Miss Percy into the position of being able to demonstrate that she had a contractual relationship with the Church; but most ministers in posts like hers had not enjoyed a legal position like hers.

The Ministries Council, long suspected by the rest of the Church to want ministers to become employees for purposes of enhanced line management of them, suddenly switched in early 2007 to a practice of giving all parish appointees[29] full contracts of employment. Contracts of employment were given for the first time to ministers occupying posts open to ministers and non-ministers alike; but the practice extended radically further, including all ministers occupying any post other than that of inducted parish minister. Whatever its merits or weaknesses, had this step been taken ten years earlier, the *Percy* case would not have taken place as it did, as there would have been very little to prevent the original Industrial Tribunal from accepting jurisdiction.

This development is one of degree not of kind. There have long been ministers subject to the spiritual jurisdiction of the courts of the Church but serving as employees. Some are employees of the Church, including all those working for its central administration. Others are employees of other agencies, and recently have come to include hospital chaplains now employed by NHS Trusts around the country. For these ministers, it has always been necessary to discover the relationship between the two legal systems to which they are subject. If it is not a condition of someone's contract of employment that he or she retains status as a minister of the Church of Scotland and if through the judicial activity of the Church that status is removed, the individual's employment must be secure.

So what has happened is that the field of parish work has been somewhat summarily added to the class of ministries which the Church no longer seeks to have regulated entirely within its own jurisdiction. It is not, after all, true to say that the boundaries of the jurisdictions are settled always by the secular authority and always in a situation of dispute between the two. For here is an example of the Church shifting – I would venture to suggest, inadvertently shifting – a large number of individuals into a position of straddling its jurisdictional boundary as both ministers and employees, individuals whom the Church had previously striven to keep firmly on its own side of that line.

If the Council of Ministries has placed the whole Church on a slippery slope, it will be because it might be difficult to argue why the regulation of the inducted parish minister needs to be preserved entirely within the Church's own powers, when other very similar ministries have been so easily abandoned to the regulation of employment law. What, after all, are the legal differences? The next major case in the sequence which begins *Ballantyne, Logan, Percy* will, I predict, feature as its Pursuer an inducted parish minister who finds some gap in the Church's laws and feels disadvantaged in comparison with his or her Associate Minister who enjoys the protection of civil employment law. The Church's attempts to duplicate these civil law provisions are described below; but the more

alike the two codes become the more some people in the
Church wonder what point there is in defending a separate
system. Why march to the beat of a different drum which
sounds no different at all?

Discussion

And so it is important not to exaggerate the direct consequences of the *Percy* case. A parish minister in a similar
situation would have to establish every part of their claim,
probably largely from scratch and currently probably
without much prospect of success, because the two cases
would be so different. This case may be used as precedent by
non-inducted clergy in other denominations: in the Church
of Scotland, the more recent events have rendered this case
largely meaningless.

And, as the following sections of this chapter will
demonstrate, the exact parameters of the spiritual jurisdiction
in areas like discrimination law are under a searching
scrutiny and an intentional review. The judgement, so far as
it delineates the authority of church and state, will soon be
largely superseded.

Already the case has attracted legal and academic analysis,
and the House of Lords judgement has generally been
regarded as leaving troublesome questions unanswered. One
tax specialist, writing before the events of 2007 in the Church
of Scotland, predicted that some religious organisations
would resort to extreme measures to ensure that their clergy
were deemed strictly self-employed. This would require
that there be absolutely no control over the individual, no
opportunity for substitution of him or her, and patently no
mutuality of obligation.[30] In a system that has any element of
superintendence or collegiality, this is bound to be virtually
impossible.

From a constitutional point of view, the alarming question
has been posed whether Miss Percy would have succeeded if

what she had been appealing had been a decision of a court of the Church. The case oscillated back and forth between the two jurisdictions, partly because her demission of status removed her from the jurisdiction of the Presbytery of Angus. Had she not taken that step, and had the Presbytery heard and issued the disciplinary case in a manner that Miss Percy felt involved sex discrimination, could the case have ended up as it did in the House of Lords? The spectre of the pre-Disruption cases looms at this thought, but it would be an entirely consistent outcome, starting from Lord Scott's view that the civil courts are entitled to review the manner of exercise of the Church's discipline. In that case, presumably, the civil courts could not question the Church's decision to make adultery a censurable offence in a minister (however unusual this might seem to the rest of society). They could, however, examine how the offence was investigated, prosecuted and adjudicated, and make a judgement in respect of her patrimonial interest (just as it had done for Mr Young in *Auchterarder*). It has to be assumed that, in the new situation of employed ministers working for local churches, that could be a reality. 'Discipline' as one of the four areas of the independent spiritual jurisdiction will come to be defined more and more narrowly as a matter of life, doctrine and therefore of ministerial status; and it will less and less be a euphemism for the Church regulating the terms and conditions of engagement of many of its professionals.

The change may have future repercussions and set very awkward precedents. That is not necessarily evidence that the change is a bad one.

A Tide of State Regulation

The European Employment Directive 2000

Clergy are not the only workers over whom the Church exercises authority. There are many hundreds of other employees – employees in the narrower, technical sense of the term – serving the Church in its parishes, Presbyteries, central agencies, statutory bodies and overseas partnerships. Some of them, as we have noted, happen to be ordained; most are not. New constraints exist for the churches, as for all employers, in exercising authority over these workers, whose status does not have the tortuous peculiarities of the parish clergy's.

Britain has been subject to European law for thirty years, but laws likely to compromise the interest of the Church as a legislative and judicial body have particularly emerged much more recently. In the summer of 2000, many European Churches engaged vigorously with the process within the European Union to introduce what came to be the European Employment Directive (2000/78/EC). The lobbying by ecumenical agencies and individual denominations concerned the possible effect upon Church life of the terms of the Directive, which addressed working conditions (including hours of work) and issues of fairness and discrimination. Many Churches anticipated that the Directive, which would be introduced to domestic law through Acts or Statutory Instruments of member states, would compromise the traditional freedoms and exemptions they had in respect of clergy; working hours, requirements of religious commitment in certain employees, and so on. After a great deal of discussion, much of it through a vast e-mail network, the Directive appeared, complete with an exemption for 'Genuine Occupational Requirements' (GORs). These were not defined with any exactness, but provided a hook upon which Churches hung their arguments as they monitored the implementation of the Directive in domestic law.

Since the adoption of the Directive, several pieces of Westminster legislation outlawing employment discrimination have come into force, and to varying degrees carry the terms of the Directive into domestic law: the Employment Equality (Religion or Belief) Regulations (SI 2003 No.

1660), the Employment Equality (Sexual Orientation) Regulations (SI 2003 No. 1661), the Employment Equality (Sex Discrimination) Regulations (SI 2005 No. 2467) and the Employment Equality (Age) Regulations (SI 2006 No. 1031). Because the ultimate origin of these regulations was the Directive, the Church of Scotland has had to ask itself whether they constitute a circumvention of the 1921 Act and an imposition on the Church of something against which the customary arguments from *Ballantyne* will not be effective. Each of the first two Regulations is particularly worthy of comment.

The Religion or Belief Regulations are meant to ensure that there is no religious discrimination except where a GOR exists, and naturally the questions are more complicated in the situation where the employer, and not just the employee, has a religious standpoint. Within the Church of Scotland there has been a difficult argument lying in the background for some years between those who think that some measurable degree of Christian activity or commitment is a GOR for all employees, and those who think it is a matter of degree, varying from role to role. For example, the former Board of Social Responsibility insisted on active Church membership for all the employees in its care homes, even people whose tasks scarcely provide opportunities for spiritual leadership. Most other boards and employing agencies did not consider such criteria at all. At the General Assembly of 2008, a motion from the floor[31] successfully affirmed that in principle the Church could declare certain types of high-profile jobs to satisfy the test for a GOR of Christian belief, albeit previously the Statutory Instrument had never been invoked by the Church for that purpose.

There were two problems in the regulations for the independent spiritual jurisdiction. First, the Church as a whole, having several employing agencies, is almost certainly incapable of deciding consistently which jobs should trigger the application of the GOR, and that throws into doubt the

Church's ability to assert where the dividing line between sacred and secular lies, with obvious implications for the 1921 Act. Second, and no doubt because the interests of other Churches had to be considered, the provisions relating to GORs were built into the regulations themselves: the protection afforded to the Church is not an exemption *from* the civil law but an exemption *within* the civil law. To this extent the 1921 Act was made redundant, because the spiritual freedom it guarantees was for this purpose provided instead by the new Statutory Instrument.

More contentious are the Sexual Orientation Regulations, which contain a further exemption recognising the offence caused to some religious organisations and their beliefs by homosexuality, and enabling such organisations to discriminate where:

> (a) the employment is for purposes of an organised religion; [and] (b) the employer applies a requirement related to sexual orientation – (i) so as to comply with the doctrines of the religion, or (ii) because of the nature of the employment and the context in which it is carried out, so as to avoid conflicting with the strongly held religious convictions of a significant number of the religion's followers.[32]

This can hardly be described as a real GOR in the sense in which the term is otherwise used in both regulations; it is instead a concession to religious sensitivity that switches off the authority of the civil law, effectively extending religious jurisdiction to areas that do not otherwise fall on the religious side of the dividing line. The provision is controversial, because many people in the Churches are horrified and fearful at the thought that the exception would be utilised in their name, and beyond the Church there is a school of thought that the Regulations go further than the Directive intends.[33] The provision grants in the secular law a form of religious freedom, and so it draws part of the

Church's claim to spiritual freedom away from the Church's own jurisdiction and locates it entirely in the civil law. If the *Ballantyne* case declared that there were non-spiritual matters that might properly be administered by Church law because they could not be naturally separated from spiritual questions, then these Regulations do the converse, by drawing into the civil law an element of the provision of spiritual freedom to the Church. Again the proposition of the previous chapter is illustrated: the Church's spiritual independence and its spiritual jurisdiction are different things and not coterminous. The blurring of the boundary between the Church's authority and the state's is made worse, albeit without any hostile intent by the civil magistrate.

On the one hand, the incorporation of the Directive into domestic law pays no regard to the existing protection the Church of Scotland thinks it enjoys, while on the other hand it makes that protection redundant to the extent by which the new law provides equivalent protection in several areas.

The Church, then, finds itself properly subject to civil law as an employer. It encounters similar levels of regulation as a charity, and as a provider of services in the public sector.

The Office of the Scottish Charity Regulator (OSCR)

Scottish charities are regulated by the Charities and Trustee Investment (Scotland) Act 2005 and consequent government regulations. It is not the purpose of this text to describe in detail the relationship between the Office of the Scottish Charity Regulator and the Church of Scotland, which in the initial phase of registration and confirmation of status has been highly complicated. There are, however, two aspects of the new regime which illustrate the extent to which secular government feels able to enquire into the inner workings of the Church.

First, and in common with all charities, the Church has to demonstrate to OSCR that the thousands of office-bearers who administer its affairs (in congregations, Presbyteries and the central agencies of the General Assembly) are competent charity trustees. They are not scrutinised individually, but the lines of accountability, and conversely the lines of superintendence, are under close and constant review. For example, the role and competence of the Presbytery as a supervisory agency has been of great interest to OSCR officials. The effect will be to remove any possibility of sloppy administration of the Church's affairs, inconsistency in dealing with the *temporalia* of the Church's assets, or discrimination or favouritism in tackling poor trusteeship, for example, through the mishandling of funds. There are many implications here for the superintendence function of the Church's courts, and for the level of expertise and diligence demanded of office-bearers, auditors, ministers and many others.

Second, the Church has been awarded what is now known as 'Designated Religious Charity' status, which will exempt it from a number of the controls imposed on other sorts of charities. This put the Church in 2007 in the interesting position of having to satisfy the state as to its religious credentials, and pass tests that exist in civil law in order to be deemed a spiritual organisation meeting the requirements of the provision. The expenditure of expert legal and administrative time to achieve this was enormous, though largely unacknowledged by the Church and invisible to its members.

As in the case of employment law, charity regulation forces the Church and the civil law to identify boundaries and allocate issues on either side of them. OSCR is entitled to scrutinise the actions of the Church where it operates as a charity, and therefore in the raising, handling and expending of its money, or in its use of the Gift Aid system. OSCR is not entitled to scrutinise those areas of the Church's life that do not impinge on its activities as a recognised charity. Early indications are that there will be cases involving both elements, and the Church will in future years have to defend its independence against this kind of secular supervision where it strays across the infamous, invisible line, just as vigilantly as it would defend the same interests in a case like *Percy*.

It is possible to imagine three reactions to these developments in charity law. The first, expressed quite often especially at Presbytery level, is disappointment and anger, a feeling that the Church's self-regulation has been prejudiced or damaged and its sphere of authority eroded, and that the Church too easily concedes this erosion in favour of the civil authority in a manner that too readily conforms to the standards of this world and not those of the gospel.[34]

The second reaction, the official line of the Church, is to comply with both the charitable test and the Designated Religious Charity (DRC) status test. By satisfying both standards, the extent of public scrutiny is minimised, and the scope for internal regulation is maximised. This is the Church's response to the critics: to be unapologetic in adopting civil law standards that serve a worthwhile aim that is perfectly consistent with the standards of the gospel, and by the same token to keep at bay excessive civil regulation by constantly earning the right to regulate its own affairs as much as possible.

There is a third, more radical, approach. If the standards and criteria imposed on ordinary charities by the 2005 Act are good and desirable, and assist charities in running well and free from possible abuse, and if DRC status exempts the Church from some of that scrutiny, it could be argued that the Church loses out on something that is meant to be a benefit and a useful control. Perhaps the Church should not jump to another conclusion, that state scrutiny of activities outwith the spiritual core must so far as possible be avoided or minimised. The Scottish Episcopal Church had not acquired DRC at the time of writing, thus arguably saving itself the administrative time and expense expended by the

Church of Scotland in this area: and it is a moot point to ask what the SEC might have forfeited as a result.

The Church as a Service Provider: The Sexual Orientation (Provisions of Goods and Services) Regulations 2007

Similar arguments apply to all the civil legislation that affects the Church acting as a public body, or providing commercial services to the public. Of the many that could be mentioned (including the Disability Discrimination Act, and the requirements of child protection legislation), one has been particularly controversial, bringing spiritual judgements into conflict with legal responsibilities.

The passing into law in 2007 of the Equality Act (Sexual Orientation) Regulations[35] extended anti-discrimination protection to the area of the provision of good and services. It was strongly resisted by parts of the Christian community, reflecting one element of the diversity of views within many of the churches on issues relating to human sexuality. Just as with the adoption four years earlier of regulations outlawing sexual orientation discrimination in the field of employment, a problem was posed by the fact that the Church is a hybrid body with spiritual and temporal activities. The government addressed this by using the same sort of exemption for religious organisations as appears as the Genuine Occupational Requirement in the employment regulations of 2003. Again, in the contemplation of the new regulations, the Church was to find itself caught by them to the extent that it was a commercial service provider but exempt from them insofar as it was a spiritual organisation.

As a service provider, the Church found itself in the position where it could avoid providing goods and services to gay people only by avoiding providing them to anyone at all. So a parish church that ran a weekday commercial enterprise, but wished not to serve gay people, could keep within the letter of the regulations simply by closing the enterprise down: by serving neither straight nor gay people, no discriminatory act would have been committed. Famously, the Roman Catholic Church has found itself compelled to consider abandoning completely its work in the area of children's adoption, as the only lawful means of avoiding placing children with same-sex couples.

As soon as the Regulations were published it became apparent that those determined to act discriminatorily on religious grounds intended to shift the apparent basis of their discrimination to avoid breaching the letter of the Regulations while continuing to defy their spirit. In the Church of Scotland in April 2007, the same month in which the Regulations came into force, a report was published[36] stating the Church's position on the general theological issue of human sexuality. In the report, which was authored by a group representing a strikingly broad range of opinion, there seemed to be conceded by the whole group an acceptance of the existence of a homosexual orientation; and by implication the debate thereafter focused entirely on questions of lifestyle and celibacy. Since those whose theology is hostile to gay partnerships tend often to be the same people who are hostile to all sex outside marriage, it was possible to develop a basis of discrimination against anyone believed to be guilty of having sex outside marriage, whether homosexual or heterosexual. Inevitably, this form of discrimination, which of course does not appear as a recognised ground in any anti-discrimination legislation, impacts more heavily upon the gay community. Anyone in a civil partnership and unwilling to be dishonest about their own sex life is regarded as having committed a sin by virtue of the fact that traditional marriage has not been made available by law to same-sex couples.[37] Time will tell whether such blatant indirect discrimination[38] will be permitted by the civil courts.

This controversy has generated more strength of feeling than has the regulation of the churches as employers or as charities, as described above. Most of the commercial enterprises run by local and national churches are regarded by them as part of their work of outreach and service to the world. Most church people would not see such activities as falling outside the spiritual life of the church, and would believe that their doctrinal standards ought to be applied to the manner in which they serve their community.

At the beginning of this book, sovereignty was defined as having two dimensions. One, which might be thought of as 'vertical', concerned the quality of authority over those subject to the ruling force. The other, described as 'horizontal', concerned the outward extent of the authority, and its limits in terms of geography or community or organisation. The new Regulations appear to be premised on a distinction between the providers and the recipients of the goods and services that may be provided by a church. The providers are themselves subject doctrinally to the teachings of the organisation (they are subject to its vertical, internal authority), and are required to modify their own behaviour in obedience to such teachings. Where goods and services are provided commercially (not as part of the core religious activities of the religion's adherents) it is forbidden to require the customer to comply with the organisation's internal standards (i.e. to try to impose one's standards horizontally to those outside). This is possibly the most delicate example so far of identifying what things properly lie inside and outside the Church's spiritual jurisdiction, and avoiding confusion between them.

If the Sexual Orientation Regulations have been the most delicate challenge to the churches, then the heaviest threat has been in the area in which this chapter began, the employment status of the clergy.

Department of Trade and Industry Clergy Working Group

Since late 2002, the Department of Trade and Industry (DTI) has consulted widely, and particularly with the Churches, about the possibility of passing regulations that would extend the rights of employees to 'office-holders'. The initial attitude of the different denominations during the conversations at the DTI was instructive.[39] The Roman Catholic contingent appeared to conduct itself as if they could not believe such a large and international institution as theirs could possibly be threatened by such a change and that the process was irrelevant to them, and they gave little practical support to the others. The Church of England, however, accepted the need for – and inevitability of – state intervention and regulation.[40] The smaller Christian denominations, especially the Reformed Churches, were very anxious lest the Roman Catholic Church and the Church of England should damage their cause. These smaller Churches believed they offered what came to be termed 'equivalence of protection',[41] in other words, provisions within their own rules and regulations that mirrored the safeguards that civil law gave to employees, and it was on the basis of this concept that the Church of Scotland made its written submission to the DTI.[42]

In March 2007 the DTI published a Model Statement of Good Practice for Faith Groups articulating the areas in which the government wished to see the churches give adequate protections to their clergy. These areas are: (1) terms and conditions of work; (2) dispute resolution; (3) development and personnel support; and (4) information and consultation.[43] Each faith group is required to use the Model Statement to produce an appropriate text for its own use, and to disseminate it throughout the organisation. Through an intended process of monitoring, and consultation through questionnaires, at the beginning and end of a two-year period, the government intended to determine whether each church has provided equivalent protection in these key areas, and whether any further regulation will have to be imposed.

The Church of Scotland responded to this challenge by establishing a Working Group straddling the Legal Questions Committee and the Council of Ministries, and co-opting expertise in the field of employment and discrimination law. Various exercises were undertaken, to tighten up the terms of the 'Ministers' Handbook' and the 'Guidelines for Nominating Committees' in vacancies, for example. The Working Group identified that the serious gap in the Church's own legal provision lay in the area of dispute-resolution, most especially where the dispute arose from bullying, harassment and discrimination. Using civil law models to provide the concepts, the Group presented to the General Assembly of 2007 legislative measures to provide remedies for ministers and others against bullying or discriminatory behaviour. The General Assembly approved these measures, which came into force in the late summer of 2007. Perhaps this supplies the want of remedy their Lordships identified: perhaps if this exercise had happened some years before, the *Percy* case would have had a different result.

An obvious question arising from the use, since 2007, of employment contracts by the Ministries Council, is whether this exercise now affects only inducted parish ministers, since all other ministers and all deacons are now employees. At the time of writing the question has not been addressed by the Church's Legal Questions Committee nor has it been tested in civil law. The sphere of independence sought in this way by the Church is probably reduced by the exact extent of the new civil law rights enjoyed by employed clergy; but these individuals remain subject to the Church's jurisdiction for matters of life and doctrine, denominational supervision and superintendence. Since that subjection in the Lord to both the superior courts of the Church can lead to removal of status or suspension from fulfilling ministerial functions,[44] it is likely that the concessions apparently offered by the former DTI do after all benefit all Church of Scotland clergy and not just those who are non-employed office-holders.

Taking BERR/DTI's attitude together with the apparent respect for the Church of Scotland's independent jurisdiction shown in the *Percy* judgement described earlier, this process cannot be interpreted as showing any intention to transgress upon the inherent spiritual jurisdiction, or diminish its scope. The list of areas mentioned in the Model Statement, even for example where they relate closely to areas of clergy discipline, refer to what Lord Scott called the manner of exercise of discipline and not its content. The best possible outcome of the current process, from the Church's point of view, would be that these areas – which the House of Lords did not regard as belonging to the inherent spiritual jurisdiction – are left to the Church to regulate internally. Could it be that the result of a process that initially appeared threatening might be to extend the authority of the Church?

There remain, though, three possible attitudes to these events, as with the developments relating to OSCR already described. The first is the resentful one, defensive of the 1921 settlement and the historical dignity of the Church. This attitude stems from the fear that the civil magistrate is forcing the Church to take steps and enact measures that are not natural to it. Its danger is that instinctive, principled resistance to these developments is bound to result in the government's resorting to the route of external regulation by default, the very reverse of the intention of those who take such an exalted view of the existing settlement.

The second attitude is probably the dominant one within the Church of Scotland, and was the one adopted by the Working Group. In its view, the Church was being prompted, largely from outside itself, to do things it ought to be considering in any case. It is perhaps slightly embarrassing that these measures were not introduced entirely on an initiative from within the Church, but at least the right thing was being done, and if successful it would have the benefit of retaining the maximum possible extent of Church authority over employment-type issues relating to the clergy.

But perhaps there is a third attitude, one to which the argument of all these chapters has been pointing. If this kind of regulation has in fact never been part of the spiritual jurisdiction – the Church only thought it was because the question had never been put to the test and the contours of that jurisdiction were always extremely unclear – why should the Church assume that it is better to regulate these things internally, and why should she presume that she should maximise her authority in this area? Might the civil law be better suited for this work, and might the resources of the Church, its time and the talents of its officials, be better not wasted on providing an equivalence of protection that does not achieve anything different from the civil law's protections? If that third approach were daringly adopted, all sorts of implications would flow.

Conclusion

In 1921, the Church of Scotland and the British state reached a settlement of their respective jurisdictions that left to the courts of the Church authority in matters of worship, doctrine, discipline and Church government, subject to no review by the civil magistrate. In the *Ballantyne* case of 1936 discussed in Chapter 3 above, a doctrine was adopted that extended the authority of the courts of the Church to include any non-spiritual matters that so adhered to spiritual ones that it would be artificial to separate their consideration into two different legal systems. Over a long period in the late twentieth century, free from litigation on these issues, the Church was largely left to regulate itself, to the extent that the whole of the internal affairs of the Church were left to its own disposition and not just those that strictly belonged to the four traditional and specific areas listed in the Fourth Article Declaratory.

In the first few years of the new century, two related things seem to have happened. First, the *laissez-faire* attitude of the previous century no longer holds sway. The civil law is no longer content to leave it to the Church to regulate all its temporal affairs as if they came within its own jurisdiction. Where issues belong not to any of the four traditional areas of spiritual authority, but primarily within the scope of the ordinary law of the land – and this is true of all the examples in this chapter – the civil courts are no longer prepared to conspire with the fiction that those are matters for the Church to deal with alone. Since the Articles Declaratory were not designed to claim that such issues were spiritual ones, it cannot be argued that the spiritual jurisdiction has been diminished by these developments. It has, rather, been clarified. It opens the possibility, probably horrifying to many constitutional conservatives within the Church of Scotland, that the judicial decisions of its courts could and should be subject to appeal – or at least to judicial review – by secular courts where the subject of the judgement falls outwith the historic core of the Church's jurisdiction.

Second, and more particularly, the concession in the 1936 judgement in *Ballantyne*, what might be termed the *Ballantyne* doctrine of kindred litigation, has been clearly set aside by the House of Lords. Lord Scott's distinction between the content of the spiritual jurisdiction over discipline and the manner of its exercise – the former belonging to the Church, the latter possibly to the state – removes any possibility that the employment status of ministers could somehow be treated as an accrual onto the vague notion of ministerial discipline, as if one were contingent on the other. Lord Nicholls's rebuttal of the presumption against ministers having legally enforceable workers' rights provides another means whereby the behaviour of the Church as a quasi-employer is placed under the review of the civil courts.

What has not been adequately addressed in case law is the possibility of overlapping jurisdictions. The House of Lords judgement has presumed that the location of any particular case within the jurisdiction of the civil law must *ipso facto* remove it from the jurisdiction of the Church's courts, and indeed that the non-application of civil law within Church law must mean that the Church cannot give an equivalent, adequate remedy. If it is possible for even just one set of circumstances to be resolved in more than one legal system, then many of their Lordships' arguments would be unnecessary; and the *Ballantyne* doctrine could be revived. Since the *Percy* case is the more recent of the two, and adjudicated in a higher court, its stark precedent prevails, until government does something that supersedes it.

However, the current exercise between faith groups and BERR/DTI would appear to constitute just such an innovation. It provides for the churches to regulate many matters that do not fall within the strictest definition of the Fourth Article, and so far has treated the Church of Scotland as being, in fact, perfectly adequate to the tasks of self-regulation. In the confusing light of this simultaneous specification (*Percy*) and expansion (by the DTI) of the Church's area of sovereignty, what should the Church do to respond adequately to new pressures and opportunities?

First, the Church must recognise that its own area of legal authority and independence cannot be read off the 1921 Act alone. Government legislation giving religious exemptions (the 2003 and 2007 sexual orientation regulations are obvious examples) extend the Church's powers in one direction. The eventual settlement reached with the DTI in areas such as discrimination and minister's terms and conditions of work, extends the sphere of self-regulation in another. The 1921 Act will always be a critical text to provide authority for the Church's entitlement to spiritual independence; but it has never provided adequately clear authority for the nature and extent of a spiritual jurisdiction.

Those two things, this chapter has illustrated several times, are not the same.

Second, the Church must learn one of the lessons of the *Percy* case. A litigant who ought to pursue his or her claim in the courts of the Church because the matter clearly does belong within its traditional jurisdiction, but who resolutely and unswervingly casts their claim in terms of civilian legislation, must be unapologetically resisted. There does remain a spiritual jurisdiction – this chapter has shown that it survives largely as it was originally defined – and the Church must defend its proper core even in the teeth of someone who is determined to pursue a more favourable outcome by defining something as secular, when plainly it is not. Next time, in a case quite different from Miss Percy's, the four traditional areas may be under threat, and so it is important not to allow a slippage of precedents.

Third, the Church has a profound decision of principle to make: whether to continue to work to maximise the amount of self-regulation it has conceded to it, or whether to entrust to the government anything that it does not strictly need to supervise for itself. This question will be picked up again in the final chapter.

Fourth and last, however extensive its own jurisdiction should be in theory, the Church must ensure in practice that its structures, courts and laws do pass the test of adequacy to task. It would be wrong of the Church to seek powers that it was hopelessly ill equipped to exercise justly and equitably. In the next chapter, the Church of Scotland's institutions will be examined, with that challenge in view.

Notes

[1] In earlier drafts the two were a single article and tend to be treated as if they were one topic, quite illegitimately. When they were properly separated in the drafting process, it could be argued that

the provision for boundary-setting should have been moved from what is now Article VI to what is now Article IV.

2 Lyall, *Of Presbyters and Kings*, ch. V.

3 *Ballantyne and Others* v. *Presbytery of Wigtown and Others*, 1936 SC 625.

4 In fact the congregation had not understood the intention of the Act, which was to ensure that no civil rights would improperly prevent a congregation calling a minister: it was not legitimate to interpret the Act to mean that a congregation had an absolute right to call when the obstacle was an internal legal matter within the Church's governance.

5 *Logan* v. *Presbytery of Dumbarton*, 1995 SLT 1228.

6 Lord Davidson and R. A. Paterson, 'Church of Scotland', in *Stair Memorial Encyclopaedia* (Edinburgh: Butterworth, 1993), vol. III, pp. 1501–1609, p. 1505.

7 The Helen Percy case: *Percy* v. *Church of Scotland Board of National Mission*, Industrial Tribunal case S/300120/98, unpublished judgement; *Percy* v. *Church of Scotland Board of National Mission*, Employment Appeal Tribunal case EAT/1415/98, unpublished judgement; *Percy* v. *Order and Judgement of the Employment Appeals Tribunal*, 2001 SC 757; Case Reports: Petition of Helen Percy, in *Volume of Reports and Papers of the Church of Scotland General Assembly of 1999* (Edinburgh: Board of Practice and Procedure, 1999); *Order of Proceedings Papers of the 2002 Church of Scotland General Assembly* (Edinburgh: Board of Practice and Procedure, 2002); 'Report of the Committee on Commissions (Bills and Overtures)', in *Supplementary Volume of Reports to 2002 Church of Scotland General Assembly* (Edinburgh: Board of Practice and Procedure, 2002); *Helen Douglas* v. *The Presbytery of Angus and The Board of National Mission*, Special Commission of the General Assembly, in *Volume of Reports to the General Assembly of 2004* (Edinburgh: Board of Practice and Procedure) pp. 34/1ff.; and the key judgement: *Percy (AP) (Appellant)* v, *Church of Scotland Board of National Mission (Respondent) (Scotland)* [2005] UKHL 73.

For commentary on the case, see: F. Cranmer and S. Peterson, 'Employment, Sex Discrimination and the Churches: The Percy Case', *Ecclesiastical Law Journal* 8 (2006), pp. 392–405; M. MacLean, F. Cranmer and S. Peterson, 'Recent Developments in Church–State Relations in Scotland', in R. M. Morris (ed.),

Church and State (Basingstoke: Palgrave Macmillan, forthcoming); D. Mathieson, 'Clergy, Offices and Employment', *New Zealand Law Journal* (March 2006), pp. 65–8; J. T. Newth, 'Changes at the Manse', *Taxation* (15 March 2007), pp. 296–9; J. Rivers, 'Law, Religion and Gender Equality', *EccLJ* 9 (2007), pp. 24–52.

8 The area of debate was the relationship of European Union legislation with the authority claimed by the General Assembly under the 1921 Act, and the implications for the Church's supposed spiritual independence. Is the sovereignty 'granted' to the Church of Scotland qualified by sovereignty held by the European Union?

It cannot be presumed that the European Union would by its own initiative grant (i.e. acknowledge) in the Church of Scotland an inherent, independent spiritual jurisdiction, since this is not something that has been granted to (i.e. acknowledged in) any other denomination in the Union. If the European Union suffers any lack of authority over the Church of Scotland, it can only be because its own sovereignty is derivative, made up of part of the sovereignty of the British Parliament transferred to the European institutions. The United Kingdom government cannot confer on someone else a jurisdiction that its own legislation denies to it. However important and powerful a state might be, the relevant question is its sovereignty (J. A. Camilleri and J. Falk, *Beyond Sovereignty?: The Politics of a Shrinking and Fragmenting World* [Aldershot: Edward Elgar, 1992], p. 83). This was the conclusion of the Employment Appeal Tribunal, despite an argument by the pursuer's counsel (EAT Report, p. 6E) that in effect contended that the state could be compelled by European law to redraw the bounds of the spiritual jurisdiction. If the judgement is correct, the European Union is obliged to recognise the spiritual independence of the Church of Scotland, just as it recognises its own lack of jurisdiction in respect of, say, a non-member state. This would be quite a different argument from one used by any other European Church to claim exemption from some part of the law; here the exemption is founded in a unique civil statute.

We have seen in respect of the *Logan* case that an argument can be made that the spiritual jurisdiction is a contingent benefit to the Church, so that in appropriate circumstances the state could withdraw its recognition and impose judicial review of the Church's activity. Brian Napier, counsel for Helen Percy, was making a different kind of 'withdrawal of recognition' argument; he was claiming that the Westminster Parliament is obliged to fulfil the directives of the

European Union and therefore that it may be obliged to interpret the 1921 Act in a manner that restricts the privilege that the Church has always had from it. The Procurator at the time, Patrick Hodge QC, appearing for the Church's Board in the Inner House, countered that it was unreasonable to infer that a European Directive was intended to modify the 1921 Act implicitly; but this sounds a little hollow in respect of an Act which we have already seen implicitly repeals other unspecified UK legislation.

9   *Volume of Reports and Papers of the Church of Scotland General Assembly of 1999*, section C, p. 7.

10   *Order of Proceedings Papers of the 2002 Church of Scotland General Assembly*, p. 40.

11   'Report of the Committee on Commissions (Bills and Overtures)', in *Supplementary Volume of Reports to 2002 Church of Scotland General Assembly*, p. 32/12–13.

12   *Supplementary Volume of Reports*, p. 32/13.

13   Sheriff John Horsburgh, who has chaired disciplinary commissions within the Church's jurisdiction; Rev. Alistair McGregor, a retired minister and former QC; and Ms Jill Bell, Director of *Spectrum*, the Discrimination Law Service of Messrs Anderson Strathern WS, who at the time had no other connection with any superior court of the Church.

14   Second Opinion of the Special Commission in Petition of *Helen Douglas v. The Presbytery of Angus and the Board of National Mission*, 24 February 2003 (punctuation original).

15   However, this case and a subsequent one have made it much more possible to interpret the situation of parish clergy in a manner that seems to be moving in this direction: see *New Testament Church of God v. Stewart EAT*, on 27 October 2006, reported at [2007] IRLR 178. It is important to note that the *Stewart* case provides authority for the proposition that it is not impossible for a church minister, by virtue of his or her ministry, to be an employee. That is not at all the same thing as saying the all ministers must be employees. The *Percy* case, it seems to me, affirms that it is possible for a church and minister to create legal relations, but those legal relations may take several forms.

16   Lords Nicholls of Birkenhead, Hope of Craighead and Scott of Foscote, and Baroness Hale of Richmond. Lord Hoffmann dissented.

17   Inner House interlocutor, para. 13.

[18] House of Lords judgement, para. 26.

[19] Ibid., para. 23.

[20] See, e.g. para. 114, in Lord Hope's judgement.

[21] Ibid., paras 56ff.

[22] Ibid., para. 76. SI 2005 No. 2467.

[23] Ibid., paras 113–15.

[24] Ibid., paras 119–35; and Lady Hale, at para. 152.

[25] Ibid., para. 41.

[26] Ibid., para. 154.

[27] Ibid., para. 138. In private conversation long after the case, one of Miss Percy's lawyers expressed to the author the opinion that this could even include some issues of substance, e.g. in examining whether there had been discriminatory behaviour by the organisation.

[28] Listed in n. 7 above.

[29] Known currently as Presbytery and Parish Workers (PPWs).

[30] Newth, 'Changes at the Manse', p. 298.

[31] It was moved by the retiring Vice-Convener of the Social Care Council, the successor body of the Board of Social Responsibility.

[32] Equality Act (Sexual Orientation) Regulations SI 2007 Section 7(3).

[33] In October 2003, the TUC attempted a legal challenge to the provision of the concept of Genuine Occupational Requirement, seeking to have the government's action judicially reviewed.

[34] This is exemplified by a number of Presbyteries who held out, in the winter of 2007–8, against implementing an arrangement for reforming congregational names to conform with the principles of transparency and consistency required by OSCR. Eventually, the General Assembly of 2008 instructed compliance.

[35] Equality Act (Sexual Orientation) Regulations SI 2007, No. 1263.

[36] Report of the Working Group on Human Sexuality, in *Volume of Reports to the General Assembly of 2007* (Edinburgh: Assembly Arrangements Committee, 2007), pp. 4/9ff.

[37] For example, see *Reaney v. Hereford Diocesan Board of Finance* ET 1602844/2006.

[38] Indirect discrimination is taken in civil law to mean treating people in such a way as impacts unequally on people who are apparently not subject to direct discrimination.

[39] Private conversation with Rev. Ann Inglis, Secretary (at the time) of the Legal Questions Committee of the Board of Practice and Procedure and the Church's representative to the DTI consultation.

The Department is now known as the Department for Business, Enterprise and Regulatory Reform, but I use here the nomenclature from the time of the Church's engagement with government on this issue.

[40] As things have worked out, this apparent appetite for state regulation has not apparently prejudiced the interests of other churches. The Church of England adopted the Statement of Good Practice for Faith Groups <http://www.dti.gov.uk/files/file38521.doc> and in 2007 enacted its own Ecclesiastical Offices (Terms of Service) Legislation, an attempt to tackle the most problematic areas they faced.

[41] Private conversation with Rev. David Cornick, General Secretary of the United Reformed Church.

[42] 'Response by the Church of Scotland to DTI Discussion Document on Employment Status in Relation to Statutory Employment Rights' (Edinburgh: Board of Practice and Procedure, 2002, unpublished).

[43] See Appendix III for the full text of the Model Statement, which appears on the website of the Department for Business, Enterprise and Regulatory Reform at <www.berr.gov.uk/files/file38521.doc>.

[44] Normally in terms of Act III 2001 (as amended) of the General Assembly.

Chapter 5

The Church of Scotland – a Sovereign Authority?

The Church of Scotland has its own legal system, complete with legislative, executive and judicial functions; a corpus of written law and a tradition of common law; and a legal literature that reflects changes and guides practitioners. Like any legal system it is based on certain premises and principles, and it would be unworkable if it did not have such an intellectual foundation.[1] Every legal system needs to have a sense of the ultimate source of its laws, which may come from a theological belief, or a Marxist philosophy, or a secular theory of justice, or some other perceived origin. Every legal system can be identified with some kind of theory of decision-making, and these may include democracy, oligarchy, meritocracy or absolute monarchy. Every legal system will develop its own culture of expectations, so that its practitioners can anticipate the place, use and relative priority of rights, duties, liberties and so on. Without these elements, usually known as 'jurisprudence' in the sense of 'legal philosophy', any body of law risks arbitrariness and rootlessness and is unlikely to form a coherent system. This chapter explores the question of what might be said to constitute the jurisprudential theory for the Church of Scotland's legal system, using the concepts developed so far, and asks what are the jurisprudential arguments that define and affirm its constitutional position in its relations with secular law.

Some legal systems contain an authority that is regarded as a 'sovereign': nation states and international empires are normally credited with sovereignty. Some systems of law serve bodies that are never described as sovereign: local authorities, professional bodies and voluntary organisations come into this category. The development of the Church of Scotland through its turbulent history and the peculiar terms of the 1921 Act leave unclear the question of how far the Church should regard itself as a sovereign institution in law; so this chapter will use the discussion of sovereignty in Chapter 1 to try to suggest some clarification.

To the extent (if any) that the Church of Scotland possesses a degree of legal sovereignty, it is important to ask whether that sovereignty needs to be defended, and it is necessary to know how to base such a defence. If, however, the Church is not sovereign but has to submit to a greater human authority, it is important to know where the Church's legal authority comes from and on what contingencies it depends. The historical narrative I have previously offered provides the resources to describe the Church's current relations with other laws and authorities.

The conclusions of this chapter consist of a network of related arguments – from theology, jurisprudence and political science – which together provide a theoretical discourse around the 1921 settlement. Such a discourse is missing in recent academic research, which has treated the settlement only as a historical event; but this discussion is much needed by the Church itself, because the implications of the settlement – and its constant slippage – are a contemporary reality in the Church's polity. With an unprecedented frequency the legal officers of the General Assembly are faced with possible challenges to the integrity of the Church's internal regulation. European, British and Scottish legislation and regulation, case law precedent within and beyond the Church, the recent growth of trade union membership among ministers and the increasing recognition within the Church of equality and discrimination issues are all examples of real pressures on Church polity and governance. What this chapter begins to address from an academic point of view is some discrimination between the responsibilities of government that the Church must not avoid or concede or forget or fail to defend, and the habits of rule that it is right to question and prise away from the Church's courts.

The Church and the Failure of Vertical Sovereignty

The Character of Vertical Sovereignty

In its vertical aspect sovereignty has two characteristics, identifiable in the survey of Scottish history previously presented. First, any sovereign power is supreme within the jurisdiction: it is the ultimate determining authority, which outranks all others and has the final say. In a dictatorship, the dictator's will prevails even in face of the will of parliament or of the people, but in a democracy the will of the people prevails either through direct consultation on an issue (a referendum) and/or through a regular electoral process (in a representative democracy). Second, any sovereign power within a piece of territory or a particular community determines its own sphere and the extent of its engagement and authority, Schmitt's *competenz-competenz*. This is an authority over questions of governance, not just authority to do the day-to-day governing. It is the power to confer power, to identify and legitimate government. These two elements are significantly different. An authority that is supreme but for some reason not sovereign (for example, if it is the supreme governing force in one territory within a larger empire) may be a moral or legal force, but it lacks the quality of being the ultimate constitutional power because it does not have the ability to change the source or location of governance. When an institution is being examined and the question is being asked whether it *is* sovereign, it is important to ask too whether it *needs* to be sovereign.

Except in an absolute dictatorship, every government – even a sovereign power – operates within limitations that have been self-imposed, or have been long recognised as part of the constitution, or – in the case of a non-sovereign power – have been imposed *de facto* by a greater power to which the government is in turn subject. The authority wielded by that governing power extends only where those limitations do not have effect, and sometimes a ruling body is thwarted from carrying out its intentions because it encounters an immoveable legal or political limitation. If a power that is meant to be sovereign finds that the number and strength of the limitations it faces increases, it may reach a point where it loses the effective ability to make decisions about governance. In that event, a sovereign power may have lost its sovereignty; and it may have happened suddenly and visibly, or subtly and unconsciously.

Several sorts of limitation may compromise a sovereign power. First, if the jurisdiction possesses a written constitution it may include a bill of rights with implications for government and law making. Even if there is no constitutional bill, government has to consider what human rights are enjoyed by its citizens, and owed by their institutions. Second, the jurisdiction may have a tradition of the principle of the 'rule of law', which means that existing provisions cannot be set aside even for constitutional purposes, and government is obliged to work within the framework of its existing legislation. Third, the principles of the traditions of Natural Law may be recognised, limited to the immutable physical laws of nature (preventing a government from legislating the impossible) or extending to moral propositions universally regarded as self-evidently normative. These would produce a corpus of law that does not require any authority in human law and is morally ring-fenced against change. Fourth, and if the institution under consideration has any constitutional recognition of religion, elements of Divine Law (e.g. the Ten Commandments) may be imported into positive law and, again, form a constraint upon the ruler. Fifth, and most likely to make the difference between a sovereign and non-sovereign regime, power may be severely limited by the sheer refusal of people to recognise or obey it. This may be a problem of vertical authority, if the ruler's subjects lose their acknowledgement of the legitimacy of the rule; and it may be a problem of horizontal freedom if competing authorities remove their recognition and their self-restraint. Not all of these are limitations in law, but each of them might apply in some way to the authority or influence of the Church as much as they do to a secular government.

Is the Church of Scotland, then, an authority that satisfies the vertical tests of sovereignty? Is its authority sufficient to survive the limitations placed on it from within its own jurisprudence? And in any case, does it need to be sovereign to achieve its ends? If the Church of Scotland has the internal mechanisms to regulate its own affairs and make administrative change, does it need a state-like power to make changes of governance, to alter its own constitution or to define afresh the scope of its authority and influence over its members? If the Church has powers that are sufficient for its purposes but not sovereign in terms of this definition, there may be no need for regret. Can the Church enforce its authority in a sovereign manner? How does Church membership compel or influence behaviour?

We saw in Chapter 1 that Reformed theology offers a pattern in which compulsion has no legitimate place within the sphere of authority of a movement founded on the mandate of the gospel. Therefore the Church cannot compel (i.e. vertically) the behaviour of those subject to its jurisdiction, and its courts have available a much more limited array of censures than the civil law has. There are in essence two kinds of punishment in the current disciplinary code: one is reprimand (which is pointless unless the offender recognises the jurisdiction and feels enough contrition for the words of the court or commission to strike home) and the other is the removal of ordained status (which does not punish the person within the system but removes him or her from it). In other words the vertical, internal aspect of the Church's sovereignty is not constructed to facilitate compulsion of behaviour, and in that respect is true to the gospel of Jesus.

Limits to the Authority of the Church: Freedom of Opinion

Even were the power of compulsion to exist, in the way it once existed in other churches, it could rarely be used, because the Church is subject to the far reaching spiritual constraint that is liberty of conscience in the interpretation of Scripture. The General Assembly has constantly to be aware where its legislative activity would compromise the legitimate beliefs of such a significant number of the Church's members that proceeding with enactment of a measure would be unwise. There are three measurements the Church must bear in mind in exercising this corporate self-discipline. First, there has to be some way of knowing that a significant number objects to a proposal, and the Barrier Act of 1697[2] and other kinds of consultation are helpful in that regard. Second, there have to be some criteria determining the sorts of things that fall within the doctrinal core of the Church's confessional identity and the sorts of thing on which it is reasonable for Church members to disagree. Third, in a Church with the ability to change and develop in the ways argued for earlier, there has to be a process to determine whether the core defined immediately above should change, and whether the fundamental beliefs required of all members (or at least all office-bearers) have expanded or contracted.

In 2006 there was a sensation in the Church when a proposal was brought to the General Assembly, which would have guaranteed to ministers and deacons that no disciplinary action could be brought against them in the event of their conducting a service of worship that recognised a recent civil partnership.[3] It was intended to affirm liberty of conscience. People seemed to approach the debate in three different ways. Many approached it as if it were an argument about the ethics of homosexuality, and appeared not to understand that they were in fact making a determination about legal liberty, which in constitutional terms was the major issue here. A few approached it with the desire to preserve appropriate liberty of conscience, even if that meant permitting others to do something they themselves would abhor. And some, hostile to the proposal for reasons of substance, approached it with the deliberate intention of removing liberty of conscience, or of separating belief from action and removing liberty of action, which would have the same effect. The measure failed to secure sufficient support during the Barrier Act process, so that no change was effected either to the Church's teaching about sexuality or to its ministers' liberty of conscience.[4] It would have been unfortunate, no matter what the outcome, if the Church had changed its standard of liberty of conscience for the sake of a single, arbitrary controversy. Liberty of individual conscience remains one of the principal limitations to the sovereign powers of the Church's courts; but the definition of that liberty is far from clear and the subject of heated debate.

Waiting in the wings of this chapter's argument is the great alternative to the Church's sovereignty of power and compulsion, and that is the diakonal sovereignty of God. The Church is not called to the exercise of vertical human sovereignty as coercive of people's beliefs and behaviour; it is called to the exercise of diakonal authority in service of the members of the Church in their dynamic relationship with God. A Church that regards any diversity of view as a necessary evil (to be tolerated only as far as external constraints require it to do so) is a Church intending to change as little as possible. It is a Church likely to take a 'Free Church case' view of its identity, conserving and preserving traditional teaching for its own sake and avoiding future doctrinal reform. A Church that serves diversity of opinion and does not enforce conformity any further than it has to is a Church that is giving God every chance to reform and transform it, understanding its traditional teaching but presuming nothing about the Divine will. It is entirely possible that God intends to maintain most of the doctrinal tradition of the Church, but the Church cannot prove that as a certainty. The former model of ecclesiastical sovereignty does not maximise God's room for manoeuvre; while the latter leaves it open to God to move the Church forward, *or not*, as the Church's reading of Scripture and wrestling of consciences allows. This conclusion is a liberal plea not for dogmatic revolution but for structured openness to the leading of God; it is a twenty-first century recasting of the New Licht[5] tradition without making any judgement as to whether any new licht happens to be shining. It is therefore a plea not to assume that the Christian authority of the Church of Scotland must always be a vertical, downward, authority of compulsion.

In its sometimes all-too-human struggles, the Church of Scotland demonstrates that it is structurally capable of achieving neither a monolithic authority nor a genuine openness to the possibility of divinely ordained change; neither a compelling and functioning human sovereignty nor a transparent obedience to the sole sovereignty of God. First, the Church of Scotland has a membership, and professional ministry, which can only be described as a loose coalition of conflicting theological viewpoints, coexisting in a single denomination but constantly in conflict with one another. On questions of scriptural interpretation and authority, and derivative arguments including many on questions of personal ethics, the Church is just too varied for it to be possible to arrive at a single authoritative position. Second, the Church cannot decide whether it is legitimate to contain this very diversity of opinion. Many people in the Church generously defend the freedom of belief of those who disagree with them on matters of substance; but many others believe the range of opinions should be narrow, coinciding of course with their own views. The Church therefore cannot agree even whether it wishes to strive for a single view on anything, because this prior debate on liberty of opinion frustrates any particular debates on individual issues of disagreement. Third, and probably not widely enough appreciated by commentators on the life of the Church, the Church does not contain two parties each with a manifesto drawing together agreed opinions on the range of debates. The Church consists of people with different attitudes to different subjects. One minister may be (1) pro-gay, (2) thoroughly disapproving of preaching being undertaken by people without professional train- ing, and (3) taking a strict view of the legislation regulating the baptism of infants.[6] Another minister may differ from him in respect of just one of those. In this example, in a group of eight different ministers there may not be any two who agree on everything.[7] Viewed over the immense range of debated topics within the Church, it becomes extremely unlikely – and completely undesirable – for the Church to fracture over one argument. The dividing groups would neither of them be monolithic, looking at all the other areas of debate also current; and they would either decline to secede together, or quickly disintegrate into many religious factions.[8] Observers of recent debates, especially over human sexuality, might regard the Church of Scotland as being already fractured beyond repair; but if that is so, then it is a 'jam-jar' fracture, the sort where the fragments are stuck together, albeit without strength or unity.

The Church of Scotland has been described in terms of a franchise operation, where individual units (congregations, ministers, Kirk Sessions) use the trading name of the whole organisation but may be quite locally distinctive in their practices.[9] Indeed, the metaphor of 'franchise' has been criticised as insufficiently pejorative, since most franchise businesses demand that their outlets provide a highly standardised product, instantly recognisable as belonging to the brand name; while the Church of Scotland allows a diversity of opinion and practice as wide as any contrast between denominations. It is the curse of many national churches that they are so broad and include such diversity, though it ought to be a glory rather than a curse. The institutional Church can speak radically while speaking inclusively, can model with courage the effect of respecting differences of opinion, and can of course find many important things on which to agree and speak out influentially to the secular realm. What it cannot manage adequately is to wield sovereign power clearly and effectively, in its present state.

There are implications of this reality, for the present discussion. The General Assembly is largely prevented from saying things as distinctive, prophetic and controversial as it would like, because it is a trumpet which sometimes has to sound an uncertain note. It represents a Church that humanly cannot make a singular authoritative proclamation. It represents God whose voice somehow has to penetrate the thick growth of many arguments, which both weave the Church together and keep it hopelessly divided. The pattern of church–state engagement has to serve difficult ecclesiastical realities that cannot be easily changed.

One thing is clear. The maddeningly broad Church of Scotland cannot exercise unfettered authority at any point in its structure, and so fails the vertical test of sovereignty.

The Church and the
Failure of Horizontal Sovereignty

In its horizontal aspect, sovereignty marks a power that is not qualified or constrained by any external power. It is difficult to say that the Church of Scotland has this external element of sovereignty in relation to civil power and law. The parts of the Church's life into which this book has shown the civil law reaches with its own sovereign power (e.g. charity law, health and safety law) are clearly the parts that cannot be described as spiritually independent, and it is increasingly difficult to be confident that there remain clear limits to that potential encroachment. It is possible to make the same point more generally about the authority of the Church in national life, and say that parts of the Church's life are compromised by a secular counter-culture that has long since lost its loyalty to the spiritual sovereignty the Church claims. The debate within the Church is over what that secular culture consists of, how far it is counter to the Church's standards, and whether either compromises the other. For example, national events that were once marked invariably by Christian acts of worship, such as the deaths of members of the Royal Family, are marked by many people in ways that are significant and meaningful to them, but not explicitly Christian or institutionally organised.

The non-coercive nature of the Church has huge implications for the contours of the Church's authority. It cannot resist by force – for it says it has none legitimately available to it – the encroachment of conflicting authority from outside, and can assert its own position only by argument. If the Church possesses power or even sovereignty that power or sovereignty must be fragile, because the Church is not an entity that can go to war against hostile threats and it is not a governmental institution that can appeal to international law against the civil authority. If it finds its horizontal sovereignty has been compromised or lost, there is nothing it can do to compel its recovery; and so its own authority becomes, in effect, contingent on the goodwill and restraints of such surrounding authorities as would possess that authority or jurisdiction in the absence of the Church. Given the civil law treatment of the 1921 settlement to date, this is exactly the situation of the Church of Scotland now.

Church and State?: The Changing Nature of the State

As fast as the authority of the Church seems still to be receding and its power to compel to be further disappearing, its partners in legal engagement beyond its own bounds seem also to be fragmenting and becoming difficult to identify, and therefore hopelessly difficult to engage with or try to control. For some purposes the point of sovereign authority is now located somewhere above the level of the nation state, as international institutions increasingly exercise powers of regulation and compulsion of behaviour by and within the older units: the regulation of trade within the European Union is the most vivid example of that from a British point of view. For other purposes the sovereign authority is located, in practice, below the level of the nation state, as different kinds of communities acquire authority of self-regulation inside the older unit: the habit of non-interference by the Westminster Government in the decisions of the current Scottish Parliament is the most vivid example from the Scottish point of view. For some purposes, any kind of purported sovereign power in law is ineffectual: the impotence of governing authorities to regulate traffic on the internet is a globally vivid demonstration. A contemporary American theologian working in the area of Church and state, Larry Rasmussen, observes that the nation state has been the chief actor with which the Church has had to deal for the past two hundred years. He points out, however, that it is no longer the only chief power, because it is too large to deal with local problems and too small to deal with global ones.[10] In the British context, a recent commentator on Church establishment pointed out:

> While historians have become accustomed to asking in the past, if inadequately, how the British State has accommodated different church–state relations within its territory – on the assumption that the State itself was stable – that assumption can now no longer be maintained.[11]

There is no point in using language that has lost its points of reference; and a phrase once useful in the analysis of church–state relations – the Two-Kingdoms theory – has to be translated into a new reality. Neither Church nor state can safely be assumed to be monolithic institutions that can relate to each other as legally competent actors, alone sufficient to exhaust the relations of the sacred and the secular. The underlying concept is not invalid, because there is still a reasonable distinction to be made between the Body of Christ (the Church) and the rest of creation (the world). For legal purposes, however, it is important to acknowledge that the powers that be on either side of that traditional divide are complex groups of authorities, not single authorities. The kingdoms are as much God's as ever they were, but to describe them as just 'two' no longer works in a discussion of laws.

In that case, the relations between Church and state might exist in all sorts of connections, not between two points of sovereign power but between two complex communities within a network of social geometry.[12] If the *societas perfecta* has lost its perfection, it is necessary to focus on the realities of *communio*. The engagement of the Church with the civil order may take place in the supra-national and local strata, and not just as a formal legal relationship between the law of a General Assembly and the law of a national parliament. For instance, the contribution made by the Conference of European Churches to the preparation of the European constitution document in the autumn of 2003 is as much an engagement between different kingdoms as are the activities envisaged by the framers of the Sixth Article Declaratory.

The Fourth and Sixth Articles Declaratory were framed to ensure that the Church of Scotland was both national and free. The Articles and the Act that acknowledged them were not framed to promote or preserve the Establishment in law of the Church, but historians and commentators tend to be unable to resist thinking in that category and they read into the Scottish church–state relationship something that is not there. In the same way legal theorists, from Figgis writing at the time the settlement was framed to MacCormick writing in our own generation, have read into the settlement a granting of legal sovereignty over an identified dominion, something that was scarcely secure to begin with and virtually impossible to argue exists any longer. The Church has conspired with this misconception, clinging to the fragile belief that the extent and nature of its jurisdiction was monolithic, unambiguous and safe from outside challenge. In a study of the relationship between theology and social theory, John Milbank puts it this way:

[A] Church which understands itself as having a particular sphere of interest will mimic the procedures of political sovereignty, and invent a kind of bureaucratic management of believers.[13]

The point is made with particular reference to the Church of Scotland in Will Storrar's article examining the relationship between the Church and what he calls the institutions of modernity.[14] Storrar argues that the contemporary decline of the Church of Scotland as a national institution can be accounted for by its close partnership with the institutions of modernity, in which he includes the nation state. By this he means that the Church in the twentieth century took on many of the characteristic social features of modern organisations, not least a rational bureaucracy that had first been developed by the Free Church through the Sustentation Fund that provided funding from congregations for national management and initiatives. The secular institutions associated with modern, rational, bureaucratic forms of management have begun to lose their power and influence; and the Church is losing its power and influence to the extent that it has made itself such an institution. The conclusion of this argument is that the Church must not try to revive what it has been, allied to a civil society that has left the old nation state model behind. Instead the Church should accept that it is changing into something else, and find new ways to relate to a different social geometry. This is a plea for the institutional Church to welcome the analyses of post-modernist thought; and it reflects the use theologians in many disciplines are making of the possibilities of new ways of thinking about language, thought, belief, metaphor, etc.[15]

One by one, the functions of the civil magistrate in supporting the life and governance of the Church of Scotland have evaporated. Some clearly vanished a long time ago: it is centuries since state legislation authorised or anathematised a Church other than the national Church, there is no longer a civil property right attached to patronage of a local congregation, and so on. Other elements of civil support remain debatable, but they do not have the relevance some people claim for them. The Church of Scotland is not an Established Church any more (either in the sense it once was on the Genevan model of Establishment or in the manner of the Established Church of England).[16] The Accession Oath probably does not constitute a barrier to change, since constitutional means would be found to recognise even a major change in Church government (provided that the Church itself legitimately chose it). In fact, the 1921 Act and the Fourth Article Declaratory are probably the only elements of the 'efficient' part of the British state that affect and secure the life of the Church of Scotland. The relationship between

Church and state is transacted at the level of the 'dignified' elements of both. In the sixteenth century Andrew Melville argued that the civil magistrate should exercise his authority in support of the Church but not over it:[17] now it is hard to see how even the former happens in any measurable way.

The way in which civil institutions support the cause of the Church is much more indirect today. In law making, the government acts against fraud, violence, dishonesty and abuse: it does so not because they are regarded as vices by Christians only but because politicians are given a mandate by the whole electorate to take those measures. The Church may benefit indirectly by the suppression in law of what are sins according to its teaching and may even take some of the credit because the Christian perspective of some of the legislators informed their voting record. In fact the government has done no more than the task that Luther believed it has, of creating the conditions in which the gospel may thrive without straying from its area of authority into that of the Church. The age of Calvin's consistory has long passed. The law may benefit the Church, but that does not necessarily mean there remains any formal state allegiance to the Church. At most, as the Catholic James Mackey suggests, the nation expects the Church to preach a philosophy that in turn will have a beneficent effect on the state's legislation.[18]

The institutions with which the Church engages are not just those from whom it asserts its independence in law, and neither are they only national institutions. The Church is elbow deep in society: from the provision of chaplaincy to the armed forces to the provision of school chaplaincy by local invitation; from the collaborative relationship between the Scottish Parliament and the Scottish Churches Parliamentary Office to the involvement of local congregations in community initiatives; from the kirking of the Parliament to the kirking of local councils – or even the kirking of a Gala Week Queen.[19] Church and society have expectations of each other based on goodwill and partnership within the network of social geometry (the more flexible definition of 'the state' offered in Chapter 1) that is the context of both parties.

Church and State?: The Church's Loss of Spiritual Monopoly

There is also a complex network of religious geometry to reduce any prospect of a meaningful horizontal 'sovereignty'. Not only is the Church of Scotland itself a network of different views and practices but also Scotland has an increasingly pluralistic religious society. There are other strong Christian denominations (especially the Roman Catholic Church, easily rivalling the national Church in size in West Central Scotland) and the growing presence of other world faiths especially in larger cities.

Even in 1921, the dignity and place of other Christian Churches was anticipated in the Church of Scotland Act itself:[20]

> Nothing contained in this Act or in any other Act affecting the Church of Scotland shall prejudice the recognition of any other Church in Scotland as a Christian Church protected by law in the exercise of its spiritual functions.

As it must now have become obvious that this book's analysis regards spiritual freedom and spiritual jurisdiction as quite different things, it is noteworthy that the civil magistrate at the time of the Church of Scotland's settlement was willing to extend the promise of the former privilege – protection of spiritual function – to all Churches and not just to what had been the Established Church of the land.

Delicate cultural and political discussion surrounds the question of finding an appropriate place in national life for the other faiths represented in Scottish society. The Scottish Inter-Faith Network works to provide for them a single voice so far as possible, and includes the Christian Churches in its membership to enhance still further the unity of purpose of everyone together. And society's institutions are gradually making space for those different expressions of religious life, for example, by the recent appointment of five civilian chaplains to the Armed Forces (Jewish, Muslim, Sikh, Hindu and Buddhist).

It is a form of limitation on horizontal sovereignty not anticipated centuries ago when Church and state were struggling for authority: other spiritual powers needing their place too, and trying to achieve the same benefits, patently with the approval of the intention of the framers of the 1921 Act.

Church and State?: The Failure of the Sphere Model

The Church appears to lack nowadays an easily demonstrated element of self-contained horizontal sovereignty *vis-à-vis* other institutions. However, this does not demonstrate a disastrous weakness on the part of the Church but, rather, a conceptual weakness in choosing a model of exclusive power to discuss the Church's kind of authority. A 'sphere sovereignty' model of mutually exclusive dominions of sovereignty is not untidy enough for the analysis of Scottish church–state relations in the past, nor for predictions for the future. Scottish Reformed political theology has never lost awareness of the belief that God is sovereign over every authority, ecclesiastical and civil alike; so the distinction of Two Kingdoms, one God's and the other the world's, is clearly troublesome. The divine sovereignty should not be confined only to the discipline of the Church: the world is God's too. Untidiness – the lack of over-narrow definition – is also necessary because sovereignties are increasingly fragmenting and shifting: the Church continues to divide into more and more self-determining denominations, while the world simultaneously splinters into more and more states and ethnic units and yet organises itself for certain important purposes into defence alliances, trading groups and cultural associations. Even as long ago as the Union of 1707, the product of the treaty was a state that was not entirely unitary, leaving behind in Scotland a distinct establishment of Church, legal system and cultural society.[21] Where a model of neat, articulated spheres of sovereignty does not work, the reality must be some element of engagement, integration or overlap. In the case of a Reformed Church seeking to engage with the world in which it is set, that should be regarded as a blessing; and the limitation it places on the Church's sovereign independence may be, after all, a price worth paying.

Perhaps those who feel frustrated by the Church's bureaucratic institutions are really experiencing the frustration of wrestling with an institution that is hitched to a model of state-like sovereignty that belongs to a passing age. The staff of the Church's central agencies do not, for the most part, believe they are regulating and constraining behaviour or imposing laws, but the popular perception is that they are a kind of civil service running a piece of legal machinery producing diktats that cannot be resisted by the rest of the Church. If the Church believes it is a sovereign institution governing a sphere of influence, what might be called a 'realm', for all purposes connected with worship, Church government, doctrine and discipline, then it is obliged to provide rules, mandates and authority throughout those areas – for its whole sphere of historic responsibility – and that adds to the weight of bureaucracy.

The question of horizontal sovereignty is one of observation: does this institution find itself subject to any external authority that it cannot resist? For the Church of Scotland the answer in law is 'yes', but there is scope in a Reformed theology to make a virtue out of what some would see as a disappointment, by recognising that the relationship between different communities may be more important than their legal separation.

The Church of Scotland does not enjoy independence of the social institutions around it, and so fails the horizontal test of sovereignty.

The Church and the Myth of Popular Sovereignty

Turning from the question of what defines sovereignty to the question of what its source is, we find that the characteristically Scottish Reformed approach developed through the thinking of John Knox, George Buchanan, Samuel Rutherford and the framers of the National Covenant of 1638. There are several elements in this Scottish tradition. First, at its root is a belief in popular sovereignty, by which is normally understood the self-determination of the whole people in the context of their relationship (individual and corporate) with God. In the immediate post-Reformation literature it is difficult to find a clear description of how an articulate and identifiable process of self-determination works, though the process of bonding or banding brought together people of like minds into groups strong enough to effect political or constitutional change. The second element in the Scottish model is 'fiduciary dominion', the ruler's power (*dominium*) to govern given by the people, who offer their trust (*fides*) but not their sovereignty, which according to the theory remains with them. The ruling power is therefore supreme but constitutionally bound, and cannot arbitrarily change the bounds of its authority or the constraints under which it is obliged to operate. The third element of the Scottish model is the presence of such constraints on the sovereign people and the holder of fiduciary dominion alike: these have normally been Natural Law and Divine Law, as understood from time to time, and the rule of law.

It is dangerously tempting to assume that this ideal, the Scottish model of popular sovereignty, must be true also of the Scottish Church and not only of the secular institutions to which it was addressed. Contrast it, though, with the constitution and operation of the courts of the Church of Scotland. The voting membership of the General Assembly is chosen by Presbyteries and consists of ministers and deacons (not necessarily still active in ministry) who are members of the Presbytery, along with elders (at least nominally still active) who are members of a Kirk Session though not necessarily also of the Presbytery.[22] The voting membership of the Presbytery is appointed in a hybrid way, consisting of active ministers (fulfilling criteria set out in the legislation) and deacons, along with elders appointed by the Kirk Sessions within the bounds or elected by the Presbytery itself.[23] The membership of a Kirk Session consists of all active and nominally active elders, and they are chosen by one of a number of methods, not all of which involve the congregation at any point, and all of which are subject to the veto of the Kirk Session itself even where the nomination has come from a congregational process.[24] The determination of who shall be the governors of the Church is therefore not a democratic decision; it is not made by the whole people of the Church and in most situations small groups of existing governors appoint from among themselves.

Neither is it possible to assert that the members of Church courts, however selected, govern in a manner that might be called 'representative democracy'. To illustrate again: the provisions of the legislation regulating appraisal of local charges sets out a process of consultation and decision-making, which includes a congregational vote in circumstances where a substantive adjustment will change the shape or resourcing of the congregation. However, this local decision is followed by a decision of Presbytery, which is at liberty to come to a conclusion at odds with the declared opinion of the congregational meeting. Members of the congregation have only a right of appeal against the final decision, but not an original right of determination of their own circumstances.[25] The people do not have the final say: Presbytery knows best.

In defence of the system, it must be said that those within it always use the rhetoric of vocation in respect of appointment or ordination to office and the discipline of prayer and intention of spiritual discernment at the point of making decisions (for example, by beginning and ending all decision-making meetings with prayer). It is difficult, however, to see what other conclusion can be reached than that the governance of the Church of Scotland is primarily a form of divine right regime and (most of the time) not a form of representative democracy.

This is a hard truth for the Church to swallow, and an even harder one for it to defend. 'Democracy' is a heavily value-laden word with entirely positive associations in virtually all its uses: it is a term whose promotion normally guarantees approval in liberal societies, and most people cannot imagine there are any circumstances in which it is not the best form of government for any institution. Some Churches even use it. Democracy, however, is basically a system for enabling the will of the people to determine issues. A sophisticated democracy is less basic, and has safeguards to ensure that the will of the majority does not override precious rights of minorities, which demonstrates that there are occasionally values that outweigh the main elements of democratic process. Presbyterianism, in contrast, is meant to be a system for discerning and applying the will of God. Its imperfections are largely the function of the imperfection of Church members' ability to discern God's will clearly, and mean that often the outcome of a process will have discerned nothing more than the will of the people. Continuing the comparison with democracy, Presbyterianism working very badly indeed will discern the will of a majority that is unconcerned to guarantee rights to legitimate minorities within the Church.

The common understanding of sovereignty that prevailed beyond Scotland, though favoured by the Stuart kings even there, was not the model of popular sovereignty; it was the idea of the Divine Right of Kings. This was the belief that the authority to govern was conferred by God directly upon the ruler and not through a sovereign populace. In its reflective versions, Divine Right theory contained the limitation of powers; so that it was absolute in the sense that no one within the ambit of authority was involved in granting it to the ruler, but it was limited in the sense that it had recognised parameters of Natural Law, natural justice, Christian duty and so on. This prevented its being an arbitrary or despotic exercise of irresistible power, and the results in terms of governance could be perfectly benign and advantageous to those who were ruled by it. In short it was not *necessarily* malign, but its potential for despotism attracted hostility and suspicion by Scottish proponents of democracy.

Presbyterianism has been regarded by some thinkers as an awkward and threatening force within the British constitution, because it has a kind of non-negotiable determination for God-given self-regulation. The mandate of the Church is to be free from any force that would compromise its ability to obey the calling of God in a dynamic, flexible way throughout human history. The Church in sixteenth- and seventeenth-century Scotland behaved rather as if its authority were a divine right granted not to the monarch but to the Church's courts.

The Church of Scotland must be aware of the true nature of its governance and must take on the near-impossible task of defending a non-democratic system if and when it serves a higher purpose. Almost a century ago the Presbyterian academic John Oman, who was the Principal of Westminster College in Cambridge and a theologian often ahead of his time in ecclesiological thought, reached exactly this conclusion:

> Christianity is not individualism tempered by the ballot-box. Christ Himself says things little flattering to majorities. A

unanimous vote leaves it still possible that God's verdict is on the other side, while the position of an oppressed minority is apparently to continue to be the lot of His real disciples. Christianity is 'ultra-democratic' not because it counts heads, but because it appeals 'to the image of God in all men' ... All authority in the Church must speak only in God's name, and that means neither an appeal to episcopal succession nor to popular election, but solely to truth and the spirit of love.[26]

What the noble tradition of Scottish democracy does offer, however, to challenge and confront the Church, is the daring suggestion that even the commonalty of the people may on occasion be capable of conveying intact the will of God. (Rutherford clearly had such faith in the populace, but then in his time the whole nation was regarded as in a self-conscious covenant relationship with God.) Certainly in the Church today there are many who would democratise decision-making as much as possible. In October 2003 the Board of Practice and Procedure of the General Assembly produced guidelines for the operation of one form of congregational constitution.[27] The drafting group agonised about whether it could recommend that congregations adopt the method of electing elders that does involve congregational election, in order to promote the most democratic method as best practice for the Church. The group felt frustrated by the fact that it had not been given any mandate or remit to innovate in this area of the law and procedure of the Church, and could do no more in their final text than list the methods of election showing the most democratic first! Whenever some part of the Church's system of governance falls to be reformed, it is arguably incumbent on the General Assembly to consider whether – all other things being equal – there is a way of discerning God's will that maximises the democratic input. The single constraint on that is that such spiritual discernment[28] always takes priority over the demands of popular opinion where the two appear to be in conflict –

where all other things are somehow not equal. As the writers of the Barmen Declaration put it: 'Church leadership activity cannot simply follow the criteria for the human exercise of power and authority.'[29]

The Church of Scotland may claim a divine authority in some areas, but fails the test of a popularly derived sovereignty authority. It is always driven back ultimately to the sole sovereignty of God.

The Church and the Sovereignty of God

Diakonia

Christianity is a monotheistic religion, and believes in God as creator, lawgiver and ultimate judge. This implies that God is sovereign in authority over all people and their human institutions, whether or not they recognise him as such. God calls his creation to recognise him and to enjoy a relationship with him; his sovereignty is relational. This does not necessarily imply that God's relationship with the world is expressed only through a system of law. In the thought system of Thomas Aquinas, for example, the phrase 'Eternal Law' was used for the overarching divine authority beyond the specific provisions of Natural and Divine Laws: such 'Eternal Law' was not something judicial but rather an expression of God's providence and rule generally.

In Church life, experiences of authority, influence and the power to affect behaviour do not come only through the structures of the Church's law. For example, in the doxological life of the Church at worship the sovereignty of God over the whole of creation is often articulated and celebrated. In the obedience of Christian service the sovereignty of God over the world is often given as the motivation of faithful people. It is important therefore to avoid conceptually limiting sovereignty to legal sovereignty alone. The possibility may exist that the spiritual freedom of the Church to live under the sovereignty of God is something far more than a technical, legal demand.

God's sovereignty is 'diakonal', as he exercises authority through sacrificial service of the world. Christ who came not to be served but to serve and the Holy Spirit sent for the comforting of the world are remarkable because they are divine figures but not figures of control. The redeeming moment, in Christian doctrine, was the moment of supreme self-sacrifice by God in Christ; and the risen Christ gave virtually no programme and no codified system of rules to the apostles. Christian belief expects judgement beyond this life, and unsurprisingly expresses that in forensic metaphor and image, but any element of coerced behaviour or punishment in this life for wrongdoing has been entirely the invention of the institutional Church, especially during the era of what was commonly known as 'Christendom' when Church and state were an alliance of coercive power.

In the last century, as theologians began to argue against the continuing existence or merit of Christendom, descriptions of the Church became common that promoted the idea of its being a non-coercive, powerless body exercising influence but not irresistible force. During the struggles of the German Confessing Church against National Socialism in the early 1930s, the Barmen Declaration asserted the principle of 'not domination but service'[30] as part of the Church's self-understanding. By the end of the century, this view was an unremarkable currency of academic ecclesiology.

Diakonal sovereignty requires the Church to be profoundly unlike the other sovereign institutions in the world with which it engages. It also severely limits the leverage the Church has over the behaviour of those subject to its authority. The Church's calling to exercise only God's diakonal sovereignty means it cannot legitimately masquerade as a miniature nation state, even though that was the constitutional model behind the events of 1921.

Covenant

The other characteristic of divine sovereignty in the Reformed theological view is that the sovereignty is expressed through a covenant relationship. Covenant theology has never regarded the relationship of the human and God as a contractual affair: it is not a bilateral deal but a number of unilateral commitments that constitute a covenant relationship. God, in entering such a relationship with Noah (the promise after the flood) or Abraham (the promise of the land) or any of the other pivotal figures in the Bible's stories, always made a promise first and then called the person or nation to commit freely to the other part of the relationship. In baptism, the Church believes that the grace conveyed in the sacrament is not conditional on the vows taken (though they are certainly expected to be taken), and the ordering of baptismal liturgy in the Church of Scotland has in recent years reflected such a covenant understanding.[31]

Again, ecclesiology has learned to reflect this idea in its modelling of the Church. A Church based on a civil law contract is not the same as one based entirely on a spiritual covenant. The main point about a contract is that the parties to it are bound by its original terms, and unless there is a universal agreement to vary its conditions it remains binding without alteration. This has implications for the constitutional freedom of a Church, again both in terms of its vertical jurisdiction and in terms of its horizontal relations. If a Church is regarded as constituted by a binding agreement of its founding members – the normal manner in which a voluntary association comes into being – the terms on which it operates and the system of beliefs on which its identity is based cannot be changed without the risk of a high price. The Free Church case that ended in 1904, and arguably was rerun just a few years ago,[32] determined that the Church founded in 1843 was defined for civil law purposes by its original constitution, so that the pecuniary interest in it belonged to any party that showed that it alone had remained faithful to the original trust purposes as the civil law understood them.

The response to the events of 1904 within the United Free Church, along with the 1921 settlement, provided a different constitutional definition for the Church of Scotland, one using the concept of covenant that enables it to change and develop without those obstructive limitations. The Church of Scotland, not founded in law on a trust deed, is able to develop its doctrinal standards and self-understanding. Whether or not that is theologically desirable is a question that will always be under debate; but in law it provides a flexibility that some other churches cannot have. It is literally vital for the Church's existence that it should have the power of dynamic self-determination. That may be because the light of revelation to which it aspires does not change but the Church needs to be able to adjust its standards to ever-improving understandings of the Word of God; or it may be because the Church's vocation does change through time, new light does shine, and God does have new demands of us.

There is growing theological hostility to the contractual, and rather static, voluntary association model of Church identity. The theologians who wrote the Barmen Declaration in the 1930s said:

> Just as the church did not come into existence as a result of the voluntary association of its members, nor is the order of the church to be seen exclusively as the contingent outcome of how the church organises itself.[33]

The theologian Stanley Hauerwas speaks of the Church resisting what he calls a temptation to be a voluntary association, whereas the Church does not associate voluntarily but under the command of God's call.[34] Pieter Coertzen, a contemporary Dutch Reformed writer on Church law and order, points out that a mark of Church law is that the Church should not be in the hands of its members; it is really God's work, only empirically taking the form of the association of believers, and it should give expression to God's will for the Church.[35] Coertzen observes Calvin's teaching that the Church council and its members must not supplant Christ.[36] All these arguments suggest that nothing must humanly obstruct the ability of God to reform the Church, to change or develop it or to enable it to relate in new ways with the world in which it is sent on its mission. The implication is that the Church's jurisprudence and constitutional theory must be based on the premise of spiritual obedience to God and never contractual dealing with any other human institution.

If that is taken seriously as the basis of the Church's legal system, however, it has to be acknowledged that only those who genuinely have an attitude of obedience to God can be asked to play any part in the system of Church governance. The non-belief of many of the officials of the civil legal system must be respected, and they cannot be expected to behave as if they had a covenanted commitment that only Christians could possibly be expected to undertake. It is not possible today to assume that there is a spiritually conscious or covenanted nation around the Church of Scotland. The Church, however, may maintain the legitimate Christian belief that God is ultimately sovereign over the whole world, even in places where he is not recognised as such. The Church has to distinguish between its doctrines (including the sovereignty of the divine over the whole of creation) and the practicalities of constitutional and social engagement (including the recognition that Christian belief cannot be assumed throughout civil society).

In a Church which, to be frank, lacks the vertical and horizontal marks of human sovereignty, and fails any test of representing some kind of popular sovereignty, what are the constitutional implications of reliance on the sole sovereignty of God?

Reform within the Articles Declaratory

In theory, the 1921 settlement remains the foundation of the constitution of the Church of Scotland as a legal institution. Because of its weaknesses and the external pressures upon it over the last eighty years, it plays little role in the lives of Church members, office-bearers and ministers, and most Church people are quite unaware of the Articles Declaratory or the events that led to the Union of 1929. Most ministers would not be able to identify most of the Articles, and tend to be much more familiar with parts of the documents that formed the Basis and Plan of Union of 1929, as these include the preamble and formula used at ordinations.

Little surprise, then, that the Church has considered the possibility of wholesale review of the Articles. A Special Commission on Structure and Change, reporting to the 2008 General Assembly, proposed that one Article should be examined and questions asked about its retention or reform. The Article selected was Article III, which describes the activity of the Church as the national church exercised through a territorial ministry; and the principal motivation for the review was the strain on physical, human and financial resources. A counter-motion in the debate argued that it was impossible to review this Article without bringing the whole set under review, and proposed that larger piece of work. The Assembly, however, accepted the argument of the Commission's Convener,[37] who asserted that it would be possible to begin with just this one and widen the review to other Articles if the conclusions of the initial review seemed to demand it.

The Articles lean on each other in groups. In writing this book I found it impossible to consider Articles IV and VI apart from each other, and the reader must judge whether it has been legitimate to examine only these two as I have done. Whether it is possible to examine Article III alone rather depends what conclusion is reached by the new Special

Commission just beginning its task at the time of writing. If that group recommends the substantial reform or repeal of Article III, the abandonment of the status of 'national Church' is bound to force a review of Articles IV and VI; and the conclusions of this book would be one possible outcome of that future review. If the Special Commission recommends no radical alteration to Article III, it is very unlikely that any examination of other Articles would follow. That might be a good outcome in respect of the Third Article, but a lost opportunity in respect of numbers IV and VI.

That is because there has been a process that might be termed 'obsolescence by a thousand cuts' afflicting the settlement, especially the Fourth and Sixth Articles. First, the terms of the settlement itself were flawed from the outset. Second, the case law of the twentieth century began to undermine the model of 'sphere' jurisdiction. Third, the partnership of Church and state changed on both sides under the pressure of forces such as ecumenism, secularisation, federalism and globalisation. Fourth, the sovereignty-based model of Church authority has been put into question theologically, casting profoundly into doubt the intention of those who framed the settlement in terms of 'spheres' of sovereignty.

The current position of the Church *vis-à-vis* civil society is not openly under threat; there is no one scheming to have the 1921 Act repealed, or another denomination particularly privileged, or the ceremonial connection between the General Assembly and the Crown dismantled. But neither is the Church's legal position entrenched in civil law, since it is no longer a matter solely in the hands of the Westminster Parliament. The Church has to recognise an increasing precariousness in its occupation of a singular place in an increasingly complex British establishment (using that term in the non-technical sense).

The Dutch Dominican theologian Edward Schillebeeckx, describing the way that God and people search each other

out, talks of God as being defenceless without necessarily
being powerless. [38] The argument of this book is essentially
the application of that idea to the institutional Church of
Scotland, by asserting: (1) that the freedom to obey God
is given by the only sovereign God and ought not to be
contingent on the provisions of civil law; (2) that the support,
protection and Establishment of the Church in Scotland
by the classic British state were mixed blessings when they
existed and no loss now that they do not;[39] and (3) that the
Church has to be a community messily engaged with the
larger community in which it is set and to which it is sent,
not a perfect legal society interested only in self-preservation
and the exercise of authority. The Church of Scotland is much
more defenceless than it appears in law, and so it has to learn
to be powerful, if at all, in rather different ways.

This chapter ends, therefore, with a suggestion of what
that rather different way of being influential would look like
translated into the terms of the Fourth and Sixth Articles
Declaratory. These Articles, brought up to date and furnished
with a theologically defensible foundation, would once again
become useful and relevant to the Church's engagement with
Scottish life – and that cannot be said for the existing version,
however tempting it was for the 2008 General Assembly to
leave them unreviewed. Neither of these Articles has been
changed since they were first framed, but the mechanism
to change them exists. It is contained in the Eighth Article
and is modelled on the procedure of the Barrier Act, except
that the innovation has to be approved by three consecutive
General Assemblies and by two-thirds of all Presbyteries in
both intervening years. The existing and proposed wordings
are set out for each Article, and are followed by some
observations about the changes to their terms.

The Fourth Article currently reads:

IV.   This Church, as part of the Universal Church wherein the
Lord Jesus Christ has appointed a government in the hands of

Church office-bearers, receives from Him, its Divine King and Head, and from Him alone, the right and power subject to no civil authority to legislate, and to adjudicate finally, in all matters of doctrine, worship, government, and discipline in the Church, including the right to determine all questions concerning membership and office in the Church, the constitution and membership of its Courts, and the mode of election of its office-bearers, and to define the boundaries of the spheres of labour of its ministers and other office-bearers. Recognition by the civil authority of the separate and independent government and jurisdiction of this Church in matters spiritual, in whatever manner such recognition be expressed, does not in any way affect the character of the government and jurisdiction as derived from the Divine Head of the Church alone, or give to the civil authority any right of interference with the proceedings or judgements of the Church within the sphere of its spiritual government and jurisdiction.

If my argument is convincing, the Article might be better worded:

IV. The Lord Jesus Christ who alone is sovereign has appointed in this Church a government in the hands of Church office-bearers. The Church receives from Him, its Divine King and Head, and from Him alone, the freedom to legislate, to reform, to declare, to administer and to adjudicate finally (recognising liberty of opinion on such points of doctrine as do not enter into the substance of the Faith)[40] in matters of doctrine, worship, government, and discipline. This freedom shall be exercised wherever no equivalent provision is made in civil law (including employment law) and otherwise wherever the teachings of Scripture and the traditions of the Church are inconsistent with the substance of civil law, of the existence of which inconsistency the Church is sole judge. The freedom to determine all questions concerning membership and office in the Church, the constitution and membership of its Courts, the mode of election of its office-bearers and the boundaries of the spheres of labour of its ministers and other office-bearers, is reserved to the Church. The jurisdiction of the Church does not extend to the enforcement of its decisions by compulsion, either directly or with the aid of the civil law. Any recognition by the civil authority of this power of separate jurisdiction of this Church in matters spiritual, in whatever manner such recognition be expressed, does not in any way affect the character of the government and jurisdiction as derived from the Divine Head of the Church alone. Civil legislatures have the responsibility to determine for themselves all questions concerning recognition of the spiritual jurisdiction and the obligations arising therefrom.

In the new text, sovereignty is attributed to Christ alone and there is no implication that it is an attribute of the Church as a legal institution. The authority exercised by the Church continues to be clearly the subject of a direct divine grant. The previous language of a right to adjudicate, subject to no civil authority, in all questions belonging to certain categories, is removed. Likewise the presumption of the old wording, that a sphere of non-interference of the civil magistrate was definable, is abandoned. The defencelessness of the Church is emphasised in several ways: by its inability to coerce the behaviour of individuals; by its inability in particular to coerce the consciences of its members; and by its inability to force the recognition of its spiritual freedom to reform, by the civil magistrate. The Article now describes spiritual freedom without legal sovereignty.

The Sixth Article currently reads:

VI.   This Church acknowledges the divine appointment and authority of the civil magistrate within his own sphere, and maintains its historic testimony to the duty of the nation acting in its corporate capacity to render homage to God, to acknowledge the Lord Jesus Christ to be King over the nations, to obey His laws, to reverence His ordinances, to honour His Church, and to promote in all appropriate ways the Kingdom of God. The Church and the State owe mutual duties to each other, and acting within their respective spheres may signally promote each other's welfare. The Church and the State have the right to determine each for itself all questions concerning the extent and the continuance of their mutual relations in the discharge of these duties and the obligations arising therefrom.

If my argument is right, this Article could be worded as follows:

VI.   This Church, as the Body of Christ within the larger community, undertakes to render homage to God, to acknowledge the Lord Jesus Christ to be King over the nations, to obey His laws, to reverence His ordinances, and to serve the Kingdom of God. The Church asserts God's divine authority over civil rulers in international and national law and in local communities. The Church of Scotland maintains its historic testimony to the duty of society to honour the Church and acknowledge its spiritual freedoms, including the freedom to be continually reformed, the freedom to criticise and the freedom to obey God even to the extent of coming into conflict in law with secular authorities. The Church calls secular society into a covenant relationship, in which the Church is the servant of society, but in which each may signally promote the other's welfare.

In this new text, spiritual obligations are entirely absorbed by the worshipping community. This is not to deny to the Church the right to call the nation to render homage to God as the existing Article says, but the formal declaration of the Church's legal constitution is not the right place to articulate that challenge. The Articles Declaratory are a declaration of legal relationships, not a homiletic text: they define what Church and society may formally require of each other, not what either might hope to inspire the other to do.

The residual elements of the old Two-Kingdoms theory remain in the assertion that the civil magistrate is – in the eyes of the Church – as much a divine appointment as is the government of the Church. The fragmentation of secular sovereignty is recognised by the transformation of the 'State' language of the old Article into the 'society' and 'community' language of the new. The new wording does not abandon entirely the element of what might be called a minimal Establishment; it retains the expectation that the civil magistrate pays some honour to the Church and concedes the non-negotiable spiritual freedoms that the Church will insist on in any case. Formal legal Establishment, either of the Genevan or of the English type, finds no place. The implication towards the end of the old Article that Church and state owed each other mutual support, as if they were bound to one another by some sort of pact, is replaced by an expression of a covenant relationship. Here the Church makes a unilateral promise to promote the welfare of the broader community and should do no more than hope that some reciprocal promotion of its own welfare matches its gesture. The language of the spheres has gone, along with the duties of secular society towards the Church and the calculation of the extent and continuance of responsibilities and relations.

The written constitution of the Church of Scotland is gradually desiccating: its usefulness is waning and the power of its terms is gradually becoming risible. Because of this, the national Church is becoming more like the other denominations in Scotland, behaving like a voluntary association and being treated like one in civil law. In turn, the doctrinal life of the Church is equally in danger of desiccation, as some ministers and office-bearers behave as if the only thing to do with the doctrinal corpus (beyond the core contained in Article I) is to preserve it and defend it from any change. A General Assembly, or rather three consecutive Assemblies, courageous enough to change the Articles Declaratory can enable the Church to redefine itself in terms of its engagement with the kingdom of God in the world and free itself from the risk that the law of the Church or the law of the land cannot keep pace with *ecclesia semper reformanda*.

Notes

1 The relative weight given to different kinds of elements (Natural Law, precedent, Christian doctrine, the classical tradition and so on) varies from system to system. This is illustrated by the difference in emphasis between the legal tradition of England, based on common law and precedent, and the civilian tradition of the Scots law system, which is more principle-based. See A. MacIntyre, *Whose Justice? Which Rationality?* (Indiana, IN: University of Notre Dame Press, 1988), pp. 226ff.

2 At the time when the constitutional settlement of 1707 between Scotland and England was under discussion, there were Presbyterian fears about the fragility of the guarantee of their forms of worship, government, doctrine and discipline. The Barrier Act is a measure that prevents the General Assembly from unilaterally innovating in these areas, by requiring that such measures be first agreed at one Assembly, then remitted by Overture to Presbyteries for their consideration and reply, and considered further at the subsequent Assembly only in the event that a majority of Presbyteries has approved the Overture. Because one of the areas is 'government', the Barrier Act is a constitutional safeguard that ensures that local voices are heard on the most momentous matters. The Catholic theologian James Mackey has described the Act as 'preventing power from coagulating at the top' of the Church of Scotland: Mackey, *Power and Christian Ethics*, p. 28.

3 *Volume of Reports to the General Assembly* (Edinburgh: Assembly Arrangements Committee, 2006), p. 6.4/9–11, section 15 of the Report of the Legal Questions Committee.

4 See the statement about the legal consequences of this exercise, given by the Principal Clerk to the General Assembly of 2007 and engrossed in its minutes: *Volume of Reports to the General Assembly, Vol. III version* (Edinburgh: Assembly Arrangements Committee, 2007).

5 In the late eighteenth and early nineteenth centuries, one of the causes of division within the Secession Churches was what is known as the 'New Licht – Auld Licht' debate over the status of the Westminster Confession of Faith. Underlying the particular debate was an argument between the belief that there could be new revelation from God for the Church and the belief that the light of divine knowledge was given once for all time.

[6] Act V 2000.

[7] Assuming two possible attitudes on each topic, we have here '2 to the power of 3' combinations of points of view, so out of eight ministers no two need agree completely. On dozens of contentious issues, the arithmetic which is theoretically possible means that if there are anything that could be called 'parties' then there are at least dozens of them.

[8] The so-called 'wiring diagram', also unkindly referred to by some as the 'drainage diagram', which was originally published in the *Evening News* at the time of the 1929 Union, illustrates the many divisions amongst the Seceders of the eighteenth century, who fragmented into Burgers and Anti-Burgers, Auld Licht and New Licht, and all combinations of these.

[9] Private conversation with Mrs Pat Holdgate, Head of Media Relations of the Church of Scotland.

[10] L. L. Rasmussen, *Moral Fragments and Moral Community: A Proposal for Church in Society* (Minneapolis, MN: Fortress Press, 1993), p. 149.

[11] K. Robbins 'Establishing Disestablishment: Some Reflections on Wales and Scotland', in Brown and Newlands, *Scottish Christianity in the Modern World*, pp. 249–50.

[12] P. G. Kauper, *Religion and the Constitution* (Baton Rouge, LA: Louisiana State University Press, 1964), ch. 1, describes the dispersal of governmental power in both kinds of institution, and prefers the more general distinction of civil and religious communities, recognising the partial overlap of membership between them.

[13] J. Milbank, *Theology and Social Theory: Beyond Secular Reason* (Oxford: Basil Blackwell, 1990), p. 408.

[14] W. Storrar, 'The Decline of the Kirk', *University of Aberdeen Alumni Association News* 18 (Autumn 1997), pp. 5–8.

[15] Many examples of the adoption of post-modernist thinking by theology are contained in K. J. Vanhoozer (ed.), *The Cambridge Companion to Postmodern Theology* (Cambridge: Cambridge University Press, 2003), especially in Part 2 of the book.

[16] For a treatment of this loose form of Establishment, see W. Carr, 'A Developing Establishment', *Journal of Theology* CII (1999), pp. 2–10.

[17] See Chapter 2, above.

[18] Mackey, *Power and Christian Ethics*, p. 127.

19 One of the more surreal aspects of ministry in my own former parish.

20 Church of Scotland Act 1921 s. 2.

21 J. Mitchell, 'Scotland in the Union, 1945–1995: The Changing Nature of the Union State', in T. M. Devine and R. J. Finlay (eds), *Scotland in the Twentieth Century* (Edinburgh: Edinburgh University Press, 1996), pp. 85–6, makes a similar point.

22 Act III, 2000, the Consolidating Act anent Church Courts (as amended by Acts VII 2001, II 2002, III and VII 2003, I 2005, I, II, XII and XIV 2006 and VII 2007) ss. 2–4.

23 Act III 2000 (as amended) ss. 11–27.

24 Act X 1932 (as amended by Acts XXVIII 1996, II 1998 and VII 2000).

25 See Act VII 2003 (as amended by Acts VIII 2004 and III 2006).

26 J. Oman, *The Church and the Divine Order* (London: Hodder & Stoughton, 1911), p. 318.

27 The Unitary Constitution, otherwise known as the *quoad omnia* constitution.

28 It is easy to be cynical about the purity or effectiveness of Church courts' methods of spiritual discernment of God's will. Some meetings are only cursorily opened and closed with a prayer, but otherwise lack any characteristic of a spiritual exercise. It must be recognised, therefore, that this part of the argument describes an ideal, and not a universal reality of experience.

29 *The Ministry of the Whole Church of Jesus Christ and the Problem of Sovereignty: Statement of the Theological Committee of the Evangelical Church of the Union on Barmen IV* (Berlin: Evangelical Church of the Union, 2001), p. 99.

30 *Ministry of the Whole Church of Jesus Christ and the Problem of Sovereignty*, p. 37.

31 The parental vows are taken after the moment of baptism.

32 *Free Church of Scotland (Continuing) v. Free Church of Scotland* [2005] CSOH 46.

33 *Ministry of the Whole Church of Jesus Christ and the Problem of Sovereignty*, p. 57.

34 S. Hauerwas, *In Good Company: The Church as Polis* (Indiana, IN: University of Notre Dame Press, 1995), p. 26.

35 P. Coertzen, *Church and Order: A Reformed Perspective*, Canon Law Monograph Series 1 (Leuven: Peeters, 1998), p. 8.

[36] Coertzen, *Church and Order*, p. 16, quoting Calvin's *Institutes* IV.III.1.

[37] The Hon Lord Brodie.

[38] E. Schillebeeckx, *Church: The Human Story of God* (London: SCM Press, 1989), p. 90.

[39] The blessings of Establishment included the financial support of the Church and especially the ministry in the period of patronage, and the guarantee of the preservation of the Presbyterian form of Church government at the time when the Union of Parliaments produced fears of an Anglican monopoly of national religion in Britain.

[40] The phrase in parenthesis is a direct quote from the Preamble used at services of ordination, being part of the texts of the Basis and Plan of Union of 1929.

Conclusion

Marching to the Beat of a Different Drum?

The Church of Jesus Christ, in any of its manifestations, cannot remain an entirely unworldly body. Every denomination is a hybrid institution, part intangible spiritual movement and part tangible legal organisation. That tangible part always has some kind of recognition, alongside all sorts of other human institutions, in civil law. The nature of that recognition varies from age to age and from country to country: pre-Constantinian Rome, post-Reformation Geneva and contemporary America illustrate the variety of experiences the Church has had with civil engagement.

Within the Church, however, it is not clear, or agreed, what the relationships should be between the two kinds of authority: that of the Church and that of the world. What does it mean to march to the beat of a different drum; to obey the law of God in preference to any other authority? And what does it mean for the Church, when as an institution it is called on to decide what that distinctive drumbeat should be, a decision needed whenever a new question is asked and needs to be answered by the Church for the first time, or afresh in the light of new understanding? The Christian response to these questions depends on whether the

drumbeats of God and of the world are really so completely
different and in conflict with each other.

In 2007, an Overture was transmitted to Presbyteries
under the Barrier Act of 1697, with a proposal that would
empower Presbyteries for the first time to impose financial
penalties, in discrimination cases brought under recent
Assembly legislation.[1] The legislation had properly been
introduced within the Church's jurisdiction, because it
clarified and articulated part of the area of 'discipline' the
Church regulates internally. However, the proposed new
financial element failed to receive sufficient support to be
brought to the next General Assembly for enactment, partly
because several Presbyteries expressed concern lest the law
of the Church would 'conform' too much to the law of the
world.[2] The gist of their complaint was that Church law
should, on principle, be distinctive and therefore different
from civil law.

Had the objectors shared the perspective of this book, they
would have rejected the proposal for a different reason; that
it would be much simpler to abandon any attempt to regulate
in this area as a Church, and instead aggrieved individuals
should be able to resort to civil law to pursue financial award.
Instead, however, their motivation was profoundly different,
so hostile to the secular provision that they were unwilling to
allow Church people to have its benefit in either jurisdiction.
Theirs was the most admirably principled determination to
cut their noses off to spite their face.

St Paul writing his letter to the Romans lived in an age
where the civil law had not been influenced by the Divine
Law. The General Assembly today, legislating in an area
like anti-discrimination law, operates in a society and
wider legal system founded and grown through centuries
of Christian influence; and against the backdrop of a legal
system consciously derived from the Eternal, Natural and
Divine Law described by Thomas Aquinas. What the 2007
proposal intended was that one provision of the Church's

law should mirror very closely a provision of civil law that seemed to have merit and chime with Christian virtues of fairness – in short, that both drums should have the same kind of beat. The Church's rejection of the proposal, whether good or bad on its merits, meant the Church was settling for an anti-discrimination provision less far-reaching than that of the civil law, which might be said to be a rather negative way to assert an independent spiritual jurisdiction.

The same kind of thinking lay behind the desire of some ministers and Kirk Sessions a decade or so earlier to be exempt from the Assembly's requirement that they must apply secular child protection/safeguarding law. They would prefer to make their own judgement of sex offenders, and determine without reference to the civil register when it was appropriate to re-admit such individuals to working with children in a parish setting. This case is slightly different from the Overture just described: there, the Church intended effectively to copy into its own law an instrument used in civil law; whereas in its safeguarding provisions the Church simply cross-refers in its law to the existing civil law and requires its courts and office-bearers to obey that civil law entirely. The objections of the reluctant are similar, though, based on the proposition that the civil magistrate's 'drum' must by definition be different, and must be undesirable, compared to the drum to which the Christian marches.

It means that anyone making the kind of suggestion that is the conclusion of this book – that the protection of the Church's freedoms through any separate jurisdiction should be as limited as it possibly can be, and the civil law play a greater part in the regulation of the Church's life – will attract some hostility from those who will feel it suggests a disloyalty to Church law. The drum analogy is, however, a useful one in defending the model that has been proposed in the previous chapters. When the Church, or the individual Christian, hears unmistakably that distinctive, challenging sound that is the call to great moral courage or prophetic witness in the face of the ways of a sometimes-hostile world, that drumbeat must be heeded. Sometimes it will involve simple disobedience of a provision of the civil law, knowing that the consequences within that law must be accepted: Christians lying down in the road outside the Faslane Naval Base on the Clyde, and being arrested, are accepting that reality. Sometimes it will involve the Church legislating for its own standard of expectations of ministers, office-bearers or members, a standard quite different from the requirements of civil law: the Church's treatment of a minister's adultery as a disciplinary offence and not merely a ground of divorce is an example of the distinctive content of a separate Church law. Sometimes it will involve the civil law itself granting scope to religious bodies to hold a different standard of judgement: the insertion of Genuine Occupational Requirements and similar exemptions into the legislation discussed in Chapter 4 above has developed that body of recognition of spiritual freedom.

But when the drumbeat is exactly the same beat, there is no need for it to be sounded on more than one drum. When the drumbeat is the insistence on fair treatment of women, or the non-negotiable protection of the innocent young, or the protection of people's patrimonial interests, nothing is gained by trying to garner these things into a separate sphere of authority. If the Church keeps those things in its own sphere but then tries to mimic the benefits of the civil law, it simply gives itself a difficult task of re-inventing a wheel, and wastes resources in the needless attempt. If the Church keeps those things in its own sphere but then deliberately eschews the merits of the equivalent civil law by refusing to provide an equivalent, it leaves a gap, an absence of protection to that extent.

Freedom without Power

> The idea that the church needs its own distinctive spiritual dispensation, which differs from the civil dispensation, as well as a judicial power as an order to maintain the spiritual dispensation ... has through the course of time continued to function to a greater or lesser extent in Reformed Church government.[3]

This study demonstrates that the boundaries between the two jurisdictions are far from clearly sketched even in quite general terms. The Church has the opportunity, I believe, to make that policy choice in favour of conceding authority to the civil magistrate (by not contending for it in cases of dispute) over parts of the Church's life that do not fall into the strictest definition of worship, government, doctrine and discipline. In particular, the word 'discipline' tends to be used very loosely, almost so that it means whatever it is convenient to the interest of the Church for it to mean. It ought to be more clearly defined as relating only to personal issues of life and doctrine peculiar to the calling of Christian leaders, and corporate issues of superintendence over Church courts and congregations.

This book has illustrated two main reasons to take this stricter attitude to the distribution of legal authority between the Church and the civil order. First, the principal Reformers, Luther and Calvin for example, did not isolate the work of the civil magistrate from the service of the Church. The prince had the potential to create social conditions that were compatible with the interests of the Church and, sometimes, explicitly to advance those interests. His task was certainly not simply to keep out of the way of the Church and stand aside from its exercise of its separate powers. In the Reformed view God is sovereign over all, including the temporal domain; so the Church must recognise and respect the civil magistrate, except when the magistrate directly opposes the standards of the gospel. This clearly supports the relatively narrow view of Church law commended above.

The second reason for reluctance to defend the sovereign sway of the Church as a legal power is the argument about the diakonal sovereignty of God. A Church that remembers it is essentially the Body of Christ should not enthusiastically pursue a legal status at odds with the divine character. A national Church that has enjoyed legal authority and social influence in the past has to take heed of the theologies of power of people like Ruth Page and Walter Wink and the Liberation Theology of the last generation. In turn, that must affect the Church's self-understanding of its dominion – or rather its lack of dominion. The Church cannot emulate the form of government exercised by civil law, because by design it does not possess the faculties of enforcement and coercion, and has always been compromised when it has pretended to have those kinds of powers over people.

The legal philosophy of the Church needs to abandon the long-used language of 'the co-ordination of jurisdictions' and the obsolete phraseology of Article IV. It was written for a time when the interference of the civil magistrate in matters of worship, church government, doctrine and internal discipline was a living memory: the Article describes the constraining of the civil law in areas it is hard to imagine fall within the scope of the civil law in any case. The civil magistrate has no mandate or motive to encroach on matters of indifference to it and will not interfere in the regulation of spiritual experience within the Church of Scotland, at least not any more than it would within other religious organisations differently constituted in law. The Church by the same token has virtually no reason to fear the elements of civil law that do apply to it and should not try to avoid secular jurisdiction by needlessly inventing an alternative provision to address a common problem. After all, in the Reformed tradition the classic Two-Kingdoms theory has, ever since Melville's exchange with James VI at Falkland, asserted that the secular as much as the sacred is subject to the ultimate sovereignty of God.

The case of Helen Percy[4] challenges some of the uses of a separate jurisdiction when the civil law is adequate to the task, a task that has no discernible need to be confined in the way it has within the spiritual authority. It is understandable that the grounds of dismissal used in relation to ministers are more demanding than they are for some other professions, because ministers take vows to live godly and circumspect lives;[5] but it is harder to understand why the Church insists on dealing internally with challenges to its decisions on grounds relating to procedural fairness or employment rights. There is a clear theological element to the question of whether women should be ordained as ministers; there is no convincing reason why the Church should be unwilling to be judged by the Sex Discrimination Act 1975 like everybody else. The problem is that the Church preserves or claims authority over issues that do not need to lie in a separated-off realm of legal governance, like a very small but quite separate state.

So my argument prefers a minimal jurisdiction of freedom before God to an extensive jurisdiction of sovereign legal power. And that claim has several immediate implications.

First, there is only one justification for refusing to recognise the writ of the civil law in any case, and that is one's prior obedience to God within a covenant relationship with God. The matter must be one in which the Church's considerations are fundamentally different from the principles of civil law, and the civil law either has nothing to say on the matter or is likely to come to a conclusion incompatible with the Church's understanding of the will or command of God. In a free and non-despotic society in which Christian people are numerous and able to express themselves in the worlds of law and politics, the resort to a separate body of Church law should not be necessary very often, especially if the sovereignty of God over the whole of life is taken seriously by Reformed theology. Where those issues arise that require the Church to insist on independent action, they should be explained and defended vigorously and unapologetically, and the Church should have the confidence to differ from the civil law when it has to.

Second, the justification for spiritual independence of action in these situations has to be from the Divine Law, that is, from Scripture and Christian tradition as understood by the Church. The other kinds of limitation on authority described earlier (Natural Law, natural justice and so on) all apply as much to civil law as to Church law, but Divine Law alone informs the Church's unique witness. If a rule or principle cannot be derived from the sources of the Divine Law, what reason is there for it to be located in the Church's legal corpus? For, if it has merit, will it not appear in the secular law, or at least in the democratic debate surrounding the development of the secular law? And if it is there, because it applies to those beyond the Church as much as to those within it, let the civil magistrate do what both Luther and Calvin believed was his God-given task, to regulate those affairs which are not uniquely the business of the Church.

Therefore, third, the Church should lose its traditional fear of exposing many of the terms and conditions of its servants to the regulation of the civil law. There is a challenge to the Church to examine the parts of its law in which it gives what it calls 'equivalence of protection' from within its own provision instead of recognising the application of the original protection of the civil law. For instance, when a minister is pregnant, she has rights that are based on a Regulation of the General Assembly, not only on a civil law right; and this is an example of what is meant by 'equivalence of protection'. It would be simpler of course if ministers were subject to the employment law of maternity rights in the first place, so that the Church need only decide on the extent of its provision within the civil framework and not have to invent a complete system of its own. Equally, the Helen

Percy/Douglas series of actions in both civil and Church law turned on the ability of the Sex Discrimination Act to provide a remedy for someone in her position, because she did not have a contract of employment. The case would have been much simpler, again, if ministers were fully subject to employment law. In each case the General Assembly would have to make a concession and let go of its insistence that the civil law should not apply.

Fourth, the Church must abhor conducting itself in a way that gives a counter-witness to its demands of secular society. The Church says what it believes are prophetic things from time to time about the way in which secular government governs, the decisions and policies it adopts and the ways it treats people and secures justice. The same Church cannot provide a poor system of justice, a corrupt administration of policy, or a legislative process that fails to consider the will of God through the prompting of the Holy Spirit. It cannot have policies that discriminate for no good reason, or devalue minorities, or remove people's personal liberties, including liberty of opinion. This is a hugely difficult standard to keep, because the breadth of opinions within the Church leads some people to regard one stance as reflecting the Divine Law while others regard the same stance as nothing more than an insulting deprivation of rights (the argument about the ordination of homosexuals is the obvious illustration of this). The difficulty of implementing the standard is not an excuse for failing to try, or forgetting the general principle.

In Conclusion

In 1921 a settlement was reached that tried to resolve some of the issues of the tension that had existed between the Church and state in Scotland, partly to settle long-existing questions and partly to facilitate the 1929 Union. The conclusions of this study suggest that the situation is far more complicated than the protagonists in 1921 thought they had made it; and so this monograph has left quite a different kind of task for the Church, as expressed by Stanley Hauerwas:

> So we have wanted to underscore that Christians are called first and foremost not to resolve the tension between church and state, but to acknowledge the kingship of Christ in their lives, which means leaving church–state relations profoundly unresolved, until the day when He comes again in glory.[6]

Notes

[1] Joint Report of the Ministries Council and the Legal Questions Committee, in *Volume of Reports and Papers of the Church of Scotland General Assembly of* 2007 (Edinburgh: Assembly Arrangements Committee, 2007), pp. 26/1ff.; and Returns to Overtures Report, in *Volume of Reports and Papers of the Church of Scotland General Assembly of* 2008 (Edinburgh: Assembly Arrangements Committee, 2008), pp. 22/1ff.

[2] One directly quoted Romans 12:2: 'Do not be conformed to this world, but be transformed by the renewing of your minds, so that you may discern what is the will of God – what is good and acceptable and perfect' (NRSV); and several others expressed the same sentiment.

[3] Coertzen, *Church and Order*, p. 91.

[4] See Chapter 4, pp. 144–53.

[5] A phrase from the Ordination vows.

[6] Hauerwas, *In Good Company*, p. 216.

Appendix 1

The National Covenant of 1638

The confession of faith of the Kirk of Scotland, subscribed at first by the King's Majesty and his household in the year of God 1580; thereafter by persons of all ranks in the year 1581, by ordinance of the lords of the secret council, and acts of the general assembly; subscribed again by all sorts of persons in the year 1590, by a new ordinance of council, at the desire of the general assembly; with a general band for the maintenance of the true religion, and the King's person, and now subscribed in the year 1638, by us noblemen, barons, gentlemen, burgesses, ministers, and commons under subscribing; together with our resolution and promises for the causes after specified, to maintain the said true religion, and the King's Majesty, according to the confession aforesaid, and Acts of Parliament; the tenure whereof here followeth. We all, and every one of us underwritten, do protest, that after long and due examination of our own consciences in matters of true and false religion, we are now thoroughly resolved of the truth, by the word and spirit of God; and therefore we believe with our hearts, confess with our mouths, subscribe with our hands, and constantly affirm before God and the whole world, that this only is the true Christian faith and religion, pleasing God, and bringing salvation to man, which now is by the mercy of God revealed to the world by the preaching of the blessed evangel, and received, believed, and defended by many and sundry notable kirks and realms, but chiefly by the Kirk of Scotland, the King's Majesty, and three estates of this realm, as God's eternal truth and only ground of our salvation; as more particularly is expressed in the confession of our faith, established and publicly confirmed by sundry Acts of Parliament; and now of a long time hath been openly professed by the King's Majesty, and whole body of this realm, both in burgh and land. To the which confession and form of religion we willingly agree in our consciences in all points, as unto God's undoubted truth and verity, grounded only upon His written Word; and therefore we abhor and detest all contrary religion and doctrine, but chiefly all kind of papistry in general and particular heads, even as they are now damned and confuted by the Word of God and Kirk of Scotland. But in special we detest and refuse the usurped authority of that Roman Antichrist upon the Scriptures of God, upon the Kirk, the civil magistrate, and consciences of men; all his tyrannous laws made upon indifferent things against our Christian liberty; his erroneous doctrine against the sufficiency of the written Word, the perfection of the law, the office of Christ and His blessed evangel; his corrupted doctrine concerning original sin, our natural inability and rebellion to God's law, our justification by faith only, our imperfect sanctification and obedience to the law, the nature, number, and use of the holy sacraments; his five bastard sacraments, with all his rites, ceremonies, and false doctrine, added to the ministration of the true sacraments, without the Word of God; his cruel judgements against infants departing without the sacrament; his absolute necessity of baptism; his blasphemous opinion of transubstantiation or real presence of Christ's body in the elements, and receiving of the same by the wicked, or bodies of men; his dispensations, with solemn oaths, perjuries, and degrees of marriage, forbidden in the Word; his cruelty against the innocent divorced; his devilish mass; his blasphemous priesthood; his profane sacrifice for the sins of the dead and the quick; his canonization of men, calling upon angels or saints departed, worshipping of imagery, relics, and crosses; dedicating of kirks, altars, days, vows to creatures; his purgatory, prayers for the dead, praying or speaking in a strange language; with his processions and blasphemous litany, and multitude of advocates or mediators; his manifold orders, auricular confession; his desperate and uncertain repentance; his general and doubtsome faith; his satisfactions of men for their sins; his justification by works, *opus operatum*, works of supererogation, merits, pardons, peregrinations and stations; his holy water, baptizing of bells, conjuring of spirits, crossing, saning, anointing, conjuring, hallowing of God's good creatures, with the superstitious opinion joined therewith; his worldly monarchy and wicked hierarchy; his three solemn vows, with all his shavelings of sundry sorts; his erroneous and bloody decrees made at Trent, with all the subscribers and approvers of that cruel and bloody band conjured against the Kirk of God. And finally, we detest all his vain allegories, rites, signs, and traditions, brought in the Kirk without or against the Word of God, and doctrine of this true reformed Kirk. To which we join ourselves willingly, in doctrine, religion, faith, discipline, and life of the holy sacraments, as lively members of the same, in Christ our head, promising and swearing, by the great name of the Lord our God, that we shall continue in the obedience of the doctrine and discipline of this Kirk, and shall defend the same according to our vocation and power all the days of our lives, under the pains contained in the law, and danger both of body and soul in the day of God's fearful judgement. And seeing that many are stirred up by Satan and that Roman Antichrist, to promise, swear, subscribe, and for a time use the holy sacraments in the Kirk, deceitfully against their own consciences, minding thereby, first under the external cloak of religion, to corrupt and subvert secretly God's true religion within the Kirk; and afterwards, when time may serve, to become open enemies and persecutors of the same, under vain hope of the pope's dispensation, devised against the Word of God, to his great confusion, and their double condemnation in the day of the Lord Jesus.

We therefore, willing to take away all suspicion of hypocrisy, and of such double dealing with God and His Kirk, protest and call the Searcher of all hearts for witness, that our minds and hearts do fully agree with this our confession, promise, oath, and subscription: so that we are not moved for any worldly respect, but are persuaded only in our consciences, through the knowledge and love of God's true religion printed in our hearts by the Holy Spirit, as we shall answer to Him in the day when the secrets of all hearts shall be disclosed. And because we perceive that the quietness and stability of our religion and Kirk doth depend upon the safety and good behaviour of the King's Majesty, as upon a comfortable instrument of God's mercy granted to this country for the maintenance of His Kirk, and ministration of justice among us, we protest and promise with our hearts under the same oath, hand-writ, and pains, that we shall defend his person and authority with our goods, bodies, and lives, in the defence of Christ His evangel, liberties of our country, ministration of justice, and punishment of iniquity, against all enemies within this realm or without, as we desire our God to be a strong and merciful defender to us in the day of our death, and coming of our Lord Jesus Christ; to Whom, with the Father and the Holy Spirit, be all honour and glory eternally.

Like as many Acts of Parliament not only in general do abrogate, annul, and rescind all laws, statutes, acts, constitutions, canons civil or municipal, with all other ordinances and practick penalties whatsoever, made in prejudice of the true religion, and professors thereof, or of the true Kirk discipline, jurisdiction, and freedom thereof; or in favours of idolatry and superstition; or of the papistical kirk (as Act 3. Act 31. Parl. I. Act 23. Parl. 11. Act 114. Parl. 12, of K. James VI), that papistry and superstition may be utterly suppressed, according to the intention of

the Acts of Parliament reported in Act 5. Parl. 20. K. James
VI. And to that end they ordained all papists and priests
to be punished by manifold civil and ecclesiastical pains,
as adversaries to God's true religion preached, and by law
established within this realm (Act. 24. Parl. 11. K. James VI)
as common enemies to all Christian government (Act 18.
Parl. 16. K. James VI), as rebellers and gainstanders of our
Sovereign Lord's authority (Act 47. Parl. 3. K. James VI),
and as idolaters (Act 104. Parl. 7. K. James VI), but also in
particular (by and attour the confession of faith) do abolish
and condemn the pope's authority and jurisdiction out of
this land, and ordains the maintainers thereof to be punished
(Act 2. Parl. 1. Act. 51. Parl. 3. Act 106. Parl. 7. Act 114.
Parl. 12. of K. James VI); do condemn the pope's erroneous
doctrine, or any other erroneous doctrine repugnant to any
of the Articles of the true and Christian religion publicly
preached, and by law established in this realm; and ordains
the spreaders or makers of books or libels, or letters or writs
of that nature, to be punished (Act 46. Parl. 3. Act 106. Parl.
7. Act 24. Parl. 11. K. James VI); do condemn all baptism
conform to the pope's kirk, and the idolatry of the Mass;
and ordains all sayers, wilful hearers, and concealers of the
Mass, the maintainers and resetters of the Priests, Jesuits,
trafficking Papists, to be punished without exception or
restriction (Act 5. Parl. I. Act 120. Parl. 12. Act 164. Parl. 13.
Act 193. Parl. 14. Act. I. Parl. 19. Act 5. Parl. 20 K. James
VI); do condemn all erroneous books and writs containing
erroneous doctrine against the religion presently professed,
or containing superstitious rights and ceremonies papistical,
whereby the people are greatly abused; and ordains the
home-bringers of them to be punished (Act 25. Parl. 11. K.
James VI); do condemn the monuments and dregs of bygone
idolatry, as going to crosses, observing the festival days of
saints, and such other superstitious and papistical rites, to the
dishonour of God, contempt of true religion, and fostering
of great errors among the people, and ordains the users of

them to be punished for the second fault as idolaters (Act 104. Parl. 7. K. James VI).

Like as many Acts of Parliament are conceived for maintenance of God's true and Christian religion, and the purity thereof in doctrine and sacraments of the true Church of God, the liberty and freedom thereof in her national synodal assemblies, presbyteries, sessions, policy, discipline, and jurisdiction thereof, as that purity of religion and liberty of the Church was used, professed, exercised, preached, and confessed according to the reformation of religion in this realm. (As for instance: Act 99. Parl. 7. Act 23. Parl. 11. Act 114. Parl. 12. Act 160. Parl. 13. K. James VI, ratified by Act 4. K. Charles.) So that Act 6. Parl. I. and Act 68. Parl. 6. of K. James VI, in the year of God 1579, declares the ministers of the blessed evangel, whom God of His mercy had raised up or hereafter should raise, agreeing with them that then lived in doctrine and administration of the sacraments, and the people that professed Christ as He was then offered in the evangel, and doth communicate with the holy sacraments (as in the reformed Kirks of this realm they were presently administered) according to the confession of faith to be the true and holy Kirk of Christ Jesus within this realm, and discerns and declares all and sundry, who either gainsays the word of the evangel, received and approved as the heads of the confession of faith, professed in Parliament in the year of God 1560, specified also in the first Parliament of K. James VI, and ratified in this present Parliament, more particularly do specify; or that refuses the administration of the holy sacraments as they were then ministrated, to be no members of the said Kirk within this realm and true religion presently professed, so long as they keep themselves so divided from the society of Christ's body. And the subsequent Act 69. Parl. 6. K. James VI, declares that there is no other face of Kirk, nor other face of religion than was presently at that time by the favour of God established within this realm, which therefore is ever styled God's true religion, Christ's true religion, the true and Christian religion, and a perfect religion, which by manifold Acts of Parliament all within this realm are bound to profess to subscribe the Articles thereof, the confession of faith, to recant all doctrine and errors repugnant to any of the said Articles (Act 4 and 9. Parl. 1. Act 45. 46. 47. Parl. 3. Act 71. Parl. 6. Act 106. Parl. 7. Act 24. Parl. 11. Act 123. Parl. 12. Act 194 and 197. Parl. 14 of K. James VI). And all magistrates, sheriffs, &c., on the one part, are ordained to search, apprehend, and punish all contraveners (for instance, Act 5. Parl. I. Act 104. Parl. 7. Act 25. Parl. 11. K. James VI). And that, notwithstanding of the King's Majesty's licences on the contrary, which are discharged and declared to be of no force, in so far as they tend in any ways to the prejudice and hindrance of the execution of the Acts of Parliament against Papists and adversaries of the true religion (Act 106. Parl. 7. K. James VI). On the other part, in Act 47. Parl. 3. K. James VI, it is declared and ordained, seeing the cause of God's true religion and His Highness's authority are so joined as the hurt of the one is common to both; and that none shall be reputed as loyal and faithful subjects to our Sovereign Lord or his authority, but be punishable as rebellers and gainstanders of the same, who shall not give their confession and make profession of the said true religion; and that they, who after defection shall give the confession of their faith of new, they shall promise to continue therein in time coming, to maintain our Sovereign Lord's authority, and at the uttermost of their power to fortify, assist, and maintain the true preachers and professors of Christ's religion, against whatsoever enemies and gainstanders of the same; and namely, against all such of whatsoever nation, estate, or degree they be of, that have joined or bound themselves, or have assisted or assists to set forward and execute the cruel decrees of Trent, contrary to the preachers and true professors of the Word of God, which is repeated word by word in the Articles of Pacification at Perth, the 23rd of Feb., 1572, approved by Parliament the last of April 1573, ratified in Parliament 1578, and related

Act 123. Parl. 12. of K. James VI, with this addition, that they are bound to resist all treasonable uproars and hostilities raised against the true religion, the King's Majesty and the true professors.

Like as all lieges are bound to maintain the King's Majesty's royal person and authority, the authority of Parliaments, without which neither any laws or lawful judicatories can be established (Act 130. Act 131. Parl. 8. K. James VI), and the subjects' liberties, who ought only to live and be governed by the King's laws, the common laws of this realm allanerly (Act 48. Parl. 3. K. James I, Act 79. Parl. 6. K. James VI, repeated in Act 131. Parl. 8. K. James VI), which if they be innovated or prejudged the commission anent the union of the two kingdoms of Scotland and England, which is the sole Act of 17 Parl. James VI, declares such confusion would ensue as this realm could be no more a free monarchy; because by the fundamental laws, ancient privileges, offices, and liberties of this kingdom, not only the princely authority of His Majesty's royal descent hath been these many ages maintained, also the people's security of their lands, livings, rights, offices, liberties and dignities preserved. And therefore for the preservation of the said true religion, laws and liberties of this kingdom, it is statute by Act 8. Parl. 1. repeated in Act 99. Parl. 7. ratified in Act 23. Parl, 11 and 14. Act of K. James VI and 4 Act of K. Charles, that all Kings and Princes at their coronation and reception of their princely authority, shall make their faithful promise by their solemn oath in the presence of the Eternal God, that during the whole time of their lives they shall serve the same Eternal God to the utmost of their power, according as He hath required in His most Holy Word, contained in the Old and New Testaments, and according to the same Word shall maintain the true religion of Christ Jesus, the preaching of His Holy Word, the due and right ministration of the sacraments now received and preached within this realm (according to the confession of faith immediately preceding); and shall abolish and gainstand all false religion contrary to the same; and shall rule the people committed to their charge according to the will and commandment of God revealed in His foresaid Word, and according to the lowable laws and constitutions received in this realm, no ways repugnant to the said will of the Eternal God; and shall procure to the utmost of their power, to the Kirk of God, and whole Christian people, true and perfect peace in all time coming; and that they shall be careful to root out of their Empire all heretics and enemies to the true worship of God, who shall be convicted by the true Kirk of God of the aforesaid crimes. Which was also observed by His Majesty at his Coronation in Edinburgh, 1633, as may be seen in the Order of the Coronation. In obedience to the commands of God, conform to the practice of the godly in former times, and according to the laudable example of our worthy and religious progenitors, and of many yet living among us, which was warranted also by act of council, commanding a general band to be made and subscribed by His Majesty's subjects of all ranks for two causes: one was, for defending the true religion, as it was then reformed, and is expressed in the confession of faith above written, and a former large confession established by sundry acts of lawful general assemblies and of Parliament, unto which it hath relation, set down in public catechisms, and which had been for many years with a blessing from heaven preached and professed in this Kirk and kingdom, as God's undoubted truth grounded only upon His written Word. The other cause was for maintaining the King's Majesty, his person and estate; the true worship of God and the King's authority being so straitly joined, as that they had the same friends and common enemies, and did stand and fall together. And finally, being convinced in our minds, and confessing with our mouths, that the present and succeeding generations in this land are bound to keep the aforesaid national oath and subscription inviolable: —

We noblemen, barons, gentlemen, burgesses, ministers, and commons under subscribing, considering divers times before, and especially at this time, the danger of the true reformed religion, of the King's honour, and of the public peace of the kingdom, by the manifold innovations and evils generally contained and particularly mentioned in our late supplications, complaints, and protestations, do hereby profess, and before God, His angels and the world, solemnly declare, that with our whole hearts we agree and resolve all the days of our life constantly to adhere unto and to defend the aforesaid true religion, and forbearing the practice of all novations already introduced in the matters of the worship of God, or approbation of the corruptions of the public government of the Kirk, or civil places and power of kirkmen, till they be tried and allowed in free assemblies and in Parliaments, to labour by all means lawful to recover the purity and liberty of the gospel as it was established and professed before the aforesaid novations; and because, after due examination, we plainly perceive and undoubtedly believe that the innovations and evils contained in our supplications, complaints, and protestations have no warrant of the Word of God, are contrary to the articles of the aforesaid confessions, to the intention and meaning of the blessed reformers of religion in this land, to the above-written Acts of Parliament, and do sensibly tend to the re-establishing of the popish religion and tyranny, and to the subversion and ruin of the true reformed religion, and of our liberties, laws and estates; we also declare that the aforesaid confessions are to be interpreted, and ought to be understood of the aforesaid novations and evils, no less than if every one of them had been expressed in the aforesaid confessions; and that we are obliged to detest and abhor them, among other particular heads of papistry abjured therein; and therefore from the knowledge and conscience of our duty to God, to our King and country, without any worldly respect or inducement so far as human infirmity will suffer, wishing a further measure of the grace of God for this effect, we promise and swear by the great name of the Lord our God. to continue in the profession and obedience of the aforesaid religion; that we shall defend the same, and resist all these contrary errors and corruptions according to our vocation, and to the utmost of that power that God hath put into our hands, all the days of our life. And in like manner, with the same heart we declare before God and men, that we have no intention or desire to attempt anything that may turn to the dishonour of God or the diminution of the King's greatness and authority; but on the contrary we promise and swear that we shall to the utmost of our power, with our means and lives, stand to the defence of our dread Sovereign the King's Majesty, his person and authority, in the defence and preservation of the aforesaid true religion, liberties and laws of the kingdom; as also to the mutual defence and assistance every one of us of another, in the same cause of maintaining the true religion and His Majesty's authority, with our best counsels, our bodies, means and whole power, against all sorts of persons whatsoever; go that whatsoever shall be done to the least of us for that cause shall be taken as done to us all in general, and to every one of us in particular; and that we shall neither directly or indirectly suffer ourselves to be divided or withdrawn by whatsoever suggestion, combination, allurement or terror from this blessed and loyal conjunction; nor shall cast in any let or impediment that may stay or hinder any such resolution as by common consent shall be found to conduce for so good ends; but on the contrary shall by all lawful means labour to further and promote the same; and if any such dangerous and divisive motion be made to us by word or writ, we and every one of us shall either suppress it or (if need be) shall incontinently make the same known, that it may be timously obviated. Neither do we fear the foul aspersions of rebellion, combination or what else our adversaries from their craft and malice would put upon us, seeing what we do is so well warranted, and ariseth from an unfeigned desire to maintain the true worship of God, the majesty of our King, and the peace of the kingdom, for the common happiness of ourselves and posterity. And because we cannot look for a blessing from God upon our proceedings, except with our profession and subscription, we join such a life and conversation as beseemeth Christians who have renewed their covenant with God; we therefore faithfully promise, for ourselves, our followers, and all other under us, both in public, in our particular families and personal carriage, to endeavour to keep ourselves within the bounds of Christian liberty, and to be good examples to others of all godliness, soberness and righteousness, and of every duty we owe to God and man; and that this our union and conjunction may be observed without violation we call the living God, the searcher of our hearts to witness, who knoweth this to be our sincere desire and unfeigned resolution, as we shall answer to Jesus Christ in the great day, and under the pain of God's everlasting wrath, and of infamy, and of loss of all honour and respect in this world; most humbly beseeching the Lord to strengthen us by His Holy Spirit for this end, and to bless our desires and proceedings with a happy success, that religion and righteousness may flourish in the land, to the glory of God, the honour of our King, and peace and comfort of us all.

In witness whereof we have subscribed with our hands all the premises, &c.

Appendix 2

Articles Declaratory of the Constitution of the Church of Scotland in Matters Spiritual (The Schedule to the Church of Scotland Act 1921 c. 29)

I. The Church of Scotland is part of the Holy Catholic or Universal Church; worshipping one God, Almighty, all-wise, and all-loving, in the Trinity of the Father, the Son, and the Holy Ghost, the same in substance, equal in power and glory; adoring the Father, infinite in Majesty, of whom are all things; confessing our Lord Jesus Christ, the Eternal Son, made very man for our salvation; glorying in His Cross and Resurrection, and owning obedience to Him as the Head over all things to His Church; trusting in the promised renewal and guidance of the Holy Spirit; proclaiming the forgiveness of sins and acceptance with God through faith in Christ, and the gift of Eternal Life; and labouring for the advancement of the Kingdom of God throughout the world. The Church of Scotland adheres to the Scottish Reformation; receives the Word of God which is contained in the Scriptures of the Old and New Testaments as its supreme rule of faith and life; and avows the fundamental doctrines of the Catholic faith founded thereupon.

II. The principal subordinate standard of the Church of Scotland is the Westminster Confession of Faith approved by the General Assembly of 1647, containing the sum and substance of the Faith of the Reformed Church. Its government is Presbyterian, and is exercised through Kirk Sessions; Presbyteries, [Provincial Synods deleted by Act V, 1992], and General Assemblies. Its system and principles of worship, orders, and discipline are in accordance with 'The Directory for the Public Worship of God', 'The Form of Presbyterial Church Government' and 'The Form of Process', as these have been or may hereafter be interpreted or modified by Acts of the General Assembly or by consuetude.

III.   This Church is in historical continuity with the Church of Scotland which was reformed in 1560, whose liberties were ratified in 1592, and for whose security provision was made in the Treaty of Union of 1707. The continuity and identity of the Church of Scotland are not prejudiced by the adoption of these Articles. As a national Church representative of the Christian Faith of the Scottish people it acknowledges its distinctive call and duty to bring the ordinances of religion to the people in every parish of Scotland through a territorial ministry.

IV.   This Church as part of the Universal Church wherein the Lord Jesus Christ has appointed a government in the hands of Church office-bearers, receives from Him, its Divine King and Head, and From Him alone, the right and power subject to no civil authority to legislate, and to adjudicate finally, in all matters of doctrine, worship, government, and discipline in the Church, including the right to determine all questions concerning membership and office in the Church, the constitution and membership of its Courts, and the mode of election of its office-bearers, and to define the boundaries of the spheres of labour of its ministers and other office-bearers. Recognition by civil authority of the separate and independent government and jurisdiction of this Church in matters spiritual, in whatever manner such recognition be expressed, does not in any way affect the character of this government and jurisdiction as derived from the Divine Head of the Church alone or give to the civil authority any right of interference with the proceedings or judgments of the Church within the sphere of its spiritual government and jurisdiction.

V.   This Church has the inherent right, free from interference by civil authority, but under the safeguards for deliberate action and legislation provided by the Church itself, to frame or adopt its subordinate standards, to declare the sense in which it understands its Confession of Faith, to modify the forms of expression therein, or to formulate other doctrinal statements, and to define the relation thereto of its office-bearers and members, but always in agreement with the Word of God and the fundamental doctrines of the Christian Faith contained in the said Confession, of which agreement the Church shall be sole judge, and with due regard to liberty of opinion in points which do not enter into the substance of the Faith.

VI.   This Church acknowledges the divine appointment and authority of the civil magistrate within his own sphere, and maintains its historic testimony to the duty of the nation acting in its corporate capacity to render homage to God, to acknowledge the Lord Jesus Christ to be King over the nations, to obey His laws, to reverence His ordinances, to honour His Church, and to promote in all appropriate ways the Kingdom of God. The Church and the State owe mutual duties to each other, and acting within their respective spheres may signally promote each other's welfare.

The Church and the State have the right to determine each for itself all questions concerning the extent and the continuance of their mutual relations in the discharge of these duties and the obligations arising therefrom.

VII. The Church of Scotland, believing it to be the will of Christ that His disciples should be all one in the Father and in Him, that the world may believe that the Father has sent Him, recognises the obligation to seek and promote union with other Churches in which it finds the Word to be purely preached, the sacraments administered according to Christ's ordinance, and discipline rightly exercised; and it has the right to unite with any such Church without loss of its identity on terms which this Church finds to be consistent with these Articles.

VIII. The Church has the right to interpret these Articles, and, subject to the safeguards for deliberate action and legislation provided by the Church itself, to modify or add to them; but always consistently with the provisions of the first Article hereof, adherence to which, as interpreted by the Church, is essential to its continuity and corporate life. Any proposal for a modification of or addition to these Articles which may be approved of by the General Assembly shall, before it can be enacted by the Assembly, be transmitted by way of overture to Presbyteries in at least two immediately successive years. If the overture shall receive the approval, with or without suggested amendment, of two-thirds of the whole of the Presbyteries of the Church, the Assembly may revise the overture in the light of any suggestions by the Presbyteries, and may transmit the overture when so revised to Presbyteries for their consent. If the overture as transmitted in its final form shall receive the consent of not less than two-thirds of the whole of the Presbyteries of the Church, the General Assembly may, if it deems it expedient, modify or add to these Articles in terms of the said overture. But if the overture as transmitted in its final form shall not receive the requisite consent, the same or a similar proposal shall not be again transmitted for the consent of Presbyteries until an interval of five years after the failure to obtain the requisite consent has been reported to the General Assembly.

Appendix 3

DTI Model Statement
of Good Practice
(www.berr.gov.uk/files/file38521.doc)

Preface

The content of this statement represents minimum standards which faith groups should aim to achieve. The expectation of the DTI is that faith groups shall disseminate this statement at all levels within their organisations to ensure awareness of the terms of the statement. It will be a matter for the leaders of faith groups how individual members are kept up to date with progress towards these standards but DTI would encourage an open and transparent approach.

Terms and conditions of work

Standard: Faith groups should make available to individuals statements of terms and conditions, (and if appropriate individual job descriptions), with the aim that individuals have a clear understanding of their responsibilities and the support they can expect. This information could also be set out in job advertisements.

Such statements might cover some or all of the following areas:

- Arrangements for special leave in cases of sickness and caring responsibilities.

- Entitlement to annual leave and rest breaks.
- Arrangements, where appropriate, for maternity, paternity, ante-natal and adoption leave.
- Provision of accommodation, where appropriate.
- Role of spouses and locums, and the division of responsibilities within team ministries.
- Agreement to provide a written statement of grounds for termination of appointment.
- Provision of time off to look for another appointment or arrange training in the event of loss of post.
- Rights to belong to and be active in a trade union.
- Minimum periods of notice.
- Pension arrangements, where appropriate.
- Availability and extent of any expenses and allowances.

Resolving disputes

Standard: There should be clear procedures for resolving disputes (including grievance and disciplinary cases and issues over appointments), and there should be a point of recourse when formal procedures and agreed good practice are not followed.

These procedures could include the following:

- Rights to be accompanied to hearings and other procedures.
- Clear timelines for all procedures.
- Appeal and review procedures.
- Pastoral advisers to give informal advice and support.
- Involvement of third parties not directly involved in disputes.

Development and personnel support

Standard: Faith groups should provide support for individuals when they apply for posts and over the course of appointments to help with ongoing development.

Such activities might include the following:

- Mentoring, coaching, and job shadowing, and support in applying for positions
- Staff annual reports, objective setting and performance appraisal.

Information and Consultation

Standard: Faith groups should aim to ensure that individuals are kept informed of and consulted about changes affecting them.

- Information about and consultation on significant changes, which will impact on faith group working conditions. This could include changes in terms and conditions, statements of practice, policy changes and financial decisions.

DTI
March 2007

The Process

Initial steps

- the DTI will publish the model statement of good practice which has emerged from discussions within the Clergy Working Group, acknowledging which faith groups have participated in the discussions and encouraging all faith groups to implement it; individual faith groups can amend the exact wording to meet individual needs but it should adhere closely to the principles in the statement and any changes should be justifiable;

- faith groups should aim to establish the current position ie the baseline, on the issues raised in the statement of good practice by:
  - ◊ mechanisms which are open to individuals to give their views freely and without detriment, for example discussion or focus groups; or
  - ◊ using a questionnaire to ascertain views, either using the DTI model questionnaire or an amended version reflecting a modified statement of good practice.

Faith groups should

- make available details of the current position on the issues raised in the statement of good practice to all individuals within faith groups and DTI within 6 months of the date of publication of the statement of good practice; and

- make it known that individuals can contact DTI direct on a non-attributable basis about the issues raised in the statement of good practice and that any views or information obtained by DTI will be taken into account and also summarised, anonymised and reflected back to individual faith groups.

- It will be a matter for the leaders of faith groups how individuals are kept up to date with progress towards implementing the statement but DTI would encourage an open and transparent approach.

The future

- Two years from the publication of the model statement of good practice, DTI will call upon faith groups to provide an update to see what steps have been taken to implement the statement (as well as other relevant changes) using a second questionnaire or other mechanisms to allow individuals to give their views freely and without detriment about progress.
- Again any updates should be freely available to all individuals within faith groups.
- As before, faith groups should make it known that individuals can contact DTI on a non-attributable basis about progress towards implementing the statement and these views will be taken into account and also reflected back to individual faith groups.
- Based on the information provided, DTI will consider if any further action is appropriate at this stage, including legislative action.

Bibliography

Primary Texts

Aquinas, St Thomas, *Summa Theologiae* 1a2ae, ed. Thomas Gilby (London: Eyre & Spottiswoode, 1966).

Bodin, J., *On Sovereignty; Four Chapters from 'The Six Books of the Commonwealth'*, ed. and trans. Julian H. Franklin (Cambridge: Cambridge University Press, 1992).

The Booke of the Universall Kirk of Scotland, ed. Alexander Peterkin (Edinburgh: Edinburgh Printing & Publishing Company, 1839).

Buchanan, G., *De Iure Regni Apud Scotos, Dialogus* (Edinburgh, 1579, facsimile edn Amsterdam: Theatrum Orbis Terrarum, 1969); for a translation see *De Jure Regni Apud Scotos; A Dialogue Concerning the Rights of the Crown in Scotland* (Edinburgh, 1799).

Calvin, J., *Institutes of the Christian Religion*, trans. Henry Beveridge (London: James Clarke, 1962).

European Convention on Human Rights, as amended by Protocol No. 11 (Strasbourg: Directorate of Human Rights, 1999).

The First Book of Discipline, with introduction and commentary by J. K. Cameron (Edinburgh: Saint Andrew Press, 1972).

Free Church of Scotland Appeals 1903–4, Authorised Report, ed. R. L. Orr (Edinburgh: Macniven & Wallace, 1904).

Hobbes, T., *Leviathan: or the Matter, Forme and Power of a Commonwealth Ecclesiasticall and Civil* (Oxford: Basil Blackwell, 1946).

Hooker, R., *Ecclesiastical Polity*, ed. Arthur Pollard (Fyfield, 1990).

James VI, *Basilikon Doron*, ed. James Craigie, 2 vols (Scottish Text Society, 1944 and 1950).

James VI, True Law of Free Monarchies, *and* Basilikon Doron: *A Modernized Edition* (Toronto: Centre for Reformation and Renaissance Studies, 1996).

Joint Report of the Ministries Council and the Legal Questions Committee, in *Volume of Reports and Papers of the Church of Scotland General Assembly of 2007* (Edinburgh: Assembly Arrangements Committee, 2007).

Knox, John, *John Knox's History of the Reformation in Scotland*, ed. W. Croft Dickinson, 2 vols (Edinburgh: Thomas Nelson, 1949).

Knox, J., *On Rebellion*, ed. R. A. Mason (Cambridge: Cambridge University Press, 1994).

Marsilius of Padua, *Defensor Pacis*, trans. and Introduction by A. Gewirth (Toronto: University of Toronto Press, 1980).

The Ministry of the Whole Church of Jesus Christ and the Problem of Sovereignty: Statement of the Theological Committee of the Evangelical Church of the Union on Barmen IV (Berlin: Evangelical Church of the Union, 2001).

Report of the Working Group on Human Sexuality, in *Volume of Reports to the General Assembly of 2007* (Edinburgh: Assembly Arrangements Committee, 2007), pp. 4/9ff.

'Response by the Church of Scotland to DTI Discussion Document on Employment Status in Relation to Statutory Employment Rights' (Edinburgh: Board of Practice and Procedure, 2002, unpublished).

Returns to Overtures Report, in *Volume of Reports and Papers of the Church of Scotland General Assembly of 2008* (Edinburgh: Assembly Arrangements Committee, 2008).

Rutherford, S., *Lex, Rex: A Dispute for the Just Prerogative of King and People* (Edinburgh: Ogle & Boyd, 1843).

A Scholastic Miscellany: Anselm to Ockham, ed. and trans. E. R. Fairweather, Library of Christian Classics X (London: SCM Press, 1956).

Scots Confession, in *The Book of Confessions* (Louisville, KY: Office of the General Assembly of the Presbyterian Church [USA]), 1999, pp. 9–25.

The Second Book of Discipline, with introduction and commentary by J. Kirk (Edinburgh: Saint Andrew Press, 1980).

Social Contract: Essays by Locke, Hume and Rousseau, with Introduction by Sir Ernest Barker (London: Oxford University Press, 1947).

White, J., Collected papers in New College library, Edinburgh, special collection.

Civil Legislation

Act anent the Abolishing of the Pape, and his usurped Authoritie 1567 c. 2.

Act anent the Jurisdiction of the Kirk 1579 ch. 69.

Act Ratifying the Presbyterian Order of the Church 1592 c. 116.

The Claim of Right 1689 c. 28.

Act Ratifying the Confession of Faith, and Settling the Presbyterian Church Government 1690 c. 5.

Protestant Religion and Presbyterian Church Act 1707 c. 6 (also known as the Act of Security 1707).

Union with England Act 1707 c. 7.

Church Patronage (Scotland) Act 1711 c. 21.

Church Patronage (Scotland) Act 1874 c. 82.

Churches (Scotland) Act 1905 c. 12.

Church of Scotland Act 1921 c. 29.

Church of Scotland (Property and Endowments) Act 1925 c. 33.

Sex Discrimination Act 1975 c. 65.

European Employment Directive 2000/78/EC.

Employment Equality (Religion or Belief) Regulations (SI 2003 No. 1660).

Employment Equality (Sexual Orientation) Regulations (SI 2003 No. 1661).

Charities and Trustee Investment (Scotland) Act 2005 asp 10.

Employment Equality (Sex Discrimination) Regulations (SI 2005 No. 2467).

Employment Equality (Age) Regulations (SI 2006 No. 1031).
Equality Act (Sexual Orientation) Regulations 2007 SI No. 1263.

Cases in Chronological Order
(*Percy* case shown last, with commentaries)

Earl of Kinnoull and Rev R Young v. *Presbytery of Auchterarder* (1838) 16S 661, (1841) 3D 778, (1843) 5D 1010 (the *Auchterarder* case).

Presbytery of Strathbogie and Rev J Cruickshank and others, suspenders, and related cases (1839) 2D 258, 585, (1840) 2D 1047, 1380, (1840) 3D 282, (1842) 4D 1298, (1843) 5D 909, (1843) 15 Juris 375 (the *Strathbogie* case).

Middleton v. *Anderson* (1842) 4D 957 (the Culsalmond case).

Cuninghame v. *Presbytery of Irvine* (1843) 3D 427 (the *Stewarton* case).

Bannatyne v. *Lord Overtoun* (1902) 4 F 1083: (1904) AC 515 (the Free Church case).

Ballantyne and Others v. *Presbytery of Wigtown and Others*, 1936 SC 625.

McDonald v. *Burns*, 1940 SC 376

Hunter v. *Chief Constable of the West Midlands Police* [1982] AC 529.

Logan v. *Presbytery of Dumbarton*, 1995 SLT 1228.

Free Church of Scotland (Continuing) v. *Free Church of Scotland* [2005] CSOH 46.

Reaney v. *Hereford Diocesan Board of Finance* ET 1602844/2006.

New Testament Church of God v. *Stewart EAT*, on 27 October 2006 reported at [2007] IRLR 178.

The Helen Percy Case

Percy v. *Church of Scotland Board of National Mission*, Industrial Tribunal case S/300120/98, unpublished judgement.

Percy v. *Church of Scotland Board of National Mission*, Employment Appeal Tribunal case EA T/1415/98, unpublished judgement.

Percy v. *Order and Judgement of the Employment Appeals Tribunal*, 2001 SC 757.

Case reports: Petition of Helen Percy, in *Volume of Reports and Papers of the Church of Scotland General Assembly of 1999* (Edinburgh: Board of Practice and Procedure, 1999).

Order of Proceedings Papers of the 2002 Church of Scotland General Assembly (Edinburgh: Board of Practice and Procedure, 2002).

'Report of the Committee on Commissions (Bills and Overtures)', in *Supplementary Volume of Reports to 2002 Church of Scotland General Assembly* (Edinburgh: Board of Practice and Procedure, 2002).

Helen Douglas v. *The Presbytery of Angus and The Board of National Mission*, Special Commission of the General Assembly, in *Volume of Reports to the General Assembly of 2004* (Edinburgh: Board of Practice and Procedure), pp. 34/1ff.

Percy (AP) (Appellant) v. *Church of Scotland Board of National Mission (Respondent) (Scotland)* [2005] UKHL 73.

Commentary on the Helen Percy case

Cranmer, F., and S. Peterson, 'Employment, Sex Discrimination and the Churches: The Percy Case', *EccLJ* 8 (2006).

MacLean, M., F. Cranmer and S. Peterson, 'Recent Developments in Church–State Relations in Scotland', in R. M. Morris (ed.), *Church and State* (Basingstoke: Palgrave Macmillan, forthcoming).

Mathieson, D., 'Clergy, Offices and Employment', *NZLJ* (March 2006), pp. 65–8.

Newth, J. T., 'Changes at the Manse', *Taxation* (15 March 2007), pp. 296–9.

Rivers, J., 'Law, Religion and Gender Equality', *EccLJ* 9 (2007), pp. 24–52.

Secondary Sources

Avis, P., *Church, State and Establishment* (London: SPCK, 2001).

Bagehot, W., *The English Constitution*, with Introduction by R. H. S. Crossman (London: Collins, 1963).

Balfour, W., *The Establishment Principle Defended: A Reply to the Statement by the Committee of the United Presbyterian Church on Disestablishment and Disendowment* (Edinburgh: Johnstone, Hunter & Co., 1873).

Barr, J., *The Scottish Church Question* (London: James Clarke, 1920).

Barr, J., *The United Free Church of Scotland* (London: Allenson, 1934).

Barth, K., *Church and State* (London: SCM Press, 1939).

Barth, K., *The Knowledge of God and the Service of God according to the Teaching of the Reformation: Recalling the Scottish Confession of 1560*, The Gifford Lectures 1937 and 1938, trans. J. L. M. Haire and I. Henderson (London: Hodder & Stoughton, 1938).

Berman, H. J., *Faith and Order: The Reconciliation of Law and Religion*, Emory University Studies in Law and Religion (Atlanta, GA: Scholars Press, 1993).

Berman, H. J., *The Interaction of Law and Religion* (London: SCM Press, 1974).

Berman, H. J., and J. Witte, 'The Transformation of Western Legal Philosophy in Lutheran Germany', *Southern California Law Review* 62.6 (September 1989).

Blank, Josef, 'The Concept of "Power" in the Church: New Testament Perspectives', in Provost and Walf, *Power in the Church*, pp. 3–12.

Bogdanor, V., *The Monarchy and the Constitution* (Oxford: Clarendon Press, 1995).

Bosanquet, B., *The Philosophical Theory of the State* (London: Macmillan, 1958).

Bradley, I., *God Save the Queen: The Spiritual Dimension of the Monarchy* (London: Darton, Longman & Todd, 2002).

Bretherton, L., 'A New Establishment? Theological Politics and the Emerging Shape of Church-State Relations', *Political Theology* 6 (2006).

Brotherstone, T., *Covenant, Charter and Party: Traditions of Revolt and Protest in Modern Scottish History* (Aberdeen: Aberdeen University Press, 1989).

Brown, C. G., *The Death of Christian Britain: Understanding Secularisation 1800–2000* (London: Routledge, 2001).

Brown C. G., 'The Myth of the Established Church of Scotland', in J. S. Kirk (ed.), *The Scottish Churches and the Union Parliament 1707–1999* (Edinburgh: Scottish Church History Society, 2001).

Brown, C. G., *Religion and Society in Scotland since 1707* (Edinburgh: Edinburgh University Press, 1997).

Brown, K. M., 'In Search of the Godly Magistrate in Reformation Scotland', *Journal of Ecclesiastical History* 40 (1989), pp. 553–81.

Brown, P. H., *George Buchanan, Humanist and Reformer: A Biography* (Edinburgh: David Douglas, 1890).

Brown, S. J., *The National Churches of England, Ireland, and Scotland, 1801–1846* (Oxford: Oxford University Press, 2001).

Brown, S. J., 'The Social Vision of Scottish Presbyterianism and the Union of 1929', *Records of the Scottish Church History Society* XXIV (1990), pp. 77–96.

Brown, S. J., *Thomas Chalmers and the Godly Commonwealth in Scotland* (Oxford: Oxford University Press, 1982).

Brown, S. J., and M. Fry (eds), *Scotland in the Age of the Disruption* (Edinburgh: Edinburgh University Press, 1993).

Brown, S. J., and G. Newlands (eds), *Scottish Christianity in the Modern World: Essays in Honour of A. C. Cheyne* (Edinburgh: T&T Clark, 2000).

Brown, T. (ed.), *Annals of the Disruption* (Edinburgh: Macniven & Wallace, 1892).

Bruce, S., *Religion in Modern Britain* (Oxford: University Press, 1995).

Bruce, S., *Religion in the Modern World: from Cathedrals to Cults* (Oxford: University Press, 1996).

Brunner, E., *Justice and the Social Order* (London: Lutterworth, 1945).

Buckroyd, J., *Church and State in Scotland: 1660–1681* (Edinburgh: John Donald, 1980).

Burgess, G., *Absolute Monarchy and the Stuart Constitution* (New Haven and London: Yale University Press, 1996).

Burleigh, J. H. S., *A Church History of Scotland* (Edinburgh: Hope Trust, 1983).

Burleigh, J. H. S., *The Scottish Reformation and the Idea of a National Church* (Edinburgh: Church of Scotland, 1960).

Burns, J. H., 'Conciliarism, Papalism, and Power, 1511–1518', in Wood (ed.), *Church and Sovereignty c. 590–1918*.

Burns, J. H., *Lordship, Kingship and Empire: The Idea of Monarchy, 1400–1525* (Oxford: Clarendon Press, 1992).

Burns, J. H., 'The Political Ideas of George Buchanan', *Scottish Historical Review* 30 (1951), pp. 60–8.

Burns, J. H., *The True Law of Kingship: Concepts of Monarchy in Early-Modern Scotland* (Oxford: Clarendon Press, 1996).

Burrell, S. A., 'The Covenant Idea as a Revolutionary Symbol: Scotland 1596–1637', *Church History* 27 (1958), pp. 338–50.

Camilleri, J. A., and J. Falk, *Beyond Sovereignty?: The Politics of a Shrinking and Fragmenting World* (Aldershot: Edward Elgar, 1992).

Campbell, W. M., 'Samuel Rutherfurd: Propagandist and Exponent of Scottish Presbyterianism: An Exposition of His Position and Influence in the Doctrine and Politics of the Scottish Church', PhD thesis (Edinburgh University, 1937).

Carr, W., 'A Developing Establishment', *Journal of Theology* CII (1999), pp. 2–10.

Chadwick, O., 'Chalmers and the State', in Cheyne, *Practical and the Pious*.

Cheyne, A. C., *The Practical and the Pious: Essays on Thomas Chalmers (1780–1847)* (Edinburgh: Saint Andrew Press, 1985).

Cheyne, A. C., *Studies in Scottish Church History* (Edinburgh: T&T Clark, 1999).

Cheyne, A. C., *The Ten Years' Conflict and the Disruption: An Overview* (Edinburgh: Scottish Academic Press, 1993).

Cheyne, A. C., *The Transforming of the Kirk: Victorian Scotland's Religious Revolution*, Chalmers Lectures 1982 (Edinburgh: Saint Andrew Press, 1993).

Clark, J. C. D., *English Society 1688–1832: Ideology, social structure and political practice during the Ancien Regime* (Cambridge: Cambridge University Press, 1985).

Coertzen, P., *Church and Order: A Reformed Perspective*, Canon Law Monograph Series 1 (Leuven: Peeters, 1998).

Coffey, J., *Politics, Religion and the British Revolution: The Mind of Samuel Rutherford* (Cambridge: Cambridge University Press, 1997).

Corecco, E., 'Ecclesiological Bases of the Code', in Provost and Walf, *From Life to Law*, pp. 3–13.

Cowan, E. J., 'The Making of the National Covenant', in Morrill, *Scottish National Covenant*.

Cowan, I. B., 'Church and Society in Post-Reformation Scotland', *Records of the Scottish Church History Society* xvii (1971), pp. 185–201.

Cowan, I. B., *The Scottish Reformation: Church and Society in Sixteenth-century Scotland* (London: Weidenfeld & Nicolson, 1982).

Cranz, F. E., *An Essay on the Development of Luther's Thought on Justice, Law, and Society*, Harvard Theological Studies XIX (Cambridge, MA: Harvard Theological Press, 1959).

Creveld, M. van, *The Rise and Decline of the State* (Cambridge: Cambridge University Press, 1999).

Cunningham, A., and M. di Maio (trans.), *The Early Church and the State*, Sources of Early Christian Thought Series (Philadelphia, PA: Fortress Press, 1982).

Davidson, Lord, and R. A. Paterson, 'Church of Scotland', in *Stair Memorial Encyclopaedia* (Edinburgh: Butterworth, 1994), vol. III, pp. 1501–1609.

Davie, G., *Religion in Britain since 1945: Believing without Belonging* (Oxford: Basil Blackwell, 1994).

Davie, G. E., *The Democratic Intellect: Scotland and Her Universities in the Nineteenth Century* (Edinburgh: Edinburgh University Press, 1964).

Davies, R. E., *The Problem of Authority in the Continental Reformers: A Study in Luther, Zwingli, and Calvin* (London: Epworth, 1946).

Davis, C., *Theology and Political Society*, The Hulsean Lectures in the University of Cambridge 1978 (Cambridge: Cambridge University Press, 1980).

Dawson, C., *Religion and Culture*, Gifford Lectures 1947 (London: Sheed & Ward, 1948).

Dawson, J., 'The Two John Knoxes: England, Scotland and the 1558 Tracts', *Journal of Ecclesiastical History* 42 (1991), pp. 555–76.

Devine, T. M., and R. J. Finlay (eds), *Scotland in the Twentieth Century* (Edinburgh: Edinburgh University Press, 1996).

Dicey, A. V., *Introduction to the Study of the Law of the Constitution*, 9th edn with Introduction and Appendix by E. C. S. Wade (London: Macmillan, 1939).

Dickinson, W. C., G. Donaldson and I. A. Milne, *A Source Book of Scottish History*, 3 vols (Edinburgh: Thomas Nelson, 1958–61).

Donald, P., *An Uncounselled King: Charles I and the Scottish Troubles, 1637–1641* (Cambridge: Cambridge University Press, 1990).

Donaldson, G., *All the Queen's Men: Power and Politics in Mary Stewart's Scotland* (London: Batsford, 1983).

Donaldson, G., *The Faith of the Scots* (London: Batsford, 1990).

Donaldson, G., *The Making of the Scottish Prayer Book* (Edinburgh: Edinburgh University Press, 1954).

Donaldson, G., 'The Polity of the Scottish Church 1560–1600', *Records of the Scottish Church History Society* xi, pp. 212–26.

Donaldson, G., *Scotland: Church and Nation through Sixteen Centuries* (Edinburgh: Scottish Academic Press, 1960).

Donaldson, G., *Scotland: James V to James VII* (Edinburgh: Oliver & Boyd, 1965).

Donaldson, G., *Scottish Church History* (Edinburgh: Scottish Academic Press, 1985).

Donaldson, G., *Scottish Historical Documents* (Glasgow: Neil Wilson, 1997).

Donaldson, G., *The Scottish Reformation* (Cambridge: Cambridge University Press, 1960).

Douglas, J. D., *Light in the North: The Story of the Scottish Covenanters* (Exeter: Paternoster Press, 1964).

Dunbar, L. J., *Reforming the Scottish Church: John Winram (c. 1492–1582) and the Example of Fife* (Aldershot: Ashgate, 2002).

Dunlop, A. I., 'The Paths to Reunion in 1929', *Records of the Scottish Church History Society* XX (1980), pp. 163–78.

Dunlop, A. I., *William Carstares and the Kirk by Law Established*, Chalmers Lectures 1964 (Edinburgh: Saint Andrew Press, 1967).

Ehler, S. Z., and J. B. Morrall, *Church and State through the Centuries: A Collection of Historic Documents with Commentaries* (London: Burns & Oates, 1954).

Ellul, J., *The Theological Foundation of Law* (London: SCM Press, 1961).

Emerson, E. H., 'Calvin and Covenant Theology', *Church History* 25 (1956), pp. 136–42.

Ferguson, W., *The Identity of the Scottish Nation: An Historic Quest* (Edinburgh: Edinburgh University Press, 1998).

Fergusson, D., *Church, State and Civil Society* (Cambridge: Cambridge University Press, 2004).

Ferrier, J., *Observations on Church and State* (Edinburgh: William Blackwood, 1848).

Figgis, J. N., *Churches in the Modern State* (London: Longmans Green, 1914).

Figgis, J. N., *From Gerson to Grotius 1414–1625* (Cambridge: Cambridge University Press, 1916).

Figgis, J. N., *The Theory of the Divine Right of Kings* (Cambridge: Cambridge University Press, 1896).

Fleming, J. R., *A History of the Church in Scotland 1875–1929* (Edinburgh: T&T Clark, 1933).

Forrester, D. B., *Beliefs, Values and Policies: Conviction Politics in a Secular Age*, The Henley Henson Lectures, 1987–8 (Oxford: Clarendon Press, 1989).

Forrester, D. B., 'Ecclesia Scoticana – Established, Free or National?', *Theology* CII.806 (March/April 1999).

Forrester, D. B., 'The Political Teaching of Luther, Calvin, and Hooker', in L. Strauss and J. Cropsey (eds), *History of Political Philosophy* (Chicago, IL: Rand, McNally, 1963).

Forrester, D. B., 'Radical Reformed Orthodoxy: Can It Be Retrieved?', *Truthful Action*, pp. 161–84.

Forrester, D. B., *Truthful Action: Explorations in Practical Theology* (Edinburgh: T&T Clark, 2000).

Forrester, D. B., *Theology and Politics* (Oxford: Basil Blackwell, 1988).

Foster, W. R., *The Church Before the Covenants: The Church of Scotland 1596–1638* (Edinburgh: Scottish Academic Press, 1975).

Gierke, O., *Natural Law and the Theory of Society 1500–1800*, trans. with introduction by Ernest Barker (Cambridge: Cambridge University Press, 1958).

Gierke, O., *Political Theories of the Middle Age*, trans. with an Introduction by F. W. Maitland (Cambridge: Cambridge University Press, 1900; repr. Key Texts series [Bristol: Thoemmes, 1996]).

Gilby, T., *Between Community and Society: A Philosophy and Theology of the State* (London: Longmans, Green, 1953).

Gladstone, W. E., *The State in its Relations with the Church* (London: John Murray, 1838).

Glassey, L. K. J., 'William II and the Settlement of Religion in Scotland, 1688–1690', *Records of the Scottish Church History Society* xxiii (1989), pp. 317–29.

Graham, M. F., *The Uses of Reform: 'Godly Discipline' and Popular Behaviour in Scotland and Beyond, 1560–1610*, Studies in Medieval and Reformation Thought LVIII (Leiden: E. J. Brill, 1996).

Greaves, R. L., *Theology and Revolution in the Scottish Reformation: Studies in the Thought of John Knox* (Grand Rapids, MI: Christian University Press, 1980).

Hart, H. L. A., *The Concept of Law* (Oxford: Clarendon Press, 1961).

Hauerwas, S., *After Christendom?: How the Church is to Behave if Freedom, Justice and a Christian Nation are Bad Ideas* (Nashville, TN: Abingdon, 1991).

Hauerwas, S., *In Good Company: the Church as Polis* (Indiana, IN: University of Notre Dame Press, 1995).

Henderson, G. D., *Heritage: A Study of the Disruption* (Edinburgh: Oliver & Boyd, 1943).

Herron, A., *Kirk by Divine Right: Church and State: Peaceful Coexistence*, The Baird Lectures 1985 (Edinburgh: Saint Andrew Press, 1985).

Hertz, K. (ed.), *Two Kingdoms and One World* (Minneapolis, MN: Augsburg, 1976).

Hill, G., *A View of the Constitution of the Church of Scotland* (Edinburgh: John Waugh, 1835).

Hinsley, F. H., *Sovereignty* (London: C. A. Watts, 1966).

Hopfl, H., *The Christian Polity of John Calvin* (Cambridge: Cambridge University Press, 1982).

Hunt, G. L. (ed.), *Calvinism and the Political Order* (Philadelphia, PA: Westminster Press, 1965).

Huntington, S. P, *The Clash of Civilizations and the Remaking of World Order* (London: Touchstone, 1998).

Jenkins, P., *The Next Christendom: The Coming of Global Christianity* (Oxford: Oxford University Press, 2002).

Johnston, C. N., 'Church Union in Scotland', *Quarterly Review* (1920), pp. 205–25.

Johnston, C. N., *Handbook of Scottish Church Defence* (Edinburgh: James G. Hitt, 1892).

Johnston, D., and C. Sampson, C. (eds), *Religion, the Missing Dimension of Statecraft* (New York, NY: Oxford University Press, 1994).

Jouvenel, B. de, *On Power: Its Nature and the History of its Growth*, with preface by D. W. Brogan, trans. J. F. Huntington (from 1945 edn) (Boston, MA: Beacon, 1962).

Jouvenel, B. de, *Sovereignty: An Inquiry into the Political Good*, trans. J. F. Huntington (Cambridge: Cambridge University Press, 1957).

Kauper, P. G., *Religion and the Constitution* (Baton Rouge, LA: Louisiana State University Press, 1964).

Kellas, J. G., 'The Liberal Party and the Scottish Church Disestablishment Crisis', *English Historical Review* 79 (1964), pp. 31–46.

Kellas, J. G., *Modern Scotland: The Nation since 1870* (London: Pall Mall, 1968).

Kelsen, H., *General Theory of Law and State*, trans. Anders Wedberg (Cambridge, MA: Harvard University Press, 1945).

Kennedy, J., *Presbyterian Authority and Discipline* (Edinburgh: Saint Andrew Press, 1960).

Kern, F., *Kingship and Law in the Middle Ages*, trans. with Introduction by S. B. Chrimes (New York, NY: Frederick A. Praeger, 1956).

Kirk, J. (ed.), *The Books of Assumption of the Thirds of Benefices: Scottish Ecclesiastical Rentals at the Reformation* (Oxford: Oxford University Press for British Library, 1995).

Kirk, J., *Patterns of Reform: Continuity and Change in the Reformation Kirk* (Edinburgh: T&T Clark, 1989).

Krieder, A., *The Origins of Christendom in the West* (Edinburgh: T&T Clark, 2001).

Kuhn, K.-C., 'Church Order instead of Church Law?', in Provost and Walf, *From Life to Law*.

Küng, H., and J. Moltmann (eds), *The Ethics of World Religions and Human Rights*, Concilium (London: SCM Press, 1990).

Kyle, R., 'The Nature of the Church in the Thought of John Knox', *Scottish Journal of Theology* 37 (1984), pp. 485–501.

Laski, H. J., *The Foundations of Sovereignty and Other Essays* (London: George Allen & Unwin, 1921).

Laski, H. J., *Political Thought in England: Locke to Bentham* (London: Oxford University Press, 1920).

Laski, H. J., *Studies in the Problem of Sovereignty* (London: Humphrey Milford, 1917).

Lee, M., Jr, 'James VI and the Revival of Episcopacy in Scotland 1596–1600', *Church History* 43 (1974), pp. 50–64.

Lee, R., *The Popery of Spiritual Independence* (Edinburgh: Myles Macphail, 1844).

Lumsden, J., *The Covenants of Scotland* (Paisley: Alexander Gardner, 1914).

Lyall, F., *Of Presbyters and Kings: Church and State in the Law of Scotland* (Aberdeen: Aberdeen University Press, 1980).

Lyall, F., 'Religion and Law', *Juridical Review* (1976), pp. 58–68.

MacCormick, N., *H. L. A. Hart*, Jurists: Profiles in Legal Theory Series (London: Edward Arnold, 1981).

MacCormick, N., 'The Kirk and the Theory of Sovereignty', unpublished lecture.

MacCormick, N., *Questioning Sovereignty: Law, State and Nation in the European Commonwealth* (Oxford: Oxford University Press, 1999).

McCrie, T., *Life of Andrew Melville* (Edinburgh: Wm Blackwood & Sons, 1856; John Menzies & Co., 1902).

MacDonald, A. R., *The Jacobean Kirk 1567–1625: Sovereignty, Polity and Liturgy* (Aldershot: Ashgate, 1998).

Macdonald, F. A. J., 'Law and Doctrine in the Church of Scotland with Particular Reference to Confessions of Faith', PhD thesis (St Andrews University, 1983).

MacDougall, N. (ed.), *Church, Politics and Society: Scotland 1408–1929* (Edinburgh: John Donald, 1983).

McFarlane, I. D., *Buchanan* (London: Duckworth, 1981).

McGrath, A. E., *Reformation Thought: An Introduction* (Oxford: Basil Blackwell, 1999).

MacGregor, J. G., *The Scottish Presbyterian Polity: A Study of Its Origins in the Sixteenth Century* (Edinburgh: Oliver & Boyd, 1926).

Machin, G. I. T., 'The Disruption and British Politics 1834–43', *Scottish Historical Review* 51 (1972), pp. 20–51.

MacInnes, A. I., *Charles I and the Making of the Covenanting Movement 1625–1641* (Edinburgh: John Donald, 1991).

McIntosh, J. R., *Church and Theology in Enlightenment Scotland: The Popular Party, 1740–1800*, Scottish Historical Review Monographs Series 5 (East Linton: Tuckwell Press, 1998).

Maclntyre, A., *Whose Justice? Which Rationality?* (Indiana, IN: University of Notre Dame Press, 1988).

MacIver, R. M., *The Modern State* (London: Oxford University Press, 1926).

Mackey, J. P., *Power and Christian Ethics* (Cambridge: Cambridge University Press, 1994).

MacLean, M. A., 'The Church of Scotland as a National Church', *Law and Justice 149* (Trinity/Michaelmas 2002), pp. 125–33.

McLear, J. F., 'Samuel Rutherford: The Law and the King', in Hunt, *Calvinism and the Political Order*, ch. 4.

McMillan, W., 'The Lord High Commissioner to the General Assembly', *Records of the Scottish Church History Society* vi, pp. 36–45, 96–114, 265–98.

McNeill, P. G. B., 'The Legal Aspects of the Scottish Reformation', *SLT News* 84 (1962).

MacPherson, H., 'The Political Ideas of the Covenanters', *Records of the Scottish Church History Society* i (1926), pp. 224–32.

Mair, W. (posthumous), *A Digest of Laws and Decisions Ecclesiastical and Civil relating to the Constitution, Practice, and Affairs of the Church of Scotland* (4th edn 1912; Edinburgh and London: Blackwood, reprint with supplement, 1923).

Makey, W., *The Church of the Covenant 1637–1651: Revolution and Social Change in Scotland* (Edinburgh: John Donald, 1979).

Mann, M. (ed.), *The Rise and Decline of the Nation State* (Oxford: Basil Blackwell, 1990).

Mansbach, R. W., and J. A. Vasquez, 'Reassessing the Past: Global History from a Changed Perspective', *In Search of Theory: A New Paradigm for Global Politics* (New York, NY: Columbia University Press, 1981).

Marr, A., *The Battle for Scotland* (London: Penguin, 1995).

Marshall, G., *Presbyteries and Profits: Calvinism and the Development of Capitalism in Scotland 1560–1707* (Edinburgh: Edinburgh University Press, 1992).

Martin, K., *The Crown and the Establishment* (London: Hutchinson, 1962).

Mason, R., 'Covenant and Commonweal: The Language of Politics in Reformation Scotland', in N. MacDougall (ed.), *Church, Politics and Society: Scotland 1408–1929* (Edinburgh: John Donald, 1983).

Mason, R. A., *Kingship and Commonweal: Political Thought in Renaissance and Reformation Scotland* (East Linton: Tuckwell Press, 1998).

Mechie, S., *The Church and Scottish Social Development, 1780–1870*, Cunningham Lectures 1957 (London: Oxford University Press, 1960).

Mechie, S., *The Office of Lord High Commissioner* (Edinburgh: Saint Andrew Press, 1957).

Milbank, J., *Theology and Social Theory: Beyond Secular Reason* (Oxford: Basil Blackwell, 1990).

Mitchell, A. F., *The Westminster Assembly: Its History and Standards*, Baird Lecture 1882 (London: James Nisbet, 1883).

Mitchell, J., 'Scotland in the Union, 1945–1995: The Changing Nature of the Union State', in Devine and Finlay, *Scotland in the Twentieth Century*.

Mitchison, R., *Lordship to Patronage: Scotland 1603–1745* (London: Edward Arnold, 1983).

Moncrieff, Lord, 'Church and State from the Reformation to 1843', in Rainy, Moncrieff and Taylor Innes, *Church and State Chiefly in Relation to the Law of Scotland*.

Morrill, J. (ed.), *The Scottish National Covenant in Its British Context* (Edinburgh: Edinburgh University Press, 1990).

Muir, A., *John White* (London: Hodder & Stoughton, 1958).

Muirhead, I. A., 'Chalmers and the Politicians', in Cheyne, *Practical and the Pious*.

Munro, C. R., 'Does Scotland have an Established Church?', *Ecclesiastical Law Journal* 20, pp. 639–45.

Murray, D. M., *Freedom to Reform: The 'Articles Declaratory' of the Church of Scotland 1921*, The Chalmers Lectures of 1991 (London: T&T Clark, 1993).

Murray, D. M., *Rebuilding the Kirk: Presbyterian Reunion in Scotland 1909–1929* (Edinburgh: Scottish Academic Press, 2000).

Murray, Lord, 'Church and State', *Stair Memorial Encyclopaedia* (Edinburgh: Butterworth, 1987), vol. 5, paras 679–705.

Murray, R. K., 'The Constitutional Position of the Church of Scotland', *Public Law* (1958), pp. 155–62.

Nicholls, D., *Church and State in Britain since 1820* (London: Routledge & Keegan Paul, 1967).

Nicholls, D., *Deity and Domination: Images of God and the State in the Nineteenth and Twentieth Centuries* (London: Routledge, 1989).

Nichols, A., *Christendom Awake: On Re-energising the Church in Culture* (Edinburgh, T&T Clark, 1999).

Niebuhr, R., *Christ and Culture* (London: Faber & Faber, 1962).

Norman, E., *Christianity and the World Order*, Reith Lectures 1978 (Oxford: Oxford University Press, 1979).

O'Donovan, O., *The Desire of the Nations: Rediscovering the Roots of Political Theology* (Cambridge: Cambridge University Press, 1996).

Oman, J., *The Church and the Divine Order* (London: Hodder & Stoughton, 1911).

Page, R., *God with Us: Synergy in the Church* (London: SCM Press, 2000).

Parker, T. M., *Christianity and the State in the Light of History* (London: A. & C. Black, 1955).

Paterson, L., *The Autonomy of Modern Scotland* (Edinburgh: Edinburgh University Press, 1994).

Percy, M., *Power and the Church: Ecclesiology in an Age of Transition* (London: Cassell, 1998).

Pfeffer, L., *Church, State and Freedom* (Boston, MA: Beacon Press, 1953).

Poggi, G., *The Development of the Modern State: A Sociological Introduction* (London: Hutchinson, 1978).

Poggi, G., *The State: Its Nature, Development and Prospects* (Cambridge: Polity Press, 1990).

Potz, R., 'The Concept and Development of Law according to the 1983 CIC', in Provost and Walf, *Canon Law – Church Reality*, pp. 14–22.

Provost, J., and K. Walf (eds), *Canon Law – Church Reality*, Concilium 185 (Edinburgh: T&T Clark, 1986).

Provost, J., and K. Walf (eds), *From Life to Law*, Concilium 1996/5 (London: SCM Press, 1996).

Provost, J., and K. Walf (eds), *Power in the Church*, Concilium 197 (Edinburgh: T&T Clark, 1988).

Pryde, G. S., *The Treaty of Union of Scotland and England 1707* (London and Edinburgh: Thomas Nelson, 1950).

Rainy, R., Lord Moncrieff and A. T. Innes, *Church and State Chiefly in Relation to the Law of Scotland* (Edinburgh: Thomas Nelson, 1878).

Rasmussen, L. L., *Moral Fragments and Moral Community: A Proposal for Church in Society* (Minneapolis, MN: Fortress Press, 1993).

Rees, W. J., 'The Theory of Sovereignty Restated', in Peter Laslett (ed.), *Philosophy, Politics and Society* (Oxford: Basil Blackwell, 1963).

Reid, D., *The Party-Coloured Mind: Prose relating to the Conflict of Church and State in Seventeenth Century Scotland* (Edinburgh: Scottish Academic Press, 1982).

Reid, J. M., *Kirk and Nation: The Story of the Reformed Church of Scotland* (London: Skeffington, 1960).

Robbins, K., 'Establishing Disestablishment: Some Reflections on Wales and Scotland', in Brown and Newlands, *Scottish Christianity in the Modern World*, pp. 249–50.

Rodger, Lord, of Earlsferry, *The Courts, the Church and the Constitution: Aspects of the Disruption of 1843*, The Jean Clark Memorial Lectures (Edinburgh: Edinburgh University Press, 2008).

Ross, K. R., *Church and Creed in Scotland: The Free Church Case 1900–1904 and Its Origins* (Edinburgh: Rutherford House Books, 1988).

Sassen, S., *Losing Control?: Sovereignty in an Age of Globalization* (New York, NY: Columbia University Press, 1996).

Schillebeeckx, E., *Church: The Human Story of God* (London: SCM Press, 1989).

Schmitt, C., *Political Theology: Four Chapters on the Concept of Sovereignty*, 2nd edn 1934, trans. George Schwab (Cambridge, MA: MIT, 1985).

Shaw, D., *The General Assemblies of the Church of Scotland 1560–1600: Their Origins and Development* (Edinburgh: Saint Andrew Press, 1964).

Simpson, P. C., *The Life of Principal Rainy* (London: Hodder & Stoughton, 1909).

Sjolinder, R., *Presbyterian Reunion in Scotland 1907–1921: Its Background and Development* (Edinburgh: T&T Clark, 1962).

Skinner, Q., *The Foundations of Modern Political Thought*, vol. II (Cambridge: Cambridge University Press, 1978).

Smart, I. M., 'The Political Ideas of the Scottish Covenanters: 1638–88', *History of Political Thought* I (1980), pp. 167–93.

Smith, D. B., 'The Spiritual Jurisdiction 1560–64', *Records of the Scottish Church History Society* xxv (1993), pp. 1–18.

Smith, J. K. A., *Introducing Radical Orthodoxy: Mapping a Post-secular Theology* (Grand Rapids, MI: Baker Academic Press, 2004).

Steele, M., 'The "Politick Christian": The Theological Background to the National Covenant', in Morrill, *Scottish National Covenant*.

Stevenson, D., *The Covenanters: The National Covenant and Scotland* (Edinburgh: Saltire Society, 1988).

Stevenson, D., 'The Covenanters and the Court of Session', *Juridical Review* 1972, 227–47

Stevenson, D., 'Cromwell, Scotland and Ireland', in J. S. Morrill (ed.), *Oliver Cromwell and the English Revolution* (London: Longman, 1990), pp. 149–80.

Stevenson, D., 'The Early Covenanters and the Federal Union of Britain', in R. Mason (ed.), *Scotland and England, 1286–1815* (Edinburgh: John Donald, 1987), pp. 163–81.

Stevenson, D., 'The General Assembly and the Commission of the Kirk, 1638–1651', *Records of the Scottish Church Society* 19 (1975–7), pp. 59–79.

Stevenson, D., *King or Covenant?: Voices from Civil War* (East Linton: Tuckwell Press, 1996).

Stevenson, D., 'The "Letter on Sovereign Power" and the Influence of Jean Bodin on Political Thought in Scotland', *Scottish Historical Review* 61 (1982), pp. 25–43.

Stevenson, D., 'The Radical Party in the Kirk, 1637–45', *Journal of Ecclesiastical History* 25 (1974), pp. 135–64.

Stevenson, D., *Revolution and Counter-Revolution in Scotland, 1644–1651* (London: Royal Historical Society, 1977).

Storrar, W., 'The Decline of the Kirk', *University of Aberdeen Alumni Association News* 18 (Autumn 1997), pp. 5–8.

Storrar, W., *Scottish Identity: A Christian Vision* (Edinburgh: Handsel, 1990).

Strehle, S., *Calvinism, Federalism and Scholasticism: A Study of the Reformed Doctrine of Covenant* (Bern: Peter Lang, 1988).

Taylor Innes, A., *Church and State: A Historical Handbook* (Edinburgh: T&T Clark, 1890).

Taylor Innes, A., *The Law of Creeds in Scotland* (Edinburgh and London: Blackwood, 1867).

Taylor, T. M., 'Church and State in Scotland', *Juridical Review* (1957), pp. 121–37.

'Theology and Political Office in Scotland since the Reformation', in *Volume of Reports to 2000 Church of Scotland General Assembly* (Edinburgh: Board of Practice and Procedure, 2000).

Thomson, D. M., '"Unrestricted Conference?": Myth and Reality in Scottish Ecumenism', in Brown and Newlands, *Scottish Christianity in the Modern World*.

Tierney, B., *The Idea of Natural Rights: Studies on Natural Rights, Natural Law and Church Law 1550–1625*, Emory University Studies in Law and Religion (Atlanta, GA: Scholars Press, 1997).

Tornay, S. C., *Ockham: Studies and Selections* (La Salle, IL: Open Court, 1938).

Torrance, J. B., 'The Covenant Concept in Scottish Theology and Politics and Its Legacy', *Scottish Journal of Theology* 34 (1981), pp. 225–43.

Torrance, J. B., 'Covenant or Contract? A Study of the Theological Background of Worship in Seventeenth-century Scotland', *Scottish Journal of Theology* 23 (1970), pp. 51–76.

Torrance, T. F., *Juridical Law and Physical Law: Towards a Realist Foundation for Human Law* (Edinburgh: Scottish Academic Press, 1982).

Torrance, T. F., *Kingdom and Church: A Study in the Theology of the Reformation* (Edinburgh: Oliver & Boyd, 1956).

Vanhoozer, K. J. (ed.), *The Cambridge Companion to Postmodern Theology* (Cambridge: Cambridge University Press, 2003).

Wade, H. W. R., 'The Basis of Legal Sovereignty', *Cambridge Law Journal* (1955), pp. 172–97.

Walker, D. M., *A Legal History of Scotland*, vols III and IV (Edinburgh: T&T Clark, 1995 and 1996).

Watt, H., *Thomas Chalmers and the Disruption* (Edinburgh: Thomas Nelson, 1943).

Weatherhead, J. L. (ed.), *The Constitution and Laws of the Church of Scotland* (Edinburgh: Board of Practice and Procedure, 1997).

Weir, D. A., *The Origins of the Federal Theology in Sixteenth-Century Reformation Thought* (Oxford: Clarendon Press, 1990).

Wilks, M., *The Problem of Sovereignty in the Later Middle Ages: The Papal Monarchy with Augustinus Triumphus and the Publicists* (Cambridge: Cambridge University Press, 1963).

Williamson, A. H., *Scottish National Consciousness in the Age of James VI: The Apocalypse, the Union and the Shaping of Scotland's Public Culture* (Edinburgh: John Donald, 1979).

Willson, D. H., *King James VI and I* (London: Jonathan Cape, 1956).

Wink, W., *Engaging the Powers: Discernment and Resistance in a World of Domination* (Minneapolis, MN: Fortress Press, 1992).

Wink, W., *Naming the Powers: The Language of Power in the New Testament* (Philadelphia, PA: Fortress Press, 1984).

Wink, W., *Unmasking the Powers: The Invisible Forces That Determine Human Existence* (Philadelphia, PA: Fortress Press, 1986).

Witte, J., and F. S. Alexander, *The Weightier Matters of the Law: Essays on Law and Religion: A Tribute to Harold J Berman*, American Academy of Religion Studies in Religion 51 (Atlanta, GA: Scholars Press, 1988).

Witte, J., and T. C. Arthur, 'The Three Uses of the Law: A Protestant Source of the Purposes of Criminal Punishment?', *Journal of Law and Religion* X.2 (1993–4).

Wood, D. (ed.), *The Church and Sovereignty c. 590–1918: Essays in Honour of Michael Wilks* (Oxford: Basil Blackwell, 1991).

Wormald, J., *Court, Kirk and Community: Scotland 1470–1625* (Edinburgh: Edinburgh University Press, 1981).

Worthington, D. H., 'Anti-Erastian Aspects of Scottish Covenanter Political Thought 1637 to 1647', PhD thesis (University of Akron, 1978).

Index

Page numbers in *italics* indicate an Appendix entry